G000168033

Microsoft® Publisher 2000

Jennifer Fulton

201 West 103rd Street
Indianapolis, Indiana 46290

SAMS

Visually in Full Color

How to Use Microsoft® Publisher 2000

Copyright © 1999 by Sams Publishing

All rights reserved. No part of this book shall be reproduced, stored in a retrieval system, or transmitted by any means, electronic, mechanical, photocopying, recording, or otherwise, without written permission from the publisher. No patent liability is assumed with respect to the use of the information contained herein. Although every precaution has been taken in the preparation of this book, the publisher and author assume no responsibility for errors or omissions. Neither is any liability assumed for damages resulting from the use of the information contained herein.

International Standard Book Number: 0-672-31571-8

Library of Congress Catalog Card Number: 99-60639

Printed in the United States of America

This book was produced digitally by Macmillan Computer Publishing and manufactured using computer-to-plate technology (a film-less process) by GAC, Indianapolis, Indiana.

First Printing: *May 1999*

02   01   00   99   4   3   2   1

Interpretation of the printing code: The rightmost double-digit number is the year of the book's printing; the rightmost single-digit, the number of the book's printing. For example, a printing code of 99-1 shows that the first pringing of the book occurred in 1999.

Trademarks

All terms mentioned in this book that are known to be trademarks or service marks have been appropriately capitalized. Sams Publishing cannot attest to the accuracy of this information. Use of a term in this book should not be regarded as affecting the validity of any trademark or service mark. Microsoft is a registered trademark of Microsoft Corporation.

Executive Editor
Mark Taber

Acquisitions Editor
Randi Roger

Development Editor
Alice Martina Smith

Project Editors
Angela Boley
Charlotte Clapp

Indexers
Kelly Talbot
Christine Nelsen

Proofreader
Mary Ellen Stephenson

Interior Design
Nathan Clement
Ruth Lewis

Cover Design
Aren Howell

Layout Technicians
Brian Borders
Susan Geiselman
Heather Miller
Mark Walchle

Contents at a Glance

	Introduction	1
1	Getting Started	2
2	Working with Text	52
3	Working with Graphics	82
4	Adding Special Elements	130
5	Tweaking Your Publication	150
6	Creating a Web Publication	176
7	Creating Specialty Publications	198
8	Printing Your Publication	224
	Glossary	242
	Index	244

Contents

 Getting Started *2*

How to Install Publisher   4

How to Start Publisher   6

How to Choose a Publication Wizard   8

How to Create a Personal Information Set   10

How to Work with the Publication Wizard   12

How to Choose a Design Set   14

How to Use a Blank Publication Design   16

How to Create a Publication from Scratch   18

How to Navigate Through a Publication   20

How to Add and Remove Pages   22

How to Use the Standard Toolbar   24

How to Use the Objects Toolbar   26

How to Use Layout Guides   28

How to Use Ruler Guides   30

How to Change the View   32

How to Use the Office Assistant   34

How to Use Contents, Answer Wizard, and Index   38

How to Get Help from Microsoft   42

How to Save and Retrieve Publications   46

How to Set Options for Publisher   48

2 Working with Text *52*

How to Replace Sample Text   54

How to Create a Text Frame   56

How to Resize and Move Text Frames   58

How to Format Text Appearance   60

How to Create Special Text Effects   62

How to Format Text Frames   64

How to Copy Formatting Quickly   66

How to Create Lists   68

How to Create Columns in Text Frames   70

How to Work with Overflow Text   72

How to Create Continued Notices   74

How to Create a Style   76

How to Import Styles from Publications   78

How to Import Styles from Word Processors   80

3 Working with Graphics *82*

How to Insert Standard Shapes   84

How to Insert Custom Shapes   86

How to Move, Resize, and Crop Shapes   88

How to Add Color and Texture to Shapes   90

How to Layer Shapes   92

How to Put Text on Shapes   94

How to Group and Ungroup Objects   96

How to Flip and Rotate Objects   98

How to Insert Clip Art   100

How to Insert Pictures   102

How to Create Picture Captions   104

How to Insert WordArt   106

How to Format WordArt   108

How to Use Microsoft Draw   112

How to Create Borders and Shadows   114

How to Align Objects   116

How to Use the Snap To Feature   118

How to Wrap Text Around Graphics   120

How to Move, Resize, and Crop Graphic Frames   122

Project 1: A Sales Brochure   124

4 Adding Special Elements *130*

How to Add a Table 132

How to Format a Table 134

How to Use the Design Gallery 136

How to Create Your Own Design Gallery 138

How to Create Background Elements 140

How to Insert Elements from Documents 144

How to Use Mail Merge 146

5 Tweaking Your Publication *150*

How to Tweak Margins 152

How to Spell Check Your Publication 154

How to Check the Design 158

How to Copyfit Your Text 160

How to Control Tracking, Kerning, and Leading 162

How to Perfect Hyphenation 164

How to Work with Bindings 166

How to Work with Crop and Registration Marks 168

Project 2: A Flyer from Scratch 170

6 Creating a Web Publication *176*

How to Set Up a Web Publication 178

How to Add Pages to a Web Publication 180

How to Add Sounds and Animation to Web Pages 182

How to Create Navigation Bars 184

How to Add Hyperlinks 186

How to Add Hot Spots 188

How to Check the Web Design 190

How to Preview Your Web Publication 192

How to Convert Publications to Web Pages 194

How to Publish Your Publication to the Web 196

7 Creating Specialty Publications *198*

How to Use Special Paper 200

How to Create Signs 202

How to Create Greeting Cards 204

How to Create Business Forms 206

How to Create a Banner 208

How to Create Calendars 210

How to Create Ads 212

How to Create an Award Certificate 214

How to Create a Gift Certificate 216

How to Create a Program 218

How to Build an Airplane 220

How to Create Origami 222

8 Printing Your Publication *224*

How to Print Your Publication 226

How to Print Special Publications 228

How to Use an Outside Printing Service 230

Project 3: A Web Site 236

Glossary *242*

Index *244*

Acknowledgements

I would like to thank Randi Roger for her drive and her vision. I'd also like to thank Alice Martina Smith for her patience and wonderful editing skills. Thanks also to Angela and Charlotte for helping to make this book a great one.

Dedication

To my husband, Scott, and my daughter, Katerina—my life, my loves.

Tell Us What You Think!

As the reader of this book, *you* are our most important critic and commentator. We value your opinion and want to know what we're doing right, what we could do better, what areas you'd like to see us publish in, and any other words of wisdom you're willing to pass our way.

You can fax, email, or write me directly to let me know what you did or didn't like about this book—as well as what we can do to make our books stronger.

Please note that I cannot help you with technical problems related to the topic of this book, and that because of the high volume of mail I receive, I might not be able to reply to every message.

When you write, please be sure to include this book's title and author's name as well as your name and phone or fax number. I will carefully review your comments and share them with the author and editors who worked on the book.

Fax: 317-581-4770

Email: office_sams@mcp.com

Mail: Mark Taber
              Associate Publisher
              Sams Publishing
              201 West 103rd Street
              Indianapolis, IN 46290 USA

How To Use This Book

The Complete Visual Reference

Each part of this book is made up of a series of short, instructional tasks, designed to help you understand all the information you need to get the most out of your computer hardware and software.

 Click: Click the left mouse button once.

 Double-click: Click the left mouse button twice in rapid succession.

 Right-click: Click the right mouse button once.

 Pointer Arrow: Highlights an item on the screen you need to point to or focus on in the step or task.

 Selection: Highlights the area onscreen discussed in the step or task.

 How to Drag: Point to the starting place or object. Hold down the left mouse button, move the mouse to the new location, and then release the button.

Drag

 Key icons: Clearly indicate which key combinations to use.

Each task includes a series of easy-to-understand steps designed to guide you through the procedure.

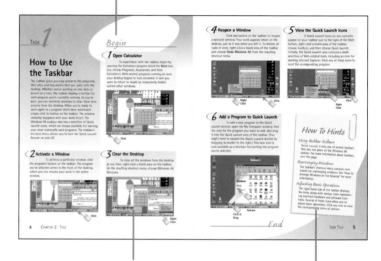

Each step is fully illustrated to show you how it looks onscreen.

Extra hints that tell you how to accomplish a goal are provided in most tasks.

Menus and items you click are shown in **bold**. Words in *italic* are defined in more detail in the Glossary. Information you type is in a **special font**.

Continues

If you see this symbol, it means the task you're in continues on the next page.

Introduction

*P*ublisher 2000 is a desktop publishing application, a unique and powerful software genre. You can use Publisher to create professional-looking publications without having to learn all the skills and jargon of the printing trade.

What is terrific about choosing Publisher 2000 for your desktop publishing chores is the amount of assistance built into the software. It's like having your own design team, including layout specialists, artists, and printing experts.

Wizards inhabit this software, and they show up for work at your beck and call. They walk you through the process of creating any of numerous preconfigured publications:

- ✓ Newsletters
- ✓ Brochures
- ✓ Greeting cards
- ✓ Business stationery
- ✓ Banners
- ✓ Paper airplanes

How to Use Microsoft Publisher 2000 is written so that you get the most out of the wizards. You travel with the wizards throughout this book in short, simple, steps; you're then taken through all the additional steps necessary to turn the wizard's preconfigured layout into your own, personalized publication.

But you don't stop there. After you've created a few publications with the wizards, you'll want to strike out on your own. This book is aimed at getting you comfortable enough to make that daunting decision. You learn how to use all of Publisher's tools and features.

Some projects are included for you to complete. Even though they're fun to do, they're also a learning experience. You put the skills presented in this book to work when working on these projects.

Feel free to read this book in whatever order you choose. *How to Use Microsoft Publisher 2000* isn't written with the thought that you'll read the pages and look at the illustrations starting with the first page and ending with the last. You can check the index to find the things you need to learn about.

In this book, you find a no-nonsense approach to learning how to perform a task, complete with illustrations, which add to your learning experience.

Task

1 How to Install Publisher 4

2 How to Start Publisher 6

3 How to Choose a Publication Wizard 8

4 How to Create a Personal Information Set 10

5 How to Work with the Publication Wizard 12

6 How to Choose a Design Set 14

7 How to Use a Blank Publication Design 16

8 How to Create a Publication from Scratch 18

9 How to Navigate Through a Publication 20

10 How to Add and Remove Pages 22

11 How to Use the Standard Toolbar 24

12 How to Use the Objects Toolbar 26

13 How to Use Layout Guides 28

14 How to Use Ruler Guides 30

15 How to Change the View 32

16 How to Use the Office Assistant 34

17 How to Use Contents, Answer Wizard, and Index 38

18 How to Get Help from Microsoft 42

19 How to Save and Retrieve Publications 46

20 How to Set Options for Publisher 48

Getting Started

*B*efore you can dive into Publisher to publish a newspaper, a book, or a birthday card for Aunt Maude, you have to install the software. Then, of course, it's a good idea to learn your way around Publisher.

Even though Publisher looks and behaves in a fashion similar to that of other Windows software you may be familiar with, there are some differences you have to get used to.

Publisher is a graphics program with robust text functions (unlike most other desktop publishing software, where text creation is onerous and you always find it easier to import text). As a result, you find more toolbars, more buttons on the toolbars, and a slew of menu commands unique to Publisher (and therefore new to you).

In this part, you learn about installing, starting, and using Publisher features. You learn how to get help as you work. You also meet the all-powerful wizard that makes creating a complicated publication a snap. ●

How to Install Publisher

Before you can work and have fun in Publisher (it *is* a lot of fun), you have to install it. This is an easy procedure, but first you should close any software programs that may be open.

If you use a virus-checking program, you must disable it before beginning the installation. (You can start it again after Publisher is installed.)

Begin

1 Put the CD-ROM in Its Drive

Most of the time, the Publisher 2000 setup process starts automatically as soon as you put the CD-ROM in its drive (that's called AutoPlay).

2 Starting Setup Manually

If AutoPlay doesn't start the setup process, click the **Start** button and choose **Run** from the **Start** menu. When the **Run** dialog box opens, enter **d:\setup** (assuming that d: is the drive letter for your CD-ROM—if not, substitute the appropriate drive letter). The opening setup window appears.

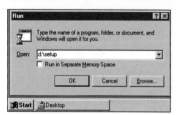

3 Enter User Information

Enter the CD key for your copy of Publisher 2000; it's on an orange sticker on the back of the CD case. Choose **Next**. Enter **User name**, **Initials**, and **Organization**.

4 Accept the License

Use the scrollbar to read through the End-User License Agreement and then choose **I accept the terms in the License Agreement**. If you don't agree, installation stops. Click **Next**.

5 Choose the Type of Installation

Setup spends a few seconds looking for previously installed versions of Publisher, and then the **Setup** dialog box asks you which type of installation you want to perform. Choose **Install Now.**

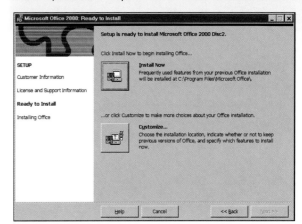

6 Restart the Computer

A message appears telling you that you must restart your computer before using Publisher. Click **Yes**. After your system restarts, you're ready to go!

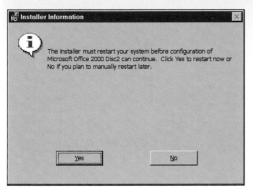

End

How-To Hints

Going Your Own Way

If you choose a custom installation, do not choose to store the Publisher clip art on your hard disk—there's just too much of it! It's better to access the clip art when you need it from the Publisher CD-ROM.

How to Start Publisher

Before you dive in to produce a book, newspaper, greeting card, or business stationery, it's a good idea to familiarize yourself with opening and closing Publisher, as well as its software window.

Begin

1 Open the Start Menu

Choose **Programs, Microsoft Publisher** from the **Start** menu.

Click

2 Introducing the Catalog

The **Publisher Catalog** opens so that you can get right to work. This Catalog is the first thing you see every time you start Publisher. Information about using the Catalog is found throughout this book, so it's not discussed here. For now, click **Exit Catalog**.

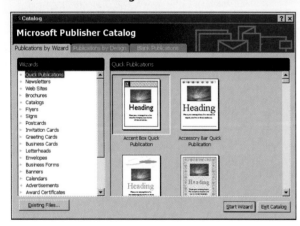

3 Close the Wizard Pane

The Quick Publication Wizard appears on the left side of the Publisher window. A wizard steps you through the process of creating a particular type of publication. You'll learn more about using wizards in the next task. For now, click **Hide Wizard**.

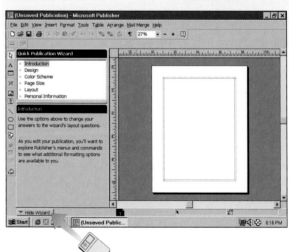

Click

4 Examine the Publisher Window

The **Publisher** window looks very much like all the Windows software you use.

Title bar | Menu bar | Standard toolbar | Minimize button | Maximize/Restore button

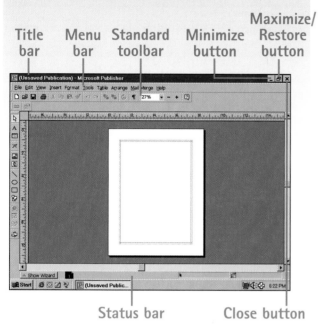

Status bar | Close button

5 The Status Bar Is Special

The Publisher status bar is unique (compared to most other Windows software). It has four elements. The **Object Position** indicator and the **Object Size** indicator are related to any selected object—if no object is selected, the **Object Position** indicator displays the mouse pointer's position, and the **Object Size** indicator is empty. The **Show Wizard** button (which displays the Wizard pane) is also on the status bar. You can use the **Page** icons to move from page to page in your project.

Show Wizard button | Object Size indicator

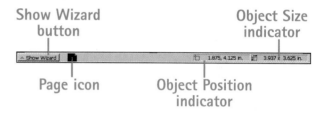

Page icon | Object Position indicator

6 Closing Publisher

To close Publisher, click the **Close** button (the **X** in the upper-right corner) or choose **File, Exit** from the **menu bar**. If you have made any changes to your publication since you last saved it, you're given a chance to save it again before the software shuts down.

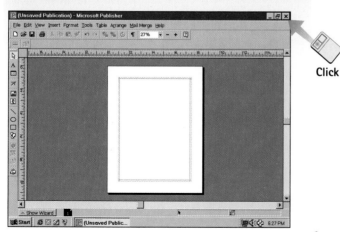

Click

How-To Hints

Make a Desktop Shortcut

Create a desktop shortcut to make launching Publisher easier: Open Explorer and find the file named **Mspub.exe**. Right-drag its icon to the desktop. When you release the mouse, choose **Create Shortcut(s) Here** from the displayed menu, and then just double-click the shortcut to open Publisher.

Custom Menus

Menus in Office 2000 show only the most common commands; to display a hidden command, point to the arrow at the bottom of the menu. To turn this option off and display full menus, see Task 20.

End

How to Choose a Publication Wizard

The easiest way to design a publication is to let a wizard do the preliminary work (for more ways to create a new publication, see Tasks 6, 7, and 8).That means the layout, color design, and other setup options are configured automatically, and all you have to worry about is writing the text.

The wizards reside in the Catalog, which is the first thing you see when you open Publisher.

Begin

1 Use the Menu Bar

If you're already working in Publisher, choose **File, New** from the **menu bar**. Don't click the **New** icon on the toolbar and don't use the **Ctrl+N** shortcut—neither of these methods brings up the Catalog (you'll only get a blank page).

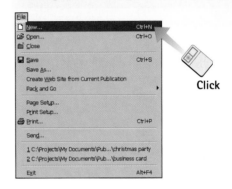

Click

2 Choose a Wizard and a Style

On the **Publications by Wizard** tab of the catalog, a list of wizards displays on the left. When you select a wizard, its set of publications displays on the right side of the window. Most wizards have quite a few publication styles to offer, and you can use the scrollbar to examine all of them.

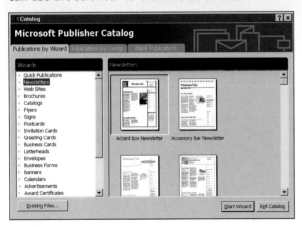

3 Understanding the Wizard

Wizards with a diamond next to the name offer a single publication type. Wizards with a right-facing arrow symbol have multiple types of publications. The list expands when you click the arrow (click again to close the list).

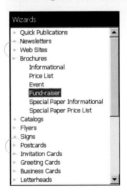

4 Choosing a Special Paper Wizard

Wizards that are named **Special Paper** display publication types that include the logo for a company named PaperDirect. Information about purchasing this paper is found in the PaperDirect catalog included in your Publisher package. The color design for PaperDirect is built into the paper; you don't have to add it graphically. This means you don't have to have a color printer to have color in your publication.

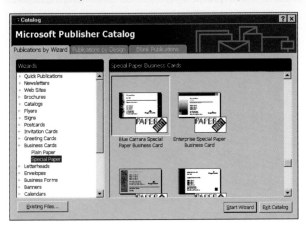

5 Start the Wizard

After you've selected a wizard and a publication type, choose **Start Wizard** to begin the process of building the publication. You may see a message telling you that the wizard must be installed first. Insert the Publisher distribution CD-ROM and click **Yes**.

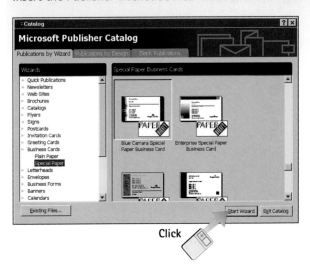

Click

6 Closing the Catalog

If you decide you don't want to use any wizard for this publication, you can close the Catalog by clicking **Exit Catalog** (or click the **X** in the upper-right corner of the catalog window).

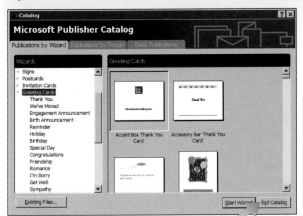

Click

How-To Hints

Eliminating the Catalog

After you've become an expert in Publisher (with the help of this book), you can eliminate the Catalog display when you open the software. Choose **Tools**, **Options** from the menu bar and check the box for the option called **Use Catalog at Startup**. Checking the box removes the check mark; hereafter, the Catalog won't load automatically on startup.

Quick Publications

If you want to create a simple, one-page publication with some text and a graphic, choose a Quick Publication wizard.

End

How to Create a Personal Information Set

The first time you select any publication wizard, you are prompted to enter some basic information. This information is saved in a Personal Information Set (PIS). Publisher automatically copies your organization's name, address, and phone numbers to the appropriate places. You can create four Personal Information Sets (PISs): Primary Business, Secondary Business, Other Organization, and Home/Family. When you create a new publication, the publication wizard will ask you to select the Personal Information Set you want to use. However, you can change to a different set later.

Begin

1 Display the PI Dialog Box

After selecting any publication wizard for the first time, you're instructed to enter your basic information into a Personal Information Set. Click OK.

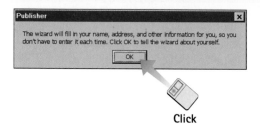

Click

2 Enter Primary Business Information

You enter information into the Primary Business set first. In addition to storing your name, business address, and phone numbers, you can also select a color scheme. This scheme is then used to color all your business publications.

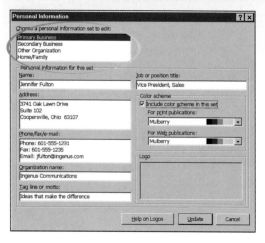

3 Enter Additional Information

You can create additional Personal Information Sets as well. For example, click **Home/Family** in the **Choose a personal information set to edit** list and enter your home address and phone number.

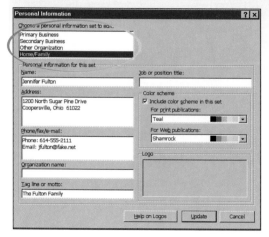

4 Select Another Color Scheme

As you create additional PISs, you can select different color schemes as well. For example, you can select a different color scheme for home use than you chose for your business publications.

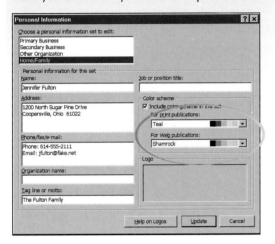

5 Close the PI Dialog Box

When you're through creating the various Personal Information Sets, click **Update**.

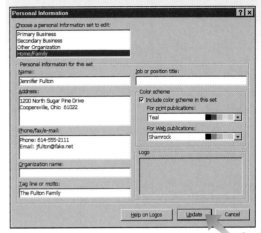

Click

6 Change to a Different PIS

When you create a new publication using a wizard, you are prompted to select a Personal Information Set. You can redisplay the wizard pane and select a different set if you like.

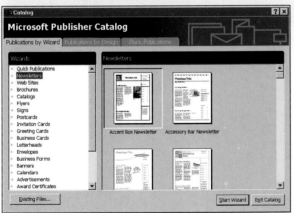

End

How-To Hints

Got a Company Logo?

The first time you insert a graphic into a publication with a logo placeholder, you'll be asked if you want to store it to the current Personal Information Set. You'll learn more about working with graphics in Part 3.

How to Work with the Publication Wizard

The wizard does a lot of work, but you can direct its efforts with your own preferences. The first preference, of course, is selecting the publication and style of publication. After that, there are other decisions for you to make; the wizard makes adjustments to the publication as you make your decisions.

Begin

1 Launch the Wizard

After you select a publication type, choose **Start Wizard**; this tells the wizard to begin putting your publication together. The wizard starts building the layout, which is based on the publication and style you selected.

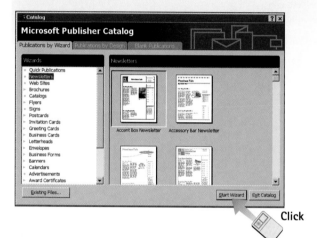

Click

2 Begin the Wizard's Questions

When the **wizard** pane opens on the left side of the screen, the wizard is ready to start. Click **Next** to begin selecting configuration options.

Click

3 Answer Each Question

The questions vary depending on the type of publication you selected. For instance, the newsletter wizard wants to know about columns, and whether you plan to print on both sides of the paper. Continue to make selections, choosing **Next** to move on through the questions.

Click

4 Choose Finish

The **Next** button is grayed out when you have answered the last query. Choose **Finish**.

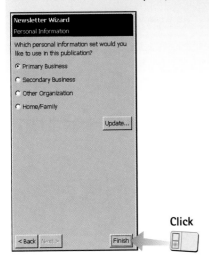

Click

5 You Can Change Your Mind

The **wizard** pane displays the question categories. To change any of your decisions, click the appropriate category; you return to that wizard page to make the necessary changes. (Options with a "no" symbol ⊘ are not available.)

6 Hide the Wizard

To have the use of your entire **Publisher** window, choose **Hide Wizard**. The **wizard** pane disappears. If you want to change your decisions, choose **Show Wizard** to bring back the pane shown in Step 5.

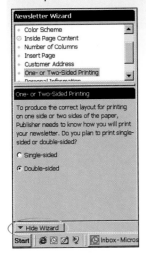

How-To Hints

Jumping to the Final Wizard Pane

You can perform a shortcut after becoming familiar with working with wizards: You can choose **Finish** as soon as the first wizard pane appears to move to the final wizard pane (with the list of categories displayed so that you can make changes to the design). If you choose this shortcut, Publisher asks you to confirm it, and also inquires whether you'd like to make this shortcut a habit.

End

How to Choose a Design Set

Another way to create a new Publication is to use **Publications by Design**. The preformatted publication layouts available in this tab of the Catalog are *design sets*, which means that they share a common design. You can use these design sets to create a variety of publication types so that all of them will share the same design elements (such as colors, fonts, and overall style). This is a great way to create matching business stationery and forms.

Begin

1 Open the Catalog

If you're already working in Publisher, choose **File, New** from the **menu bar** to open the Catalog. (The Catalog appears automatically if you're just starting Publisher.)

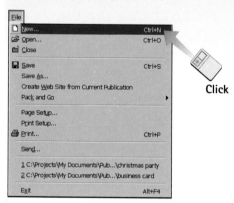

Click

2 Move to the Designs Tab

Click the **Publications by Design** tab.

Click

3 Choose a Design Set

The Catalog's left pane contains a list of design sets, each of which can be expanded by clicking the right-facing arrow next to the name. When you expand a design set, the list of designs contained in that set is displayed.

4 View the Available Publications

Select a design in the left pane to display the available publications in the right pane.

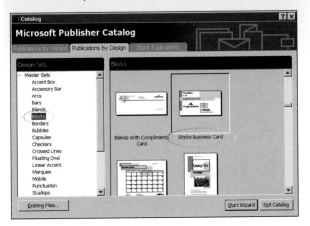

5 Select a Publication

Choose the publication you want to create by clicking its picture in the right pane; then choose **Start Wizard**.

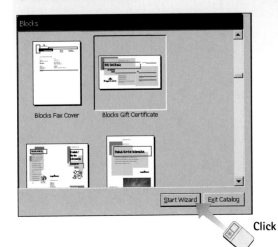

Click

6 Answer the Wizard's Questions

Choose **Next** in the **wizard** pane to move from window to window, answering the wizard's questions. When you get to the last wizard window, the **Next** button is grayed out. Choose **Finish**. The wizard displays the list of options; you can choose the appropriate one if you want to change any of your decisions.

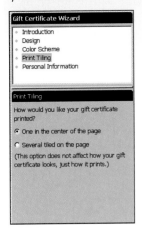

How-To Hints

Hide the Wizard

It's easier to work in the **Publisher** window if you hide the wizard by clicking the **Hide Wizard** button (found on the bottom of the wizard pane). If you want to make changes to the design, click **Show Wizard** to bring back the wizard pane.

End

How to Use a Blank Publication Design

The Publisher Catalog offers a host of designs and layouts in the **Blank Publications** tab. These designs are commonly used for publications you want to create from scratch; they limit you to a particular paper size or to some paper-folding pattern.

Begin

1 Open the Catalog

If you're already working in Publisher, choose **File**, **New** from the **menu bar** to open the Catalog. (If you're just starting Publisher, the Catalog appears automatically.)

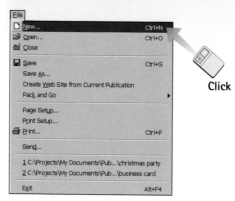

Click

2 Select the Blank Publications Tab

Click the **Blank Publications** tab at the top of the Catalog window.

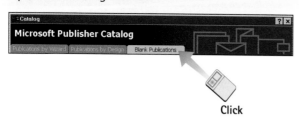

Click

3 Choose a Publication

Select a publication type. You can either click its name in the left pane or click its picture in the right pane. Click **Create**.

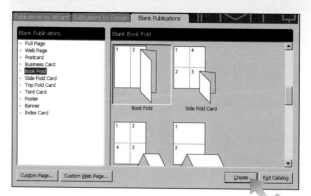

Click

4 Design a Custom Page

If the paper size or folding pattern you need isn't available, choose **Custom Page**. The **Page Setup** dialog box appears.

Click

5 Select a Custom Layout

In the **Page Setup** dialog box, choose the layout type you need from the top section of the dialog box. The bottom section of the dialog box changes to reflect your selection's options. Make changes to the specifications at the bottom of the dialog box as needed.

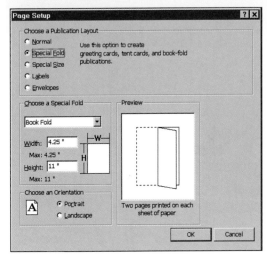

6 Labels Are Supported Too

If you choose **Labels** as the publication type in Step 5, the dialog box displays the full range of labels available from Avery. Select the one you plan to use, and Publisher displays a page that's laid out to match the labels you selected.

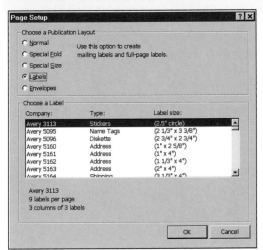

How-To Hints

Printing Labels

When you use labels in a laser printer, it's a good idea to send them through the printer in a straight path (you may have to flip down a back door to generate the straight-path feeding mode). Labels sometimes peel if they go around the roller. In addition, never put a label page back through the printer for a second run—you run the risk of destroying the printer's mechanism. If you don't use all the labels on a page, throw the page away anyway.

End

How to Create a Publication from Scratch

Publisher offers all sorts of opportunities to use pre-formatted layouts, but after you're comfortable with all the Publisher features and tools, you're likely to want to try working without a net.

Starting with a blank page can be a bit intimidating because there aren't any preset frames or margins. But with some careful planning, you can create a publication just as slick and professional as the pre-designed templates.

Begin

1 Close the Catalog

To get to a blank page when you first launch Publisher, click the **Exit Catalog** button, which is at the bottom of the **Catalog** window.

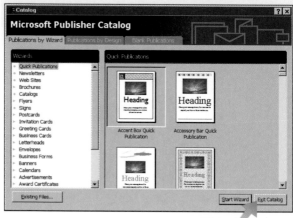

Click

2 Use the New Icon

If you're already working in Publisher, you can open a blank page by clicking the **New** icon on the **Standard** toolbar (or by pressing **Ctrl+N**).

Control + N

3 Open the Page Setup Dialog Box

Because you don't have a predefined page layout, you must set up your page manually. Choose **File, Page Setup**.

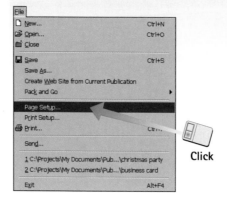

Click

4 Configure the Page

Use the options in the **Page Setup** dialog box to configure the page size, along with any other options you need for this publication. Click **OK** to save your choices.

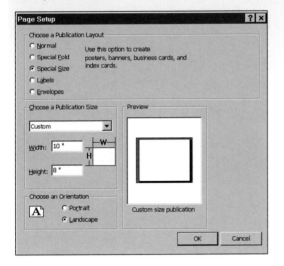

5 Configure the Layout

To establish margins and other layout options, choose **Arrange**, **Layout Guides** from the **menu bar**. When the **Layout Guides** dialog box appears, specify the margins you need and insert columns and row guides if you require them. See Part 1, Task 13, "How to Use Layout Guides," for more information about using this dialog box.

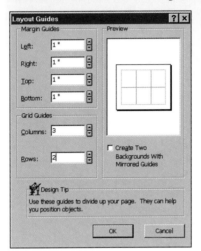

6 Add the Elements

Now you're ready to create a masterpiece. Add text frames, pictures, and other elements to your page as described throughout this book.

How-To Hints

About Page Sizes

If you create a page layout of a custom size, Publisher assumes that you'll print it on standard size paper. If you have paper that matches your layout's size, you must tell the printer about it by using the **File**, **Print Setup** command.

End

How to Navigate Through a Publication

Working with Publisher is a bit different than working with your word processor. For example, you can't use the scrollbar to move from the first page to any additional pages. Instead, the scrollbar controls the view of the current page.

Because Publisher is a desktop publishing application, it's important to see a full-page view to keep an eye on the layout. Each page in a publication is an individual object and is displayed by itself. However, if you're printing on both sides of the paper and your publication will be bound like a book, you can also view a two-page spread.

Begin

1 Use the Page Controls

Pages in your publication are represented by page icons on the status bar. To move to a particular page, click the appropriate page icon.

Show Wizard | 1 2 3 4 5 6 7 8 9 10 11 12 13 ▶

2 Display More Page Icons

To display additional page icons, click the right-facing arrow.

Show Wizard | 1 2 3 4 5 6 7 8 9 10 11 12 13 ▶

3 Display Previous Button

To display the set of page icons, click the left-facing arrow.

Show Wizard | ◀ 4 5 6 7 8 9 10 11 12 13 14 15 16

4 View Double Pages

To see adjacent pages the way they will print, choose **View, Two-Page Spread** from the **menu bar**. This command is a toggle, and when you want to return to a single-page view, select it again to remove the check mark.

5 Zoom In and Out

To zoom in (helpful when you're working in a frame) or zoom out (to see the overall layout), click the arrow next to the **Zoom** box in the Standard toolbar and select the zoom percentage you require. You can also click in the **Zoom** box and type a percentage.

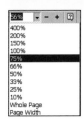

6 Quick Zoom

Use the **plus** and **minus** icons to the right of the Zoom box to zoom in and out in graduated steps. Each time you click, the zoom percentage changes in a pattern that matches the zoom percentages shown in Step 5. For instance, click the plus sign to move from **33%** to **50%**. You can also press **F9** to toggle between the current view and 100% view.

End

How-To Hints

About Two-Page Spreads

When you view a two-page spread, the odd page is always on the right and the even page is on the left. This means that if you move to the first or last page of your publication, only one page will display. Page 1 has nothing to the left of it, and the last page (which is an even-numbered page) has nothing to the right of it.

How to Add and Remove Pages

If you are creating a publication from scratch, you start with a single blank page and then you must add pages as you need them. Even if you use a wizard design, however, you may find that the original layout didn't provide enough pages.

As you perfect your publication by editing the stories and resizing the frames, you may find it necessary to delete a page.

Begin

1 Insert a Page Within the Publication

If you want to insert a page anywhere in the publication, move to the page either immediately before or immediately after the new page location; then choose **Insert**, **Page** from the menu bar.

2 Specify the New Page Options

Enter the number of pages you want to add and choose where you want these pages added—before or after the current page. Choose whether you want to add blank pages or copies of the current page. Click **OK**.

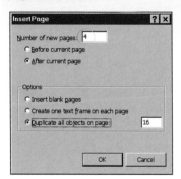

3 Adding Two Pages at a Time

If you're working with a **Two-Page Spread** view of your publication, Publisher understands that you need to add two pages at a time to make sure that your publication can be bound or folded correctly. The **Insert Page** dialog box makes the proper adjustments in the options offered. If you specify an odd number of new pages, Publisher issues a warning (but doesn't stop you).

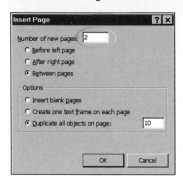

4 Delete a Page

If you want to delete a page, be sure that the page is in the **Publisher** window and choose **Edit**, **Delete Page**; the page disappears. If you are working in the **Two-Page Spread** view, the **Delete Page** dialog box appears and offers a default option of deleting both pages (to keep your publication pages at an even number). Choose the option you need and click **OK**.

End

How-To Hints

Keep Two-Page Publications Even

If you ignore Publisher's recommendation to delete two pages at a time from a publication that you're going to bind or fold, add another page somewhere else.

How to Use the Standard Toolbar

Working with the menu system can be tedious because you have to click the menu item, position your mouse just so over a command, and then click again to invoke the command. If there's a submenu, you have to position your mouse a second time and then click.

To make life easier (your life in Publisher, at least), the commonly used menu commands have been placed on buttons (also called *icons*) on a toolbar called the **Standard** toolbar. It sits right below your **menu bar**.

One click on an icon produces the same result as going through the menu system. It's amazing how many people never really take a careful look at this toolbar to see what it offers and, therefore, never use it. To make sure that you don't fall into this category, let's go over the **Standard** toolbar buttons.

Begin

1 File Tools

The first three icons on the left edge of the **Standard** toolbar are for working with files (publications). From left to right the buttons are **New**, which opens a new blank publication; **Open**, which brings up a dialog box from which you can select an existing publication to open; and **Save**, which saves your publication.

2 Print

Clicking the **Print** icon sends the current publication to the printer with the last set of options you selected in the **Print** dialog box. If this is the first time you're printing in this Publisher session, your entire document is printed. No dialog box appears to ask you whether you want to change printers, print only specific pages, or make any other choices.

3 Move and Copy Elements

The next four buttons are used to move and copy your publication's contents. From left to right, they are **Cut**, which removes the selected element (text, graphic, or the like) from your publication and places it on the Windows Clipboard; **Copy**, which places a copy of the element on the Windows Clipboard (but doesn't remove it from the publication); **Paste**, which inserts the contents of the Windows Clipboard in the location of your pointer; and **Format Painter**, which copies the formatting of a frame (rather than copying the elements in the frame) and then pastes that formatting on another frame.

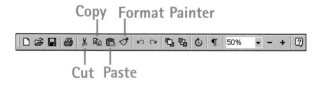

4 Oops!

Next in line are the **Undo** and **Redo** buttons. You can undo your last action, and after you do so, you can redo the previous undo if you change your mind again. If you can't remember what you did last (or undid last), hold your mouse pointer on either button to see a ScreenTip reminder.

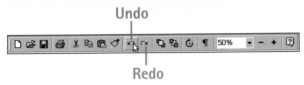

Undo

Redo

5 Manipulate Frames

Use the next three buttons to manipulate frames in your publication. **Bring to Front** moves the selected frame to the top of a set of layered frames. **Send to Back** moves the selected frame to the bottom of a pile of layered frames. Click **Custom Rotate** to rotate a frame by so many degrees. See Part 3, Task 5, "How to Layer Shapes," for more information on working with layers.

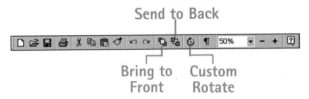

Send to Back

Bring to Front   Custom Rotate

6 Change the View

Use the next four buttons to change the way your publication looks in the window. The **Show Special Characters** button changes text frames so that each space, tab, and paragraph marker is displayed with special characters. To return to plain text, click the button again (that changes its name to **Hide Special Characters**). Use the **Zoom** box and **Zoom In** and **Out** buttons to zoom the page view, as described in Task 9.

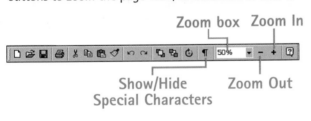

Zoom box   Zoom In

Show/Hide   Zoom Out
Special Characters

7 Summon the Office Assistant

The last button on the **Standard** toolbar looks like a question mark, and it's named **Microsoft Publisher Help**. However, it doesn't bring up the **Help** files—it calls the **Office Assistant**. See Task 16, "How to Use the Office Assistant," later in this part, for more information.

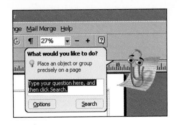

End

How-To Hints

What Exactly Are ScreenTips?

Can't remember what all those icons on the toolbars stand for? ScreenTips take care of that! Just position your cursor over a button/icon and wait for the name to appear.

What Are Frames?

Every item (object) in a publication (such as a graphic, title, or plain text) is contained within a frame that's moveable and resizeable.

How to Use the Objects Toolbar

Everything you enter into a publication is stored within a frame, and the frames you need are created with the **Objects** toolbar.

This toolbar is positioned vertically on the left side of your screen, but you can move it by placing your pointer on the ridge at the top of the toolbar and dragging it to a different location.

Begin

1 Pointer Tool

The first (topmost) button on the **Objects** toolbar is the **Pointer Tool** button. Click it when you need to have your mouse pointer work in its usual fashion instead of displaying a special pointer indicating some task that's in process. You can click anywhere in the **Publisher** window, outside the pages, to accomplish the same thing.

——Pointer Tool

2 Text Frames

Use the **Text Frame Tool** and **Table Frame Tool** buttons to create plain text frames and table text frames.

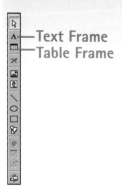

——Text Frame
——Table Frame

3 Graphic Frames

The next three buttons are for creating graphic frames. Use the **WordArt Frame Tool** button to create WordArt. (See Part 3, Tasks 12 and 13.) The **Picture Frame Tool** button is used to insert a picture file, usually something you've scanned, downloaded, or received from a friend. The **Clip Gallery Tool** button is used to create a frame that holds clip art or other objects from the Microsoft Clip Gallery. (See Part 3, Tasks 9 and 10.)

——WordArt Frame
——Picture Frame
——Clip Gallery

4 Shapes

The four Shapes buttons are **Line Tool**, **Oval Tool** (also used for circles), **Rectangle Tool** (also used for squares), and **Custom Shapes**. Click any of the first three to create a standard shape. Click the **Custom Shapes** button to open a selection of shapes you can choose from.

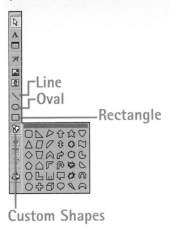

—Line
—Oval
—Rectangle

Custom Shapes

5 Web Tools

The three Web tool buttons are accessible only when you're working on a Web publication (these buttons are grayed out for standard publications). The **Hot Spot Tool** button is used to create a spot on a graphic into which you insert a hyperlink. The **Form Control** button is used to create forms on your Web pages. The **HTML Code Fragment** button creates frames that hold HTML code. Information about all these Web tools is found throughout Part 6, "Creating a Web Publication."

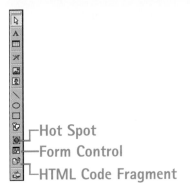

—Hot Spot
—Form Control
—HTML Code Fragment

6 Standard Design Gallery

When you're working on a regular publication (as opposed to a Web publication), use the **Design Gallery Object** button to open the **Design Gallery** window. You'll find a host of special elements, including calendars, coupons, and tons of elaborate, professional designs you can use for headlines and attention-getters. Learn about using the Design Gallery in "How to Use the Design Gallery," which is Task 3 in Part 4.

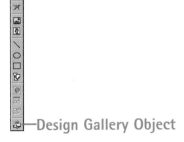

—Design Gallery Object

7 Web Design Gallery

Clicking the **Design Gallery Object** button when working on a Web publication brings up the Design Gallery; lots of objects that are designed specifically for Web pages are included.

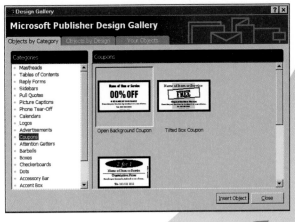

End

How to Use Layout Guides

Every publication you create has to be designed and printed around a set of margins, which mark the edges of the page. In addition to the margins, you can establish imaginary (non-printing) lines on every page for use as alignment guides. Using these guides (which do not print but appear light blue on-screen) you can lay out the publication's various elements in a professionally aligned manner.

The margins and guide lines you set for your publication are called *layout guides*, and they affect every page.

Begin

1 Use the Layout Guides Command

To change or add layout guides, choose **Arrange, Layout Guides** from the **menu bar**.

2 Set the Margins

In the **Layout Guides** dialog box, use the **Margin Guides** section to specify the margin you need for each side of the page. You can enter the numbers directly or use the **arrows** to change the defaults.

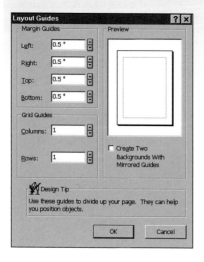

3 Set Vertical Guide Lines

If you need vertical alignment guides for the elements on your page(s), add **Columns** (one additional column for each vertical line you need). You can move these vertical lines to any position on the page after you close the dialog box.

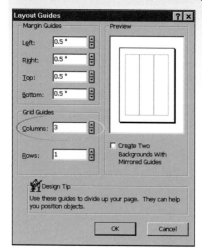

4 Set Horizontal Guide Lines

To use horizontal alignment guides, add more **Rows**. You can change the position of the guide lines after you close the dialog box.

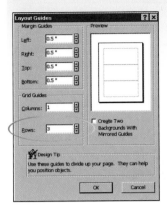

6 Fine-Tune the Layout

By default, layout guides divide your page into perfectly equal parts. To form a pleasing composition, you'll often want to move the guides so that the parts of the page are different sizes. Begin by choosing **View**, **Go to Background** from the menu. (See Part 4, Task 5, "How to Create Background Elements," to learn more about the background.) Hold the **Shift** key as you position your pointer over the line you want to move (the pointer turns into an **adjust** pointer) and drag the line where you want it. When finished, choose **View**, **Go to Foreground** to return to the foreground and work with the text and graphics on the page.

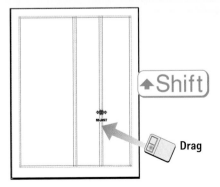

5 Create Mirrored Guide Lines

If your publication is going to be printed on both sides of the paper and then bound (binding can include staples), select the **Create Two Backgrounds With Mirrored Guides** option. Notice that the **Left** and **Right Margin Guides** are now named **Inside** and **Outside**. Make sure that the **Inside** margin specification allows enough room for your binding device. Choose **OK** to save your specifications and close the dialog box.

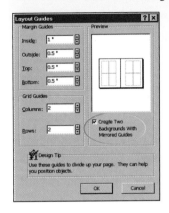

End

How to Use Ruler Guides

Sometimes you have specific pages filled with elements that should be aligned in an attractive and professional manner. Aligning those elements is easy if you employ ruler guides for each page that needs this attention. A ruler guide lines up with a specific position on a ruler, and you can use the guide line to determine the placement of frames.

These guides are created with the help of the rulers that appear on your Publisher window.

Begin

1 Select a Ruler

Select a ruler by holding down the **Shift** key as you position your pointer over a ruler. Your pointer turns into an **adjust** pointer. If you need a vertical guide, use the ruler on the left side of the **Publisher** window. For a horizontal guide, use the ruler at the top of the document window.

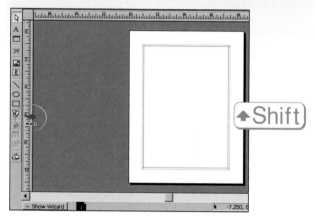

2 Drag the Ruler Guide

Drag your pointer to the appropriate position on the page. A **green line** indicates a ruler guide. (Don't worry, it doesn't print.)

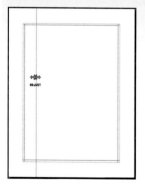

3 Adjust the Ruler Guide

You can adjust the position of any ruler guide by holding down the **Shift** key and positioning your pointer over the **green line** until your pointer turns into the **adjust** pointer. Drag the guide to a new position. When you release the **Shift** key and the mouse button, the ruler guide is in the new position (the original **green line** disappears).

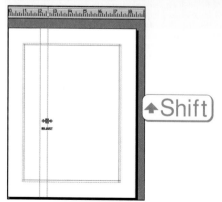

4 Add Ruler Guides Quickly

You can use menu commands if you don't want to drag a ruler guide from the ruler. Choose **Arrange**, **Ruler Guides** from the **menu bar** (you'll have to drop down the complete menu to find this command). Select **Add Horizontal Ruler Guide** or **Add Vertical Ruler Guide** from the **submenu**.

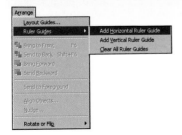

5 Position the Ruler Guide

The ruler guide is placed in the center of the page when you use the menu commands. Follow step 3 to adjust its position.

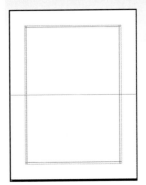

6 Delete a Ruler Guide

To delete a single ruler guide, hold down the **Shift** key and position your mouse pointer over the guide until you see an **adjust** pointer; then drag the guide back to its ruler.

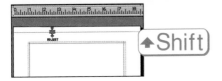

7 Delete All Ruler Guides

If you want to remove all the ruler guides you've placed on a page, choose **Arrange**, **Ruler Guides**, **Clear All Ruler Guides** from the **menu bar**.

End

How-To Hints

Take a Ruler to Work

You can move the ruler into the work area to help you resize and position objects precisely. See Task 15 in this part for help.

How to Change the View

You can change the way your Publisher window looks, or you can change the way your publication appears in the window. This can make it easier to work and can even help you work faster.

Begin

1 Hide and Show Guides

As you work, having the guide lines visible makes it easy to position elements correctly. However, if you want to view your publication's elements without the distractions of those lines, you can eliminate them from the Publisher window. Choose **View**, **Hide Boundaries and Guides** from the **menu bar**. To use the guides again, choose **View** from the **menu bar** and you'll see that the command has changed to **Show Boundaries and Guides**.

2 View the Actual Size

You can view the page and its elements in actual size. To display the page in actual size, select **100%** from the Zoom box. To return to full-page view, select **Whole Page**.

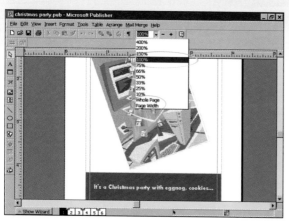

3 Grab a Ruler

Whenever you're working with a page element that must be a specific size, you can bring the ruler to the element. To do this, position your pointer over the ruler until the pointer becomes a **double-headed arrow**. Drag the ruler to the frame you want to measure.

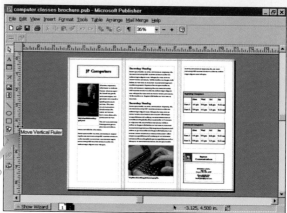

Click & Drag

4 Use the Ruler to Resize

The ruler appears when you release the mouse. You can move or resize the frame to match the measurements you need. For information on moving and resizing frames, see Part 2, Task 3, "How to Resize and Move Text Frames," and Part 3, Tasks 3, "How to Move, Resize, and Crop Shapes," and 19, "How to Move, Resize, and Crop Graphic Frames." (Drag the ruler back to its original spot when you're finished using it.)

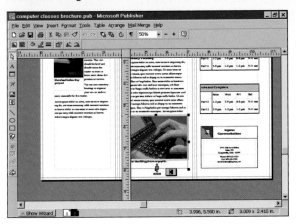

5 Change the Display of Pictures

If you have complicated, busy pictures (graphic images with a lot of elements and details), moving through your document can become a slow process. That's because Publisher has to draw the picture(s) on the page as you move to each page. To change the way pictures display, choose **View**, **Picture Display** from the **menu bar**.

6 Choose a Picture Display Mode

When the **Picture Display** dialog box opens, select a new display mode. You might want to try each alternative to see which one works best for you. Choose **OK** to save your selection.

End

How-To Hints

Viewing and Hiding Toolbars

Just like most Windows software, Publisher has choices on the **View** menu for viewing and hiding toolbars and the ruler. If you don't need one or more of these elements (at least for the moment), getting rid of them gives you more room to work in the **document** window.

How to Use the Office Assistant

I haven't met anyone with a mild reaction to the Office Assistant—people either love it or hate it. This animated character appeared first in Office 97 and has been a part of Office ever since. It's available whenever you want a hint about your current task, or if you have a specific question.

Begin

1 Call the Assistant

The Office Assistant is so eager to help that there are a wide choice of ways to call on it: Press **F1**; choose **Help, Microsoft Publisher Help**; or click the **question mark** on the **Standard toolbar**.

Click

2 Enter a Question

The Office Assistant shows up with a **bubble**, ready for you to enter a question. As soon as you begin typing, the Office Assistant's message is deleted in order to make room for your characters.

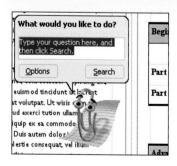

3 Start the Search

Click **Search** (or press **Enter**) to have the Office Assistant search the Help files for Help pages that contain your query.

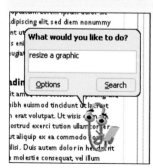

4 Choose a Help Topic

Most of the time, the Office Assistant offers a choice of Help topics related to your query. Select the one that seems to be on target. Click the **See more** arrow to see the additional topics that don't fit on the balloon.

5 Read the Help Page

The **Help Contents** window opens so that you can see the Help topic. If you want to view another Help topic, click it in the Office Assistant's bubble.

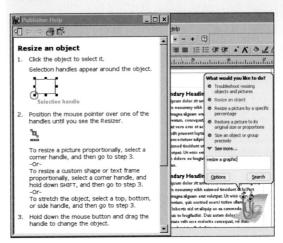

6 Browse the Help Window

Related topics, appearing as blue, underlined text, are often listed at the bottom of the Help window. To view one of these topics, click its name. (When you move the mouse pointer over one of these hyperlinks, it changes to a hand.)

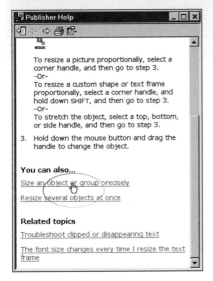

7 Close the Help Window

You can return to a previously viewed Help topic by clicking the **Back** button as many times as necessary. Return to your original topic by clicking the **Forward** button. When you're through viewing Help, click the Windows **Close** button (the **X**).

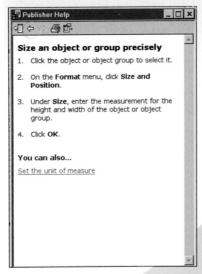

Continues

9 Configure the Office Assistant

To change the Assistant's options, right-click the image and select **Options** from the shortcut menu. You can also click the balloon's **Options** button to configure the behavior of the Office Assistant.

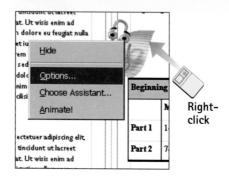

Right-click

8 Hide the Assistant

After closing the Help window, notice that the Office Assistant remains on-screen. If you want to ask another question, just click the Assistant to display the help bubble. To hide the Assistant, right-click the image and select **Hide** from the shortcut menu.

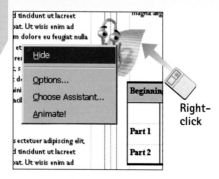

Right-click

10 Setting Options

Select the options you want from the **Options** tab of the **Office Assistant** dialog box.

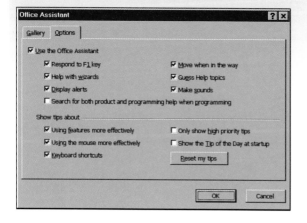

11 Change the Office Assistant Persona

You can select a different Office Assistant (perhaps you have a problem with paper clips). Click the **Gallery** tab in the **Office Assistant** dialog box.

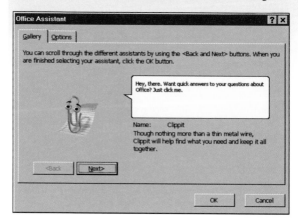

12 Move Through the Gallery

Click **Next** to move through the Office Assistant characters available to you in the gallery and choose the one you like best; then click **OK**.

End

How-To Hints

Navigating Help

For more information on how to navigate from one Help window to another and how to use the Contents window, Answer Wizard, and Index, see Task 17.

Retire the Assistant

To turn off the Assistant so that you can access Help directly, select the **Use the Office Assistant** option (turn it off) in step 10.

How to Use Contents, Answer Wizard, and Index

In addition to the Office Assistant, there are other ways you can get help from Microsoft: the Contents page, the Answer Wizard, and the Index.

Begin

1 Display the Help Tabs

In the Help Window, click the **Show** button (the leftmost icon at the top of the window) to display the Help tabs.

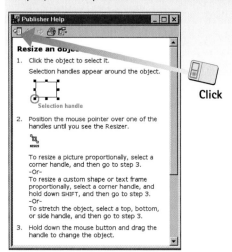

Click

2 Use the Contents

Click the **Contents** tab to display the Contents list. To expand a category, click its **plus sign**. To hide the topic, click the **minus sign** that appears. When you find a topic that interests you, click it; the topic description appears in the right pane.

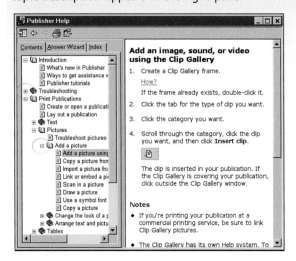

3 Use a How? Link

Some topics contain a **How?** hyperlink; when you click this link, another Help window opens. After reading the detailed how-to directions, click the **Close** button (the **X**) to close the window and return to the main Help window.

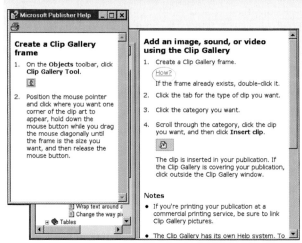

4 Ask a Troubleshooting Question

Many topics in the Troubleshooting category can help you if you encounter a problem. Expand the Troubleshooting category by clicking its **plus sign**, then click a **related topic**. A list of associated pages appears in the right pane. Click a **link** to a page to display that information.

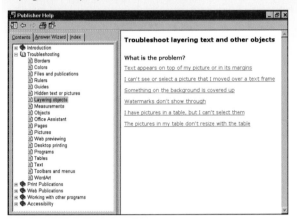

5 View a Tutorial

Some topics may include a link to a **tutorial**. To play the tutorial, click the link.

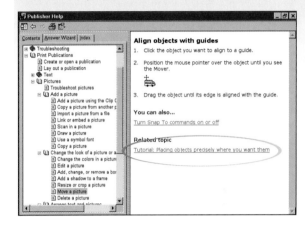

6 Navigate the Tutorial

Use the **page icons** to move from page to page in the tutorial. To view a list of additional tutorials, click the **Contents** icon (to the left of the page 1 icon). Click the **Close** button to close the Tutorial window when you're through.

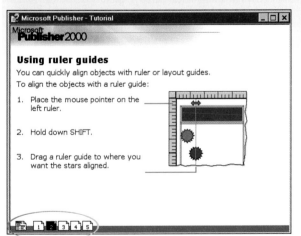

7 Use the Answer Wizard

The Answer Wizard is similar to the Office Assistant. Click the Answer Wizard tab, then type your question or keywords in the text box and press **Enter**.

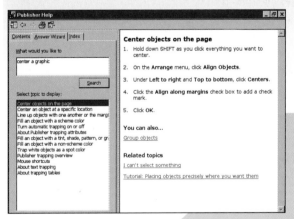

Continues

8 Display a Topic

Click a topic in the **Select Topic to Display** list, and it appears in the right pane.

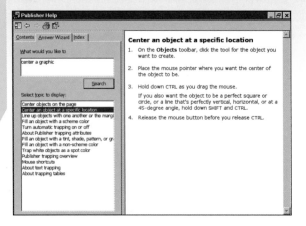

9 Use the Index

The **Index** allows you to search topic contents. Click the **Index** tab, and type a keyword or click one in the list. Click **Search**.

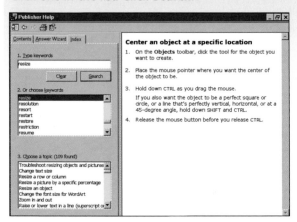

10 Display a Topic

Click a topic in the **Choose a Topic** list, and it appears in the right pane.

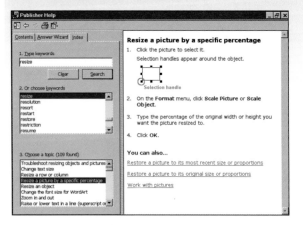

11 Close the Help Window

When you're through using Help, click its **Close** button.

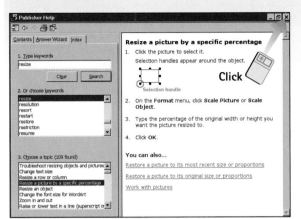

End

Print a Topic

You can print a Help topic by displaying it and then clicking the **Print** button at the top of the Help Window.

Bypass the Assistant

You can bypass the Assistant and go directly to Help when you click the **Microsoft Publisher Help** button if you select the option that turns the Assistant off. See Task 18 in this part for more information.

How to Get Help from Microsoft

Microsoft maintains a Web site for Publisher and you can go there without closing the software.

If your browser doesn't automatically connect to your Internet service provider when you launch it, you have to establish the connection before you use the steps discussed here.

Begin

1 Choose the Command

Choose **Help, Microsoft Publisher Web Site** from the **menu bar**. This command launches your browser and points it to the Publisher Web site.

2 Get Support

Click **Assistance** to get help on Publisher.

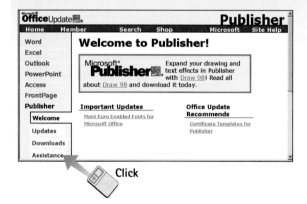

3 Search the Knowledge Base

To search for help, click **View Popular Topics for Publisher**.

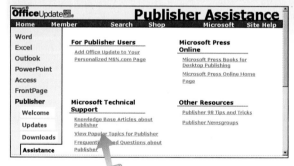

4 Personal Support Center

The Personal Support Center can serve as a "home base" as you search for help. Click **Search Support** at the top of the page.

Click

5 Enter a Query

Under step **3** on the screen, type a word or short phrase related to the Help topic you're looking for. The text that Microsoft placed in the box is deleted as soon as you start typing your own text. The default options for searching work best, so don't bother to change them. Click **go** to begin your search.

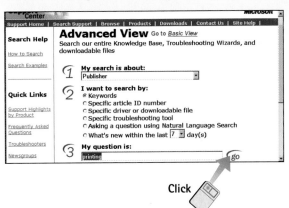

Click

6 Scan the Articles

A list of articles related to your query is displayed in the window, along with a reminder of the word(s) you entered. The first couple of lines from each article are displayed to give you an idea of the contents. Click any article that seems to provide the help you need.

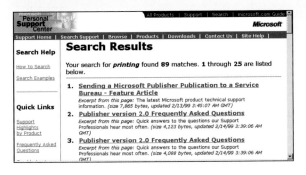

7 Using the Article

If a helpful article is available, click your browser's **Print** button to print it. You can also use the tools on your browser to select it and then you can copy it to a word processor (or to Notepad to save it to your hard disk). Use the **navigation** buttons on your browser to return to the list of articles. Continue until you have found all the available information on the topic.

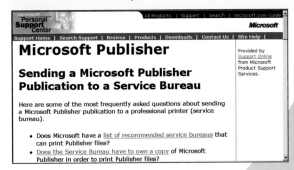

Continues

8 Return to "Home Base"

Return to the Personal Support Center by clicking your browser's **Back** button as many times as needed. Click **Frequently Asked Questions**.

Click

9 View the FAQs Page

Frequently Asked Questions (FAQs) are a collection of questions asked by other users like you. Click your version of Publisher to view a list of FAQs for that version.

10 Select a Question

Choose an area of interest from the list that appears. Then choose a question. The answer to that question appears.

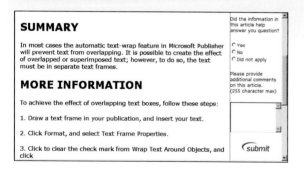

11 Return to Office Update

Click your browser's **Back** button as needed to return the Office Update page for Publisher

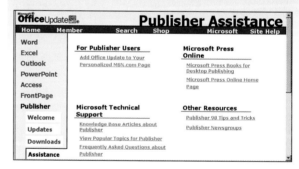

12 View Recommended Updates

On the **Updates** tab, you'll find links to files that will update your version of Publisher.

Office Update					Publisher Updates
Home	Member	Search	Shop	Microsoft	Site Help

Word	**Draw 98 for Office 97 and Publisher**
Excel	Filesize: 959 kb Last Updated: 09-Feb-98 Est. Download Time @ 28.8: 6 min(s)
Outlook	The Draw 98 Update for Microsoft® Office enhances the drawing
PowerPoint	features on Microsoft Word 97, and makes those features available in all of the Office programs.
Access	
FrontPage	**More Euro Enabled Fonts for Microsoft Office**
Publisher	Filesize: 2436 kb Last Updated: 10-Feb-99 Est. Download Time @ 28.8: 15 min(s)
Welcome	The More Euro Enabled Fonts for Microsoft® Office package adds
Updates	additional fonts with the euro glyph.
Downloads	
Assistance	

13 View Available Downloads

On the **Downloads** tab, you'll find files of interest. To download a file, click its **Add** box. Click as many files as you want, then click **Go to Basket**.

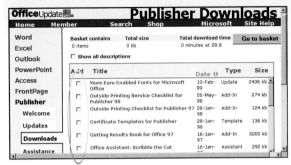

End

How-To Hints

Stop Fumbling Around

Each Web page you visit has a **Search** button on the **navigation bar**. Click it to avoid wandering aimlessly through the Microsoft support site.

How to Save and Retrieve Publications

Saving and retrieving documents are necessary processes, no matter what software you're using.

Begin

1 Choose a Save Command

You have several choices for issuing the Save command: Click the **Save** button on the **Standard** toolbar; press **Ctrl+S**; or choose **File, Save** from the **menu bar**. The first two options are easier and faster than the **menu bar** option.

Click

2 Saving for the First Time

The first time you save a publication, the **Save As** dialog box appears so that you can enter a name for the file. Click **Save** after entering that name. As you continue to work, you can use any of the methods enumerated in Step 1 to continue to save your work.

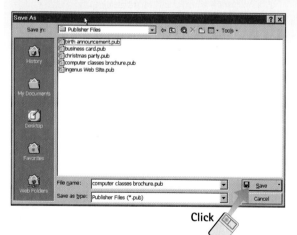

Click

3 Publisher Reminders

Publisher automatically reminds you to save your work every 15 minutes. This nagging message is really a form of insurance for you. To save your work when this message appears, click **Yes**.

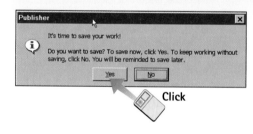

Click

4 Close a File

Choose **File**, **Close** to close a file so that you can work on another file. (Publisher permits only one open file at a time, unlike other Windows software.) If you've made changes since the last time you saved the file, you're given an opportunity to save the file before it's closed.

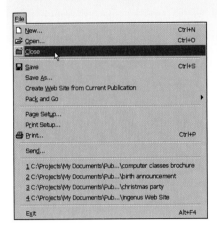

5 Open a File

After a file has been saved, you can open it to make changes anytime you want. Click the **Open** button on the **Standard toolbar** (or, if you prefer the long way, choose **File**, **Open** from the **menu bar**). When the **Open** dialog box appears, select the file you want to work on and click **Open**.

Click

6 Save with a Different Name

If you want to save a file under a different filename, choose **File**, **Save As** from the **menu bar**. This method is useful for making a copy of a file in which you've made changes, but you're not sure whether you like the changes. Now you have a copy of the file with and without your experimental elements.

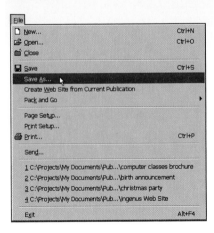

How-To Hints

Custom Saves

You can change the interval at which Publisher prompts you to save your work with the **Tools**, **Options** command. You can also change the directory you use to save your files. See Task 20 for help.

End

How to Set Options for Publisher

As you use and become comfortable with Publisher, you should change its behavior to match the way you want to work. There are plenty of customization options available to accomplish this goal.

Begin

1 Changing Options

Choose **Tools**, **Options** from the **menu bar**.

2 Set General Options

When the **Options** dialog box appears, the **General** tab is in the foreground. There are quite a few important customizations you can effect in this tab.

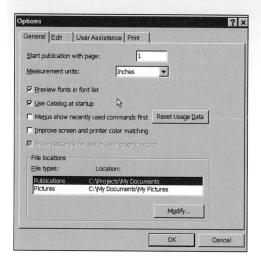

3 Change the Font List

By default, Publisher shows you its font list with each font displaying its appearance. If you find this annoying, click the **Preview fonts in font list** option on the **General** tab to remove the check mark. Now your font list appears in plain type (which you may find easier to read).

4 Start with a Blank Page

After you've been using Publisher for a while, you may prefer to start every publication from scratch. To open Publisher and see a blank page, click the **Use Catalog at startup** option to remove the check mark. (If you occasionally need the Catalog, just choose **File**, **New** from the **menu bar** to view the Catalog.)

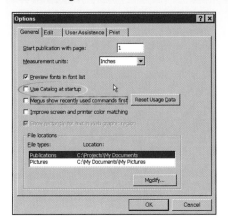

5 Customizable Menus

Menus in Office 2000 display only those commands you use most often. To display full menus, deselect the **Menus show recently used commands first** option.

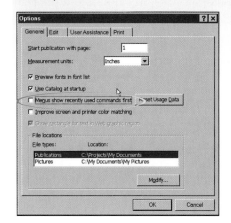

6 Other General Options

At the top of the General tab, there are a few options that aren't commonly changed, but you may find either (or both) necessary for the way you work. You can specify a new number in the **Start publication with page** box if you don't want your first page number to be 1. This is useful if the publications you create are inserted in predesigned covers that use Page 1 (and Page 2 if printed on both sides). Change the **Measurement units** to **Centimeters**, **Picas**, or **Points** if you don't want to work with inches. You can also change the default location of your files.

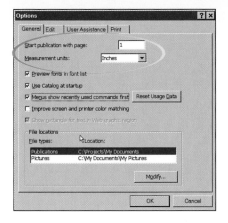

7 Set Edit Options

Move to the **Edit** tab in the **Options** dialog box to choose editing options. Start with the dialog box's **Text editing** section, where the options are self-explanatory (and are the same as word-processing software options).

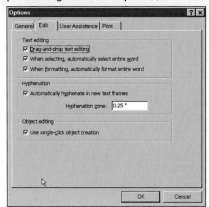

Continues

8 Set Hyphenation

You can turn off automatic hyphenation or change the hyphenation zone to alter the way automatic hyphenation works. The *zone* is the amount of space between the last character on a line and the right margin. Making the zone smaller increases the number of hyphens (and vice versa). For more information about hyphenation, read Part 5's Task 6, "How to Perfect Hyphenation."

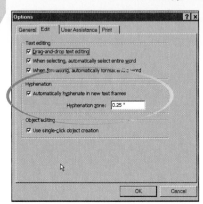

9 Create Frames with a Click

If you click the box next to the **Use single-click object creation** option to deselect it, frames won't pop into your publication with a mouse click. Instead, you must drag each frame to create it (which means that you size it to your specifications as you create it). Some people find this easier because they accidentally click and then have to resize the frame. Read Task 2, "How to Create a Text Frame," in Part 2, and Task 9, "How to Insert Clip Art," Task 10, "How to Insert Pictures," and Task 12, "How to Insert WordArt," in Part 3.

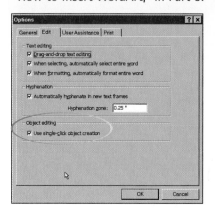

10 Set Assistance Options

The top section of the **User Assistance** tab has options you can change to increase or decrease the amount of unasked-for help that Publisher provides. For example, you can change the interval at which Publisher prompts you to save your work.

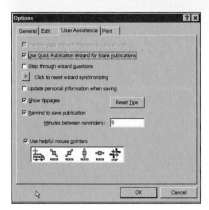

11 Reset Synchronization

Click the button named **Click to reset wizard synchronizing** to reset the current document's synchronization (this option isn't a global option). *Synchronization* is a Publisher feature that coordinates special data such as personal information to make sure that everything in the document agrees. See Task 4, "Creating a Personal Information Set," for more details about this special data.

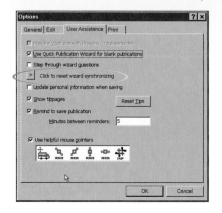

12 Set Up Pointers with Messages

When you are dragging, sizing, moving, or otherwise manipulating frames, your mouse pointer displays a different shape and also displays text to indicate its current status. If you deselect the **Use helpful mouse pointers** option, the pointers still change to a different shape, but there's no text reminder.

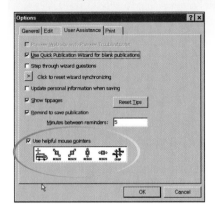

13 Configure Printing for Publications

Move to the **Print** tab in the **Options** dialog box to set the global options for printing (these options are self-explanatory).

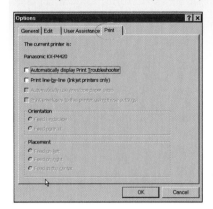

14 Configure Printing for Envelopes

If the current document is an envelope, more choices become available in the **Options** dialog box's **Print** tab. Select **Print envelopes to this printer using these settings**, and then specify the way you handle envelopes for the printer.

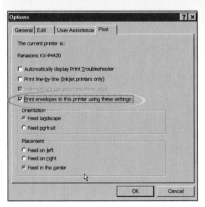

15 Save Your New Options

When you have finished selecting and deselecting options on all the tabs in the **Options** dialog box, click **OK** to save your settings.

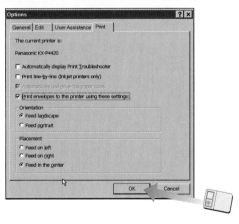

Click

End

Task

1 How to Replace Sample Text 54

2 How to Create a Text Frame 56

3 How to Resize and Move Text Frames 58

4 How to Format Text Appearance 60

5 How to Create Special Text Effects 62

6 How to Format Text Frames 64

7 How to Copy Formatting Quickly 66

8 How to Create Lists 68

9 How to Create Columns in Text Frames 70

10 How to Work with Overflow Text 72

11 How to Create Continued Notices 74

12 How to Create a Style 76

13 How to Import Styles from Publications 78

14 How to Import Styles from Word Processors 80

PART 2

Working with Text

You'll probably devote a great deal of space to text in most of your publications. You have a message, a story, an article—you have something to say—and that's frequently the most important part of your publication. In fact, if all you needed to do was show a bunch of images, you'd probably be using different software (such as Microsoft PowerPoint, which is designed to make slide shows instead of publications).

The text you present in your publication will have more impact if it's professionally presented. That means you must pay attention to the size of text as well as to the way it lays out. Headlines have a purpose, as do body text and lists. Laying out your document so that each text element has the right effect on the reader is part of learning to create slick publications.

Whether you're making an announcement with a headline, drawing attention to a picture, or telling a story that crosses several pages, Publisher has tools to assist you. In this part, you learn how to use those tools.

How to Replace Sample Text

When you create a publication using a wizard, the wizard places sample text in key locations, such as the heading area. To complete the publication, you must replace this sample text with your own text.

Begin

1 Select the Sample Text

Click the frame that contains the text you want to replace. All the text is automatically selected (highlighted).

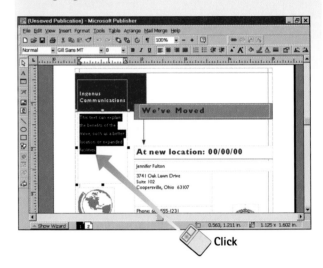

Click

2 Replace Sample Text

Type your text—what you type replaces the selected sample text. Click outside the frame when you're through.

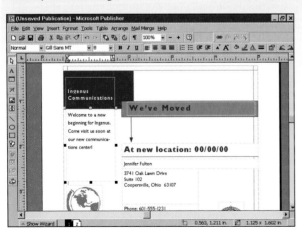

3 Make Corrections

If you make a mistake, press **Backspace** to erase it and then type the correction.

←Backspace

4 Delete Text

You can also use the mouse to drag over text to select it; then press **Delete** to remove the text.

5 Move the Cursor

To correct existing text, click at the point where you want to move the **cursor** (the vertical blinking line). Then press **Backspace** to erase characters to the left of the cursor or press **Delete** to erase characters to the right. You can also use the **arrow key** to move the cursor within a text frame.

6 Undo a Typing Correction

If you make a correction you don't like, click the **Undo** button on the Standard toolbar to undo it. You can click Undo multiple times if necessary.

Click

7 Undo an Undo

To undo an Undo, click the **Redo** button as many times as needed.

Click

End

How-To Hints

Correcting Spelling Errors

If you misspell a word, Publisher underlines it with a red wavy line. You can correct these errors as you type, or you can have Publisher check them when you're through. See Part 5, Task 2 for help.

How to Create a Text Frame

All text in a publication must be entered into a **frame**. If you start a publication from scratch, or if you want to add additional text to a predesigned page, you must insert a text frame before you can insert text.

1 Click Text Frame Tool

To add text to a publication, click the **Text Frame tool** on the **Objects** toolbar.

Click

2 Start a Text Frame

Place your pointer at the location where you want the upper-left corner of your text frame to be. Notice that your pointer has changed to a crosshair.

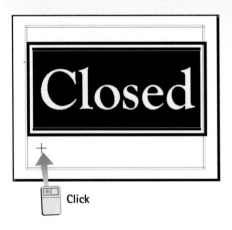

Click

3 Drag Out a Frame

Hold down the left mouse button as you drag down and to the right to form the text frame. Release the mouse button when the frame is the proper size and shape.

Drag

4 Enter Text

After you release the mouse button, notice that the cursor appears inside the frame. To enter text, just type. Click outside the frame when you're through.

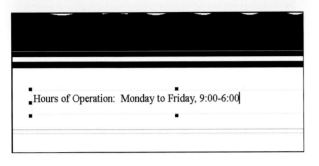

5 Creating a Vertical Rectangle

If you want a vertical rectangle (or you're not comfortable dragging the mouse), click the **Text Frame tool,** position your mouse where you want the center of the text frame to be, and click to create the text frame..

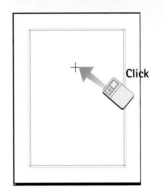

Click

6 Undoing Mistakes

If you don't like the text frame or its position on the page, click the **Undo** button on the **Standard** toolbar. Then start again.

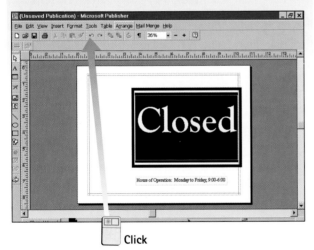

Click

End

How-To Hints

Make Room

If you used a wizard to design your publication, text frames are already in place. However, many times you'll want to insert additional text frames to hold special information such as headings. You'll probably have to make room for a new frame by changing the size of existing frames. See "How to Resize and Move Text Frames" in the following task.

How to Resize and Move Text Frames

There are a slew of reasons to resize or move text frames: If you use the one-click method of creating text frames, you almost always have to change the size—Publisher can't read your mind. Sometimes you have too much text and have to make the frame larger (or too little text and you want a smaller frame). Then there are those times you have to decide whether a heading should appear above or below an illustration, so you move the frame up and down until you like what you see.

Begin

1 Select a Frame

Click the frame to select it, which causes sizing handles (small black squares) to appear around the frame.

2 Move Any Side of a Frame

To move any side of a frame to make it either larger or smaller, place your pointer on one of the sizing handles along the side. Your pointer turns into a **Resize** pointer.

3 Drag to Resize a Frame

Press and hold the left mouse button as you drag the sizing handle in the appropriate direction. Release the mouse button when the side is where you want it.

Drag

4 Resize Proportionately

To change two sides at the same time, place your mouse pointer on one of the corner sizing handles. Your pointer turns into a **Resize** pointer again, but this time it's on an angle. Drag the corner and watch both sides adjust.

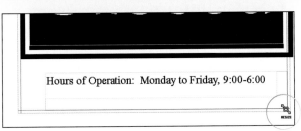

5 Text Automatically Adjusts

When you resize a frame, text automatically adjusts to fit the boundaries of the frame.

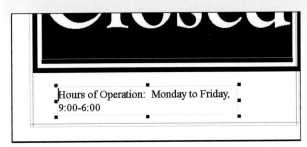

6 Change Opposite Sides Equally

To keep the center of the text frame centered (which means an equal movement on the opposite side), hold down the **Ctrl** key while you drag.

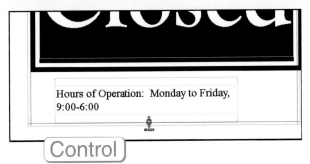

7 Move the Frame

To move a text frame, place your pointer on the outside edge of the frame between any two sizing handles. Your pointer turns into a moving van. Press and hold the left mouse button as you drag the text frame to a new location.

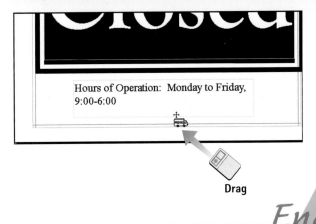

Drag

End

How-To Hints

Cancel Your Dragging Action

If you change your mind while you're dragging, press the **Esc** key to cancel the drag.

Too Much Text

If you resize a frame so that the text it contains cannot be fully displayed, an **overflow symbol** appears (the letter **A** followed by three dots). See Task 10 in this part for help.

How to Format Text Appearance

There's nothing more boring (and unprofessional) than plain, unformatted text. Bleh! No matter what your message is (even if it's on a boring topic), it's more effective to use special formatting to add pizzazz.

Notice that as soon as you click anywhere in a text frame, the frame is selected and the **Formatting toolbar** appears in your **Publisher** window.

2 Change Fonts

To change the font, click the **arrow** to the right of the Font box in the **Formatting** toolbar and choose a new Font. As a shortcut, you can begin entering the characters of the font name to move to that section of the Font list quickly. To change the font size, click the arrow to the right of the **Font Size** box and select a new size. You can also increase or decrease the font by one size with the Decrease/Increase Font Size buttons.

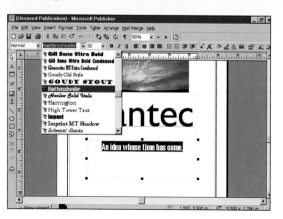

1 Select Text

Select the text you want to format. You can drag your mouse across the text to select it or use the keyboard shortcuts listed in the How-To Hints on the next page.

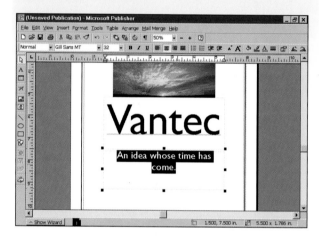

3 Add Bold, Italic, or Underline

To add bold, italic, or underline formatting (or any combination of these attributes), click the appropriate button on the **Formatting** toolbar.

Italic

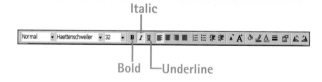

Bold   Underline

4 Change Text Alignment

Text is normally left-aligned (placed against the left edge of the frame). To center text within its frame, click the **Center** button. To right-align text or fully justify it (so that text touches both the left and right margins), click the appropriate button.

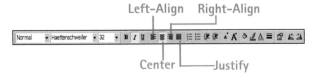

Left-Align   Right-Align

Center   Justify

5 Adjust Spacing Between Letters

You can adjust the spacing between letters (also known as **kerning**) in the **Character Spacing** dialog box, which you open by choosing **Format**, **Character Spacing** from the **menu bar**.

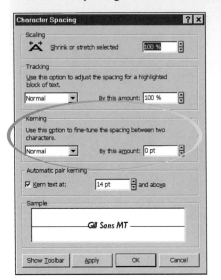

6 Adjust Spacing Between Lines

Change the spacing between lines (very effective if you have lists) with the **Line Spacing** dialog box. Choose **Format**, **Line Spacing** from the **menu bar**. You can also add a blank line before or after a paragraph using this dialog box.

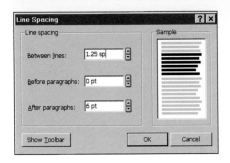

End

How-To Hints

Quick Shortcuts for Selecting Text

All text in a frame	**Ctrl+A**
One character	**Shift+Right Arrow/Left Arrow**
One word	**Ctrl+Shift+Right Arrow/Left Arrow**
To the end of the line	**Shift+End**
To the start of the line	**Shift+Home**
To the start or end of the paragraph	**Ctrl+Shift+Up Arrow/Down Arrow**

Too Much Text?

If your formatting adjustments prevent all the text from appearing in a frame, you can resize the text or the frame. See Task 10 in this part for help.

How to Create Special Text Effects

In addition to the common formatting changes that alter the appearance of characters, you may want to create some special effects for your text. These effects are frequently employed as attention-getting techniques.

Begin

1 Select Text

Select the text you want to format.

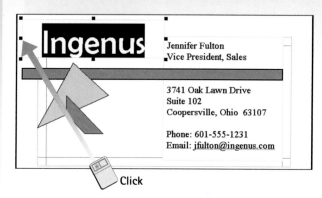

Click

2 Colorizing Text

To colorize the text, click the **Font Color** button on the **Formatting** toolbar. The colors that fit into your selected color scheme are displayed, and you can click the color you want for this text.

Click

3 Additional Text Colors

Choose **More Colors** from the drop-down menu to see a larger palette, then select the color you want to use. Choose **OK** to return to your page, where your text is still highlighted (so you can't see the color). Click anywhere outside the text frame to see the effect.

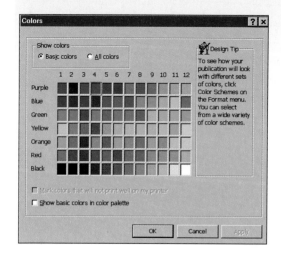

4 Rotating Text 90 Degrees

To rotate the text frame 90 degrees, click the frame to select it and click the **Rotate Left** or **Rotate Right** button on the **Formatting** toolbar.

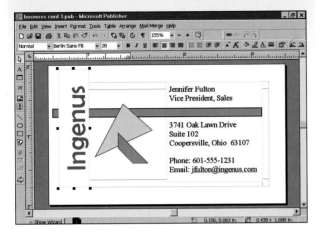

5 Rotating Text Manually

To rotate the frame by a different number of degreesthan 90, select the frame and click the **Custom Rotate** button on the **Standard** toolbar. In the **Custom Rotate** dialog box, specify the degrees and direction. Rotating text frames usually requires a further step: You must resize, move, or both.

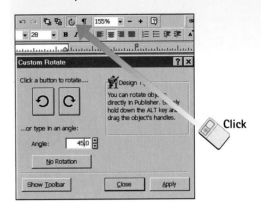

Click

6 Adding Drop Caps

To add a drop cap, select the frame and choose **Format**, **Drop Cap** from the **menu bar** to open the **Drop Cap** dialog box. Choose a drop-cap style and see the effect in the **Preview** frame.

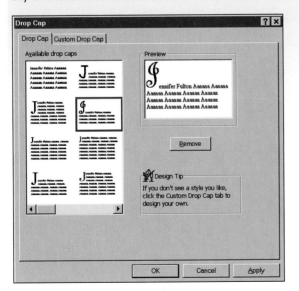

7 Customizing Drop Caps

To design your own drop cap, click the **Custom Drop Cap** tab and select the settings you want. Choose **Apply** to see the effect, then tweak until it's perfect. Choose **OK** to save the drop cap.

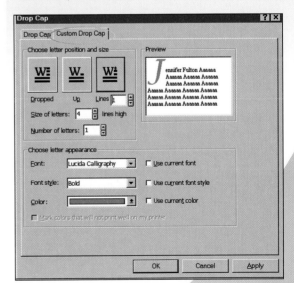

End

How to Format Text Frames

In addition to formatting the text that resides in your text frames, you can format the frame itself. This adds to the eye-catching appeal of frames and is especially effective for headings, captions, and short lists.

1 Colorizing the Frame

Select the frame to begin decorating it. You can preformat the text that's in the frame, or wait until you've formatted the frame. To colorize the frame, click the **Fill Color** icon on the **Formatting** toolbar.

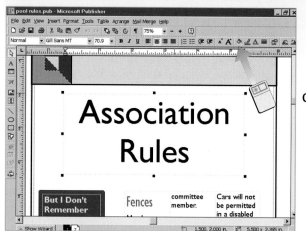

Click

2 Choose More Colors

Only a few color choices appear on the **Fill Color** menu, so choose **More Colors** to see a larger palette.

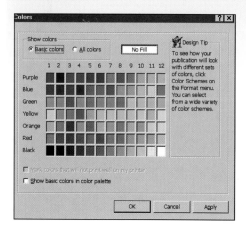

3 Add Depth/Texture to Text Frames

To add depth, texture, or both to the look of the frame, choose **Fill Effects** from the **Fill Color** menu. Then either select **Patterns** to add an interesting textured background, or select **Gradients** to add a more subtle feeling of depth.

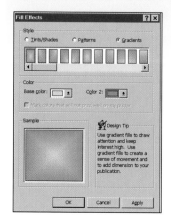

4 Align Text in a Frame

To position the text within the top and bottom margins of the frame, choose **Format**, **Align Text Vertically**, and then choose an alignment pattern from the menu. To align text horizontally, click the appropriate button (such as **Align Left**) on the **Formatting** toolbar.

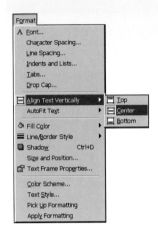

5 Add Shadows to a Text Frame

Press **Ctrl+D** to add a shadow to the text frame. (It's a toggle, so if you change your mind, press **Ctrl+D** again.)

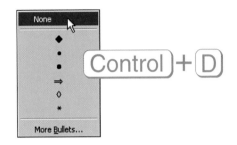

6 Add Borders to a Text Frame

Click the **Line/Border Style** icon on the **Formatting** toolbar to select a quick border from the **drop-down menu**.

7 Format Borders

Choose **More Styles** from the **Line/Border Style** drop-down menu to configure a border with the settings you prefer. While you're there, look at the **BorderArt** tab, where you can find fancy, artistic borders you might want to add to the frame.

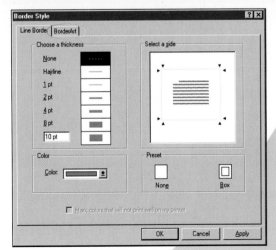

How-To Hints

Plan for Black-and-White Printing

It's tempting to add all sorts of colorful formatting gizmos to text frames, but remember that colors print as shades of gray when you don't have a color printer. That rich, deep, green background you add may print as such a dark gray that your black text disappears.

End

How to Copy Formatting Quickly

Many times, you'll create a terrific, complicated format for a particular section of text. Perhaps it's a heading or a fancy caption under a picture. You will probably want to use it again in the publication. In fact, you might want to use it many times to format similar text. This gives your publication a consistency that is slick and professional.

If you create a formatting example that is useful for many publications, consider turning it into a style. See Part 2, Tasks 12 and 13 for help.

Begin

1 Click Format Painter Tool

Select the text you've formatted to the point of perfection. Then click the Format Painter tool on the Standard toolbar.

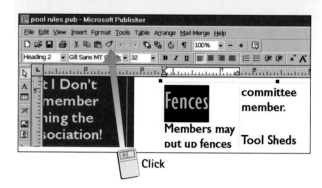

Click

2 Drag Over Text to Copy

Your mouse pointer turns into a paintbrush. Move to the text you want to format and drag your mouse pointer over the text.

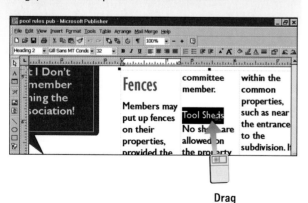

Drag

3 The Format Is Copied

The text changes to look like the text whose formatting you copied.

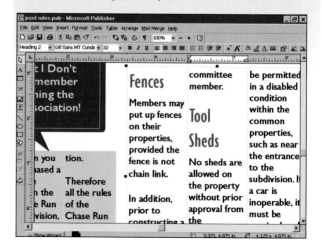

4 Copy Over and Over

If you have multiple sections of text you want to copy the formatting to, select the original text and double-click the **Format Painter** button.

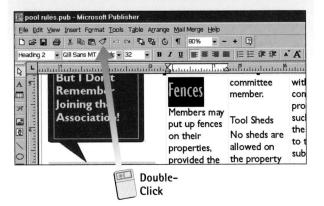

Double-Click

5 Copy Multiple Times

Drag over multiple sections of text to copy the formatting. When you're through, click the **Format Painter** button again.

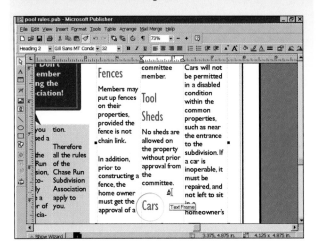

6 Copy Frame and All

You can quickly copy a frame and all its formatting, including fill, border art, columns, and so on. Just click the frame you want to copy and then click the **Format Painter** button.

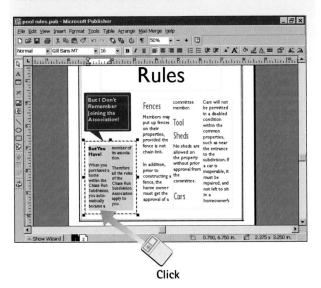

Click

7 Copy to Another Frame

Click on the other frame to copy the formatting to it.

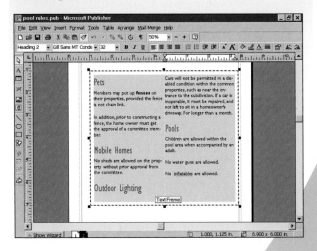

End

How to Create Lists

Sometimes important information stands out more effectively if you create a list. Since there's nothing more boring than a list of sentences on a page, Publisher provides ways to make your lists more interesting. Even better, Publisher automates the work involved so that you really don't have much to do (except tweak the formatting to make it suit your own taste).

You can create bullet lists or numbered lists with equal ease. Of course, you must create a text frame before using lists.

If you've already entered a list and want to change it to a bullet or numbered list, select the text and then use the tools described here to convert the text to lists.

Begin

1 Begin a List

To begin entering a list, position your pointer where the list starts and click the **Bullets** button on the **Formatting** toolbar. To create a numbered list, click the **Numbering** button instead.

Click

2 Enter Text

The bullet or number character appears in your text frame. Enter your text, which is automatically indented from the character. When you press **Enter**, the next bullet or number appears, and you can enter the next list item.

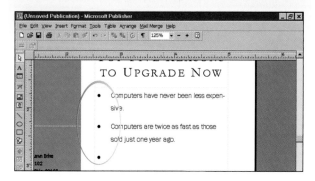

3 End a List

When you want to end the list and resume normal text, click the **Bullets** or **Numbering** button on the **Formatting toolbar** again.

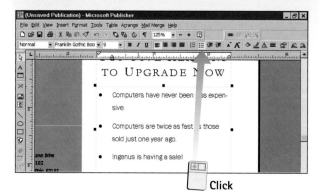

Click

4 Changing Bullet Appearance

Open the **Format** menu and select **Indents and Lists**. Bullet size, indentation, and alignment can be altered in this dialog box. Choose **Line Spacing** to see the **Line Spacing** dialog box, where you can make further changes to the appearance of the list.

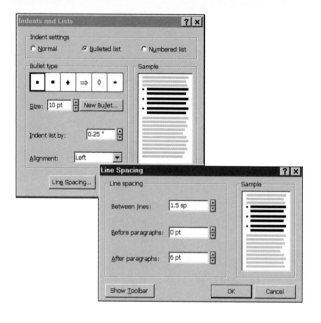

5 Change the Bullet Character

You can select a bullet character from those listed in the **Indents and Lists** dialog box, or you can import your own by clicking **New Bullet**. Select a **Font**, click the bullet you want, and click **Insert** to add it to your bullet list. In the **Indents and Lists** dialog box, click **OK**.

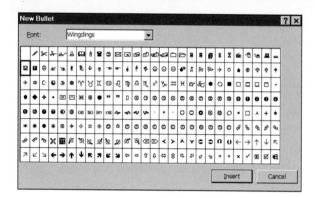

6 Change Numbered List Appearance

If you're creating a numbered list, the **Numbered List** options appear in the **Indents and Lists** dialog box. You can change the **Format** of numbers, specify **Line Spacing**, and insert a **Separator** (such as a period, comma, bracket, colon, and the like) after the number.

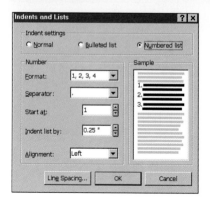

How-To Hints

Change the Start Number

If you interrupt a numbered list with regular text and want to pick up the numbering where you left off, use the **Start At** field in the **Indents and Lists** dialog box to specify the new starting number.

End

How to Create Columns in Text Frames

If you need columns in a text frame, you can create them manually, without changing your whole publication to a column format.

By default, all columns are the same width and are separated by the same amount of space when you establish columns for a text frame. However, this task provides some tricks to override that default configuration.

Begin

1 Click Text Frame Properties Icon

Click the text frame to select it, then click the **Text Frame Properties** button on the **Formatting** toolbar.

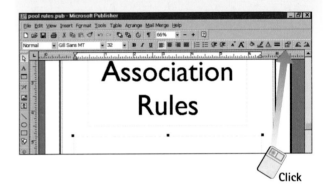

Click

2 Specify Number of Columns

In the **Text Frame Properties** dialog box, specify the **Number** of columns and the **Spacing** between them.

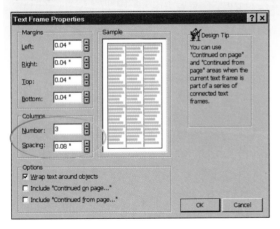

3 Enter Text

Begin entering text. As you reach the bottom of a column, the text wraps to the next column automatically.

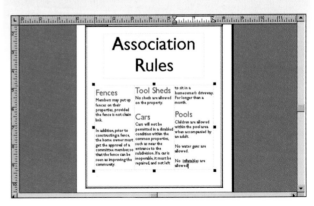

4 Resize Frames

You can drag to resize the text frame to tweak the appearance of the frame and the page. As the frame is resized, text in the columns is rearranged so that the bottom of each column touches the bottom of the frame.

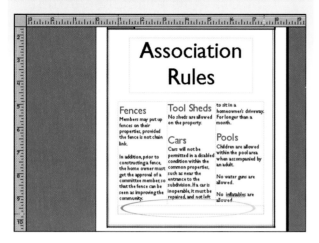

5 Create Uneven Columns

If you want to place two stories on the same page, or if you want to use uneven columns for one story, then create multiple text frames of different sizes and connect them (see Tasks 10 and 11 for help).

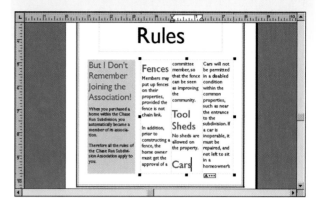

6 Create More Columns

You can create columns within the second text frame if your design warrants it.

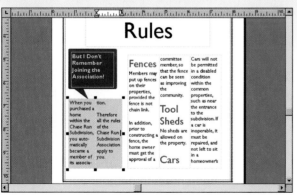

End

How-To Hints

Forcing Text to Another Column

To force text to move to the top of the next column, position the cursor at the appropriate place in the text and press **Ctrl+Shift+Enter**.

How to Work with Overflow Text

When you have a great deal to say, there may be too much text to fit in your text frame. If there's a small amount of extra text, you can probably resolve the problem with one of these easy methods:

- ✓ Edit the text to remove extraneous words. (Get rid of those multiple adverbs or use shorter adjectives.)
- ✓ Change to a smaller font size.
- ✓ Enlarge the text frame.

Frequently, however, you'll want to continue your story or article in a different frame (especially if you're designing a newsletter and want to continue a story on another page).

Begin

1 Text Overflow Indicator Button

To notify you that overflow text exists, a **Text in Overflow** indicator button appears at the bottom of the text frame.

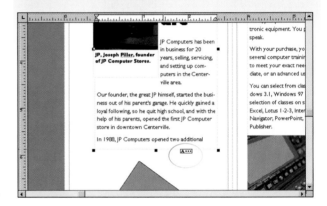

2 Inserting Text from Clipboard

If you insert text from the Clipboard (perhaps you copied it from your word processor), Publisher warns you if there's too much text. Choose **No** to refuse the offer to handle the problem automatically; you'll have far more control by using the manual steps you're learning here.

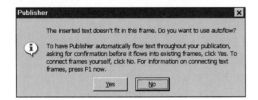

3 Create a New Text Frame

Create a text frame in the page on which you want to continue the story. Return to the original text frame and click it to select it. Choose **Tools**, **Connect Text Frames** from the **menu bar**.

4 Connect Text Frames

The **Connect Frames toolbar** appears. (The toolbar may appear at the right end of the **Standard** toolbar). Click the **Connect Text Frames** button. Your pointer turns into a **pitcher**. (The pitcher is "holding" all the text in the overflow area.)

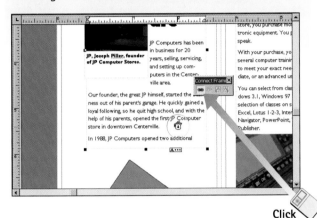

Click

5 Pouring Text into a Frame

Move to the frame you created to hold the overflow text. When you position your mouse over the frame, the **pitcher** tilts. (It's getting ready to pour the text into the frame.) Click anywhere in the frame to pour text into it.

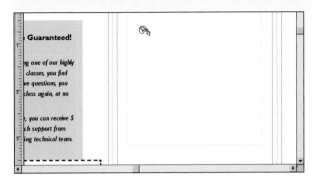

6 Add A Continued Notice

A message appears telling you that Publisher can add a **"Continued..."** notice in the previous text frame, guiding your readers to the current frame. You'll learn more about this option in Task 11, so press **Esc** to continue.

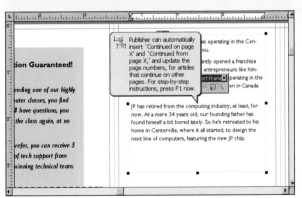

7 Go to a Previous Frame

A **Go to Previous Frame** button appears at the top of the frame; you can click it to move to the frame that holds the beginning of your story (which now has a **Go to Next Frame** button). Click the **X** in the upper-right corner of the **Connect Frames toolbar** to close it.

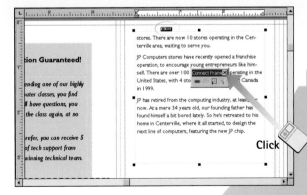

Click

End

How to Create Continued Notices

If a story or an article is continued on a different page, you can add instructions for the reader to go there. The phrases "Continued on page whatever" and "Continued from page whatever" let the reader move through your story smoothly. Publisher takes care of everything automatically, and even inserts the right page numbers.

Begin

1 Select a Frame

Click the first frame of the story to select it, then click the **Text Frame Properties** button on the **Formatting** toolbar.

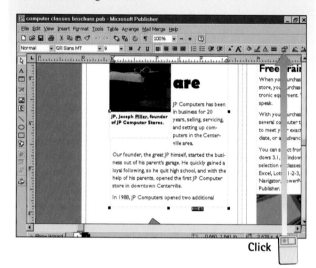

Click

2 Select Continued on Page

In the **Text Frame Properties** dialog box, select **Include "Continued on page..."** and choose **OK**. Move to the text frame on which the article is continued and do the same thing, except select **Include "Continued from page..."** in the dialog box.

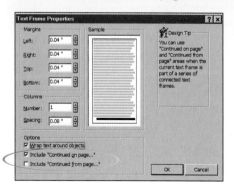

3 Auto-Insert a Page Number

Publisher automatically inserts the appropriate text and the page number.

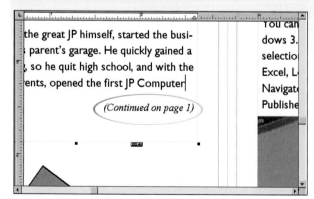

4 Change the Wording of Notice

To change the wording of the notice, remove the text and enter your own phrase. Be careful not to remove the page number code.

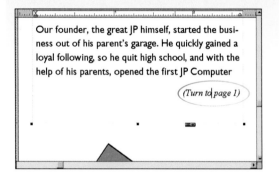

Our founder, the great JP himself, started the business out of his parent's garage. He quickly gained a loyal following, so he quit high school, and with the help of his parents, opened the first JP Computer

(Turn to page 1)

5 Change the Formatting of Notice

To change the formatting of the notice, select it and use the formatting tools on the **Formatting** toolbar or the **menu bar** to change the appearance. In this example, the font had been changed.

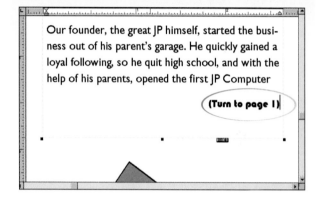

Our founder, the great JP himself, started the business out of his parent's garage. He quickly gained a loyal following, so he quit high school, and with the help of his parents, opened the first JP Computer

(Turn to page 1)

6 Accidentally Deleting a Page

If you accidentally delete the page number (which is really a code, not a number), you can replace the code. Position your pointer where you want the page number to appear in the notice and choose **Insert**, **Page Numbers** from the **menu bar**.

End

How-To Hints

Create Your Own Style

If you change the formatting of a **Continued** notice and you want all the notices in your publication to look the same, select the changed notice text and click the **Format Painter** button on the **Standard** toolbar to copy the formatting to the other notices. You can also change the style of **Continued** notices permanently (see Task 12 for help).

How to Create a Style

If you have a bunch of formatting characteristics you want to apply to text, it's silly to reinvent the wheel each time you have to format. Instead, create a *style* that's composed of all those formatting commands and apply the style to any text that should be formatted with them.

Publisher provides only a few preset styles for special types of text (such as the **Continued** notices discussed in the previous pages), so you have to create styles if you want them. Styles are created *by example*, which means that you have to format text before you can create a style.

1 Format a Sample

Apply formatting characteristics to the appropriate text to create the example you need for a style. You only have to format a single word; you don't have to select the entire paragraph. (For instance, if you want to create a style for a section heading, select a heading and format one of the words within it.)

2 Click In the Style Box

Select the word you've formatted and click the **Style** box on the **Formatting** toolbar. As soon as you click, the default style (**Normal**, which is probably the only style) is highlighted.

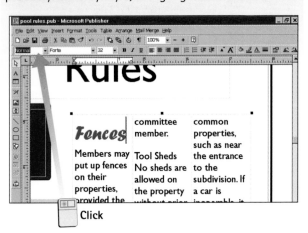

Click

3 Enter New Style Name

Enter the name for the new style (as soon as you begin typing, the highlighted text disappears and your new characters appear).

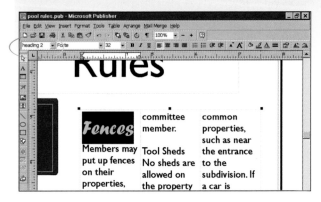

4 Save the New Style

Press **Enter**, which brings up the **Create Style by Example** dialog box. You can change the name of the style here if you want. Choose **OK** to save the style.

5 Apply the New Style

To use the style on other paragraphs you want to format with the same characteristics, select the paragraph. Choose the style by clicking the **arrow** to the right of the **Style** box and selecting the style.

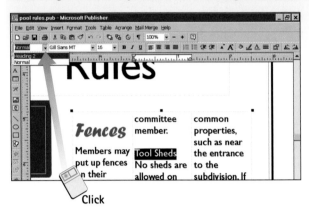

Click

6 Edit the New Style

To change the characteristics of the style, select any word that has been formatted with the style and make the formatting changes you need. Select the style from the **Style** box to bring up the **Change or Apply Style** dialog box. Select **Change the style using the selection as an example** option.

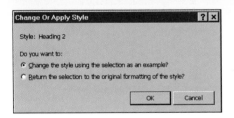

How-To Hints

You Can Import Your Styles

Styles you create are saved only in the current publication. If you want to use the style in other publications, you must import it. See the next task, "How To Import Styles from Publications," to learn how to import styles.

End

How to Import Styles from Publications

After you go to the trouble of creating styles in a publication, you can import those styles into other publications. This means, of course, that you aren't constantly reinventing the wheel. However, what is more important is the fact that having styles available in multiple publications gives your publications consistency. That's an important concept as you strive to make your output as professional as possible.

Begin

1 Choose a Text Style

Be sure that the publication into which you want to import the styles is the current document. Then choose **Format**, **Text Style** from the **menu bar**.

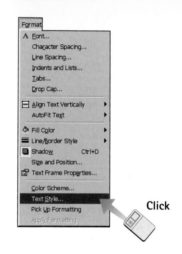

Click

2 Choose Import New Styles

In the **Text Style** dialog box, choose **Import new styles**.

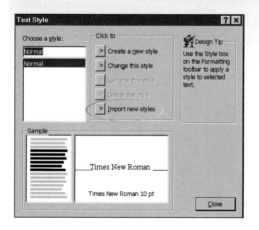

3 Double-Click to Import

When the **Import Styles** dialog box appears, make sure that the **Files of type** field is set for **Publisher Files** (which is the default). Then move to the folder where you keep your publications and double-click the file that has the styles you want to import.

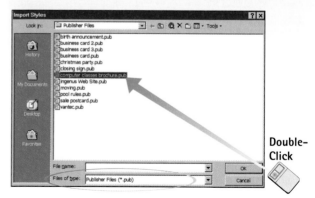

Double-Click

4 Copy Styles to Current Publication

All the styles that exist in the selected publication are copied to the current publication, as shown in the **Text Style** dialog box.

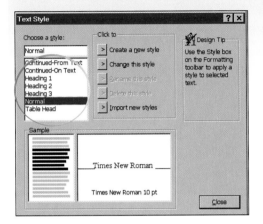

5 Check Imported Style

Check each imported style by looking at it in the **Sample** box. (It's common to find that the color scheme of an imported style doesn't match the color scheme of the current document.) If everything is fine, choose **Close** to import the styles.

6 Changing Imported Styles

If you need to adjust a style for a current publication, choose **Change this style** from the **Text Style** dialog box. When the **Change Style** dialog box opens, select the appropriate category to effect your changes. For instance, to change color, select **Character type and size**. Choose **OK** to return to the **Text Style** dialog box, and choose **Close** to import the changed styles into the current publication.

7 Apply Imported Styles

Now you can use the **Style** box on the **Formatting** toolbar to apply your newly imported styles to your publication.

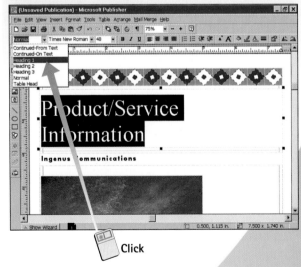

Click

End

How to Import Styles from Word Processors

Most of us use word processing software; you may have created or tweaked some styles in your word processor that you'd like to use in Publisher. You can! You can import styles from your word processing documents to take advantage of all that special formatting.

The important thing to remember is that you're not importing styles from the word processing software, but that you're importing styles from a specific document that was created in that software. Of course, once you understand this, you should open your word processor and create a document that has all sorts of styles.

Begin

1 Load Publication Needing Styles

Load the publication that needs the styles into your **Publisher** window. Then choose **Format**, **Text Style** from the **menu bar**.

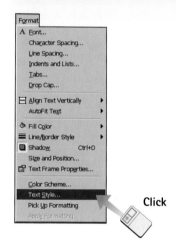

Click

2 Import the Styles

In the **Text Style** dialog box, choose **Import new styles**.

3 Locate Your Word Processor

When the **Import Styles** dialog box appears, click the **arrow** next to the **Files of type** field to see the list of supported word processors. Select your word processor.

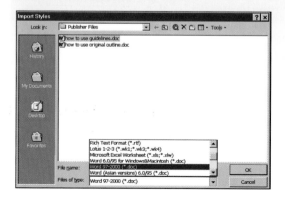

4 Locate Your Document

Use the toolbar in the dialog box to move to the folder in which you save your word processing documents. Select the document that has the styles you want to import and choose **OK** (alternatively, double-click the document icon).

Double-Click

5 Delete Unnecessary Styles

The **Text Style** dialog box now displays all the styles that were attached to the document you chose. Examine the styles you're importing. Choose **Delete this style** to remove any you don't need. You may want to tweak one or more of the styles to make them more useful in Publisher. You can accomplish that by choosing **Change this style** and making the necessary alterations.

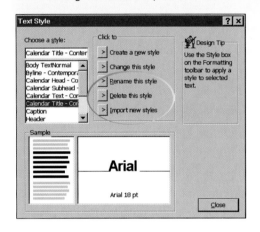

6 Apply Styles to Publication

Choose **Close** to close the **Text Style** dialog box and import the styles. Then use the **Style** box on the **Formatting** toolbar to apply the style to the text in your publication.

End

How-To Hints

Add More Templates to Get More Styles

If you use Microsoft Word, you can continue to attach templates to a document; as you do, all the styles in those templates are added to the document template. This is a great way to get a lot of styles attached to one document.

Your Word Processor Must Be Supported

If your word processor isn't listed in the **Import Styles** dialog box (see Step 3), you cannot import styles from one of its documents.

Task

1 How to Insert Standard Shapes 84

2 How to Insert Custom Shapes 86

3 How to Move, Resize, and Crop Shapes 88

4 How to Add Color and Texture to Shapes 90

5 How to Layer Shapes 92

6 How to Put Text on Shapes 94

7 How to Group and Ungroup Objects 96

8 How to Flip and Rotate Objects 98

9 How to Insert Clip Art 100

10 How to Insert Pictures 102

11 How to Create Picture Captions 104

12 How to Insert WordArt 106

13 How to Format WordArt 108

14 How to Use Microsoft Draw 112

15 How to Create Borders and Shadows 114

16 How to Align Objects 116

17 How to Use the Snap To Feature 118

18 How to Wrap Text Around Graphics 120

19 How to Move, Resize, and Crop Graphic Frames 122

Project 1: A Sales Brochure 124

Working with Graphics

Part of the fun of working in Publisher is adding graphics to your publication. It's a chance to be creative, innovative, and original. Text creation is full of rules such as spelling and grammar, but graphics offer an opportunity to do whatever you want to do, in any manner you prefer.

However, the robust graphics tools built into Publisher aren't there just so that you can have a few moments of enjoyment; they serve a real purpose. You can use graphics to help emphasize the message in your text or to send a message independently, without text. Graphics help you produce a publication that's slick and attractive.

In this part, you learn how to access graphics and then tweak them into a state of absolute perfection. ●

How to Insert Standard Shapes

Publisher provides some preset graphic shapes, called *standard shapes*, and there are a gazillion uses for them. You can put text on them, pile them on top of each other to create pictures, or use them to add a splash of color to your page.

These standard shapes are the oval/circle, square/rectangle, and line. Publisher calls them *standard shapes* to differentiate them from a group of other shapes called *custom shapes* (which are covered in the following pages).

Begin

1 Select Oval Tool Button

To place an oval shape into your publication, click the **Oval Tool** icon on the **Objects** toolbar.

Click

2 Create Oval by Dragging

Drag your mouse to create the oval, stretching it as much as you want to. You can also click the page to let Publisher insert the oval with a preset size and shape.

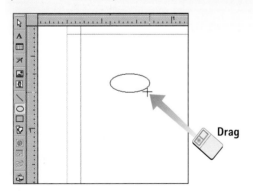

Drag

3 Create Circle with Shift Key

To create a circle, follow the instructions in steps 1 and 2, but hold down the **Shift** key as you drag the oval shape.

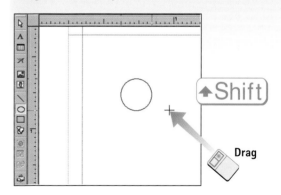

Shift

Drag

4 Select Rectangle Tool Button

Click the **Rectangle** tool on the **Objects** toolbar to create a rectangle or a square.

Click

5 Create Rectangle by Dragging

Position your mouse where you want the rectangle to start; drag to create. To create a perfect square, press and hold the **Shift** key as you drag.

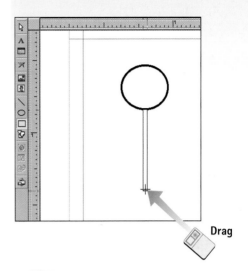

Drag

6 Select Line Tool Button

To draw a line, click the **Line** tool on the **Objects** toolbar.

Click

7 Create Line by Dragging

Position your mouse where you want one end of the line; drag to create a line of the proper length.

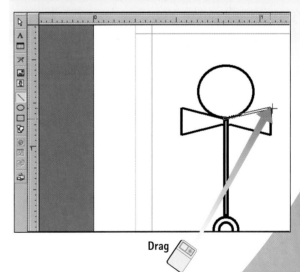

Drag

End

How to Insert Custom Shapes

Wait until you see the custom shapes in Publisher! As soon as you look at all the choices, your creative genes will go on full alert. The possibilities are endless, and you'll probably start inventing headlines and snappy phrases just to have a reason to use some of these shapes.

The real fun with custom shapes comes with "creative mouse dragging." You can manipulate your mouse as you're creating these shapes to produce weird and unusual graphics.

Begin

1 Select Custom Shapes Tool

Click the **Custom Shapes** button on the **Objects** toolbar.

Click

2 Select a Shape

The assortment of custom shapes displays. Click the shape you want to work with.

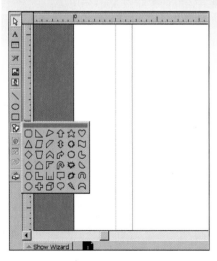

3 Drag Mouse to Create a Shape

Drag your mouse to create a custom shape in the size and proportion you require. It's best to drag diagonally to maintain a reasonable facsimile of the original shape.

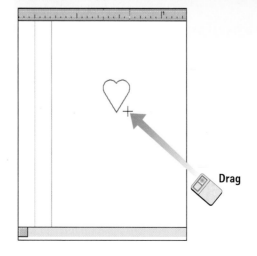

Drag

4 Hold Shift Key for Proportional Shapes

To keep the shape's form as you create it (which means that you don't change its proportions), hold down the **Shift** key while you drag.

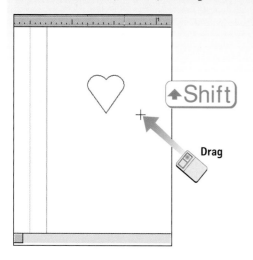

5 Drag Mouse for Disproportional Shapes

On the other hand, it's fun to distort a shape for a special effect. Just drag the mouse disproportionately, more downward or to the side than diagonally.

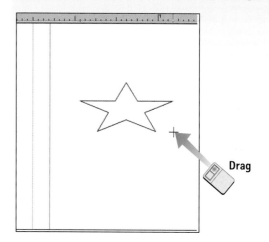

6 Click to Simply Insert Shape

You can select a shape and then click your page to insert the shape in its default size. The center of the shape is placed at the location of your mouse pointer when you click.

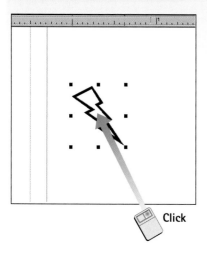

End

How-To Hints

In Bad Shape?

If you don't like your shape after drawing it, try resizing it (see the next task for help). If you still don't like the shape, click it and press **Delete** to remove it.

How to Move, Resize, and Crop Shapes

Luckily, if you're not an accomplished "mouse drag-ger," you can tweak and correct the appearance and size of a shape after you've inserted it in your publi-cation. In fact, the ability to manipulate shapes after they're placed on the page means that you can click to insert a shape instead of dragging it.

Begin

1 Select a Shape

Click the shape to select it. When an object is selected, sizing handles appear around it.

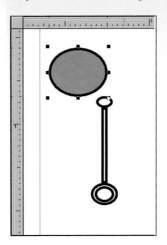

2 Position Mouse Pointer Over Shape

Position your mouse pointer anywhere over the shape. Your pointer turns into a moving van.

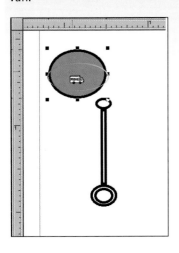

3 Move Shape to New Location

Press and hold the left mouse button and drag the shape to another location.

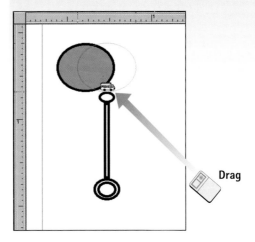

Drag

4 Position Mouse on Sizing Handle

Position your mouse pointer on a sizing handle to see the pointer turn into a **resize** pointer.

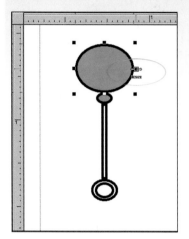

5 Drag to Resize

To resize the shape, press and hold the left mouse button and drag the resizing handle in the appropriate direction. Because you're working with shapes, this action changes the shape's appearance.

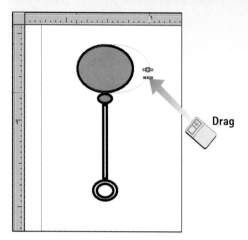

Drag

6 Control Key for Proportional Resize

To force an equal movement on the opposite side as you resize, hold down the **Ctrl** key while you drag a resizing handle. (Actually, what's happening is that the center of the shape is being forced to remain where it is.)

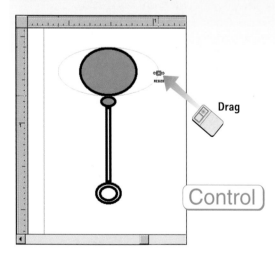

Drag

Control

7 Use Corners to Resize Proportionately

To resize a shape proportionately, use the corner sizing handles. Notice that even round shapes have corner sizing handles.

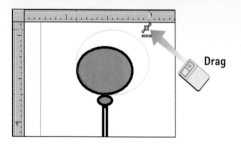

Drag

End

How-To Hints

Stop Mid-Stream if You Need To

If you're dragging a resizing handle and change your mind, just press the Esc key to cancel the action.

How to Add Color and Texture to Shapes

Most shapes, especially the standard shapes, need some help before they add much to your publication. The thin outline of a shape isn't much of an attention-getter.

You can add pizzazz to your page by changing the look of a shape, which is quite easy to accomplish.

1 Click a Shape

Click a shape to select it.

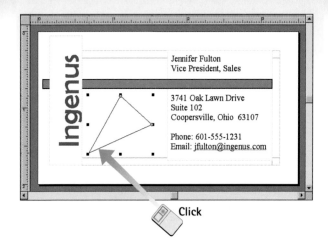

Click

2 Click Fill Icon

To add color to the shape, click the **Fill Color** icon on the **Formatting** toolbar.

Click

3 Change a Color

The **Fill Color** menu displays the colors that make up the color scheme for this publication. The bottom line of color swatches displays any colors you've recently used (which makes it easy to use the same colors throughout the publication). Click a color swatch to fill the shape with that color.

4 Choose More Colors

Choose **More Colors** from the menu to see a full palette. Select the color you want to use and choose **OK**.

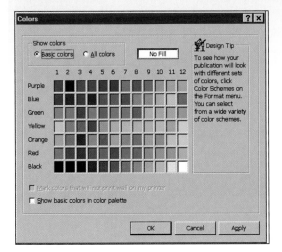

5 Choose Fill Effects

Choose **Fill Effects** from the **Fill Color** menu to add patterns or texture to your shape with the **Fill Effects** dialog box. Select **Patterns** and then scroll through the available patterns to pick the one you like. Don't forget to select your colors. If you want to work with only one color, make both the base color and the second color the same, or click **Tint/Shades**.

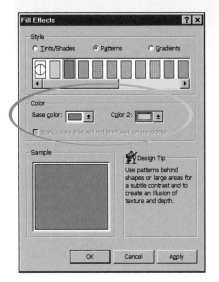

6 Choose Gradients

From the **Fill Effects** dialog box, select **Gradients** to fill your shape with a color that has an air-brushed effect. Pick the gradient pattern you like and select a color. Choose a second color to put behind the gradient.

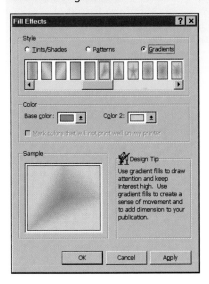

7 Tweak to Perfection

Click **OK** to check the effect. If you have to tweak the colors or fills, repeat these steps until everything looks terrific.

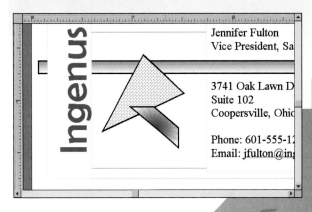

End

How to Layer Shapes

One of the nifty things you can do with shapes is to put them together to make entirely new shapes. You can stack them or overlap them to create interesting graphics.

There's a trick to all this, however, because *layering* automatically occurs according to the order in which the shapes are placed on your page. The first shape you create is on the bottom of a layer (even if you aren't layering). Then each additional shape assumes its position in the next higher layer.

Begin

1 Create Some Shapes

Create the shapes you want to put together.

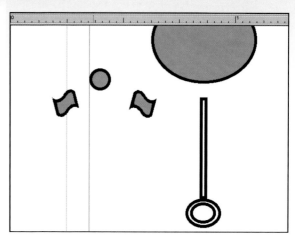

2 Select and Drag a Shape

Select a shape and drag it to put it on another shape.

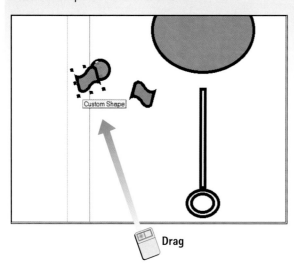

Drag

3 Notice One Shape Disappears

Uh-oh. When you move one shape on top of another, you may obscure part or all of one shape.

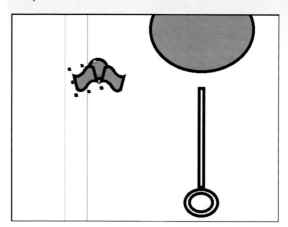

4 Choose Bring Forward

If you have more than two shapes, you might want to layer a shape on top of another shape. To move shapes through the layers by degrees, select a shape and choose the **Bring to Front** button on the **Standard** toolbar.

Click

5 Press F6 For Quick Layering

Bring a shape to the front layer quickly by selecting it and pressing the **F6** key.

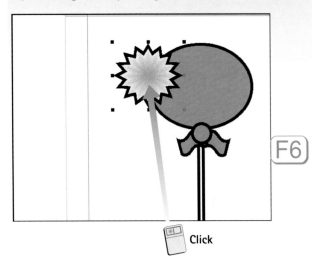

Click

6 Press Shift+F6 for Back Layering

Send a shape to the back layer quickly by selecting it and pressing **Shift+F6**.

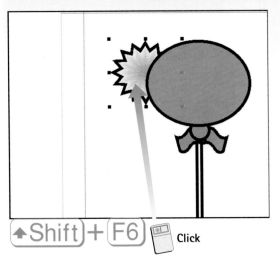

Shift + F6 Click

End

How-To Hints

Layers Work the Same Everywhere
The rules for layering apply to all types of frames in Publisher; it's just easiest to illustrate these rules with shapes.

How to Put Text on Shapes

One of the best uses you can make of a shape is as a background for important text. The shape draws the reader's eye to the text and adds zest to your page.

Begin

1 Click Text Frame Tool

Create the shape and add color or texture to it. Then click the **Text Frame** tool on the **Objects** toolbar.

Click

2 Create a Text Frame

Drag your mouse to create a text frame that fits in the shape.

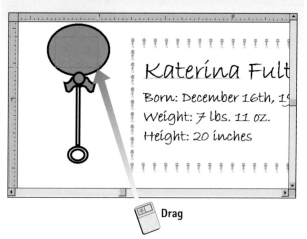

Drag

3 Enter Text in Frame

Enter the text in the text frame. (It's easier to work if you press **F9** to zoom in.)

F9

4 Format Text

Format the text. Usually it's a good idea to center text in a shape.

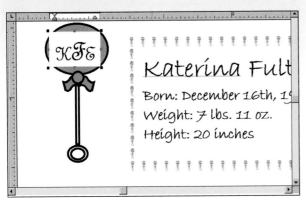

5 Zoom Out with F9 Key

Press **F9** to zoom out. Click anywhere outside the page to deselect the objects on the page so that you can see the effect.

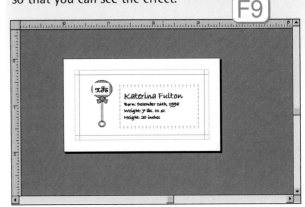

6 Press Ctrl+T for Transparent Frame

To make the text frame transparent (so that it looks as if the text were directly on the shape), select the text frame and press **Ctrl+T**.

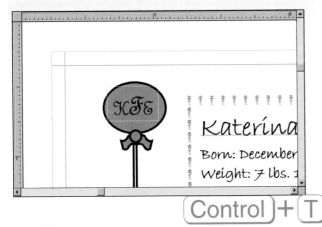

Control + T

7 Color or Texturize Frame

If you want to use the text frame for additional color or effect, select it and add color or texture.

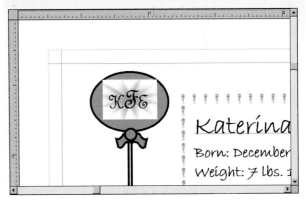

End

How-To Hints

Where to Go for More Information

See Task 4 in Part 3, "How to Add Color and Texture to Shapes."

See Task 3 in Part 2, "How to Move and Resize Text Frames."

See Task 4 in Part 2, "How to Format Text Appearance."

How to Group and Ungroup Objects

After you put a text box on a shape, a caption under a picture, or a graphic in a text frame, what do you do if you have to move all that stuff around? It's a real chore to move the shape and then move the text box, replacing it in exactly the same position. In fact, resizing a frame that has something on it or in it means that you also have to resize the interior frame to keep the proportions correct.

Luckily, Publisher has a feature that makes all this easier. You can group objects together and then manipulate the group.

Begin

1 Lasso Objects to Group

Drag your mouse to lasso the objects you want to group. Dragging creates a virtual box around the elements. (If your box crosses an object but doesn't completely encompass it, that object won't be included in the group.)

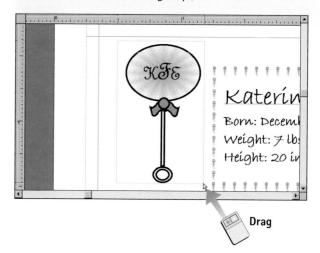

Drag

2 Hold Shift to Select

Alternatively, you can select multiple elements by holding down the **Shift** key as you click each object.

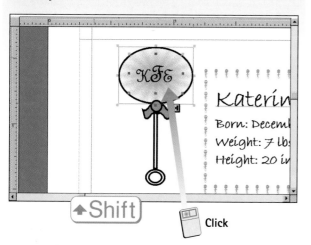

⬆Shift

Click

3 Group Objects Button Appears

A frame appears around all the objects in the group, and a **Group Objects** button is displayed at the bottom of the frame. The group exists temporarily (until you click anywhere outside the group) and you can manipulate it as a single unit.

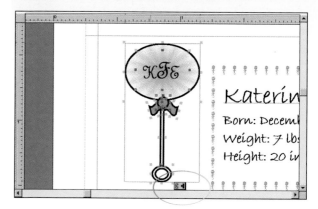

4 Click Group Objects Button

Click the **Group Objects** button to make the group permanent. The button and buttonhole come together.

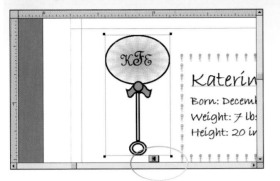

5 Move Group

To move the group, position your pointer over any element in the group and drag to bring all the objects along.

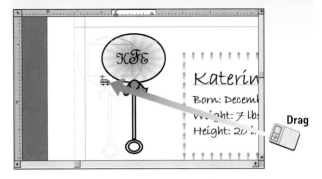

Drag

6 Resize Group

If the group is permanent (the buttonhole is closed), sizing handles appear around the group frame. When you resize the group, each element in the group changes its size proportionately.

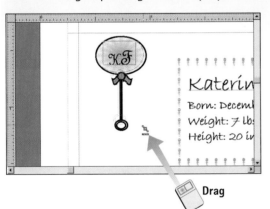

Drag

7 Format Group

You can also apply formatting changes to the group, such as colorizing or rotating the frames.

8 Deselect Group

Ungroup the objects by clicking the **Group Objects** button. Then click anywhere outside the group to restore the individual frames.

End

How to Flip and Rotate Objects

One of the many fun things to do when creating a publication is to turn frames topsy-turvy. Apart from being fun to do, you can use the results as eye-catching graphics. This is a nifty way to draw attention to a message.

You can rotate all graphics and text frames. You can flip shapes and WordArt. You can group objects and rotate them together or rotate each object individually.

Begin

1 Select a Frame

Select the frame you want to manipulate by clicking it.

Click

2 Flip a Shape Horizontally

To flip a shape horizontally, select it and then click the **Flip Horizontal** button on the **Formatting** toolbar. The shape swivels as if you had moved it with a hinge running along the side.

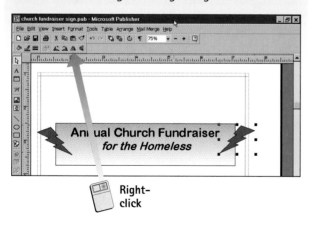

Right-click

3 Flip a Shape Vertically

To flip a shape vertically, select it and then click the **Flip Vertical** button on the **Formatting** toolbar. The shape swivels as if you had swung a hinge attached to its bottom edge.

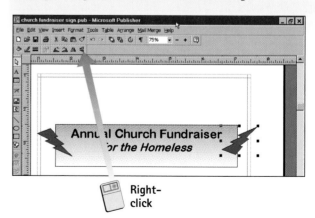

Right-click

4 Rotate an Object Manually

To control the rotation manually, hold down the **Alt** key and position your pointer over a sizing handle. The pointer becomes a rotation tool and you can drag to rotate the frame.

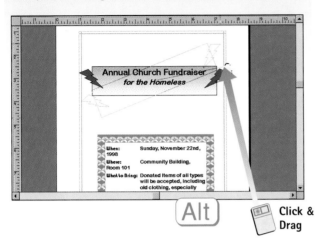

[Alt]

Click & Drag

5 Choose Arrange

To rotate a frame by a specific number of degrees, click the **Custom Rotate** button on the **Standard** toolbar.

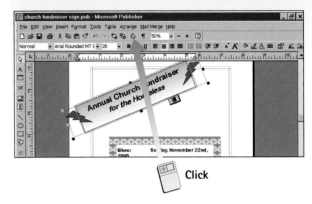

Click

6 Specify Number of Degrees

Specify the number of degrees in the **Angle** box of the **Custom Rotate** dialog box. You can also click the **Rotate** buttons and watch as the object is rotated by small amounts.

7 Flip WordArt

To flip WordArt, use any of the techniques discussed here. Be aware that flipped WordArt tends to be a bit strange and may be hard to read. You should probably adjust the font and character spacing. You can learn more about using WordArt in Task 13 of this part, "How to Format WordArt."

End

How to Insert Clip Art

Clip art is a picture, such as a drawing, that is usually a simple line drawing with lots of color. Publisher provides an enormous collection of clip art in the Clip Gallery, and you can open the gallery when you need an illustration.

Because the collection is so large, the majority of the clip art files are kept on the Publisher CD-ROM. When you want to select clip art, you must make sure that the CD-ROM is in its drive.

Begin

1 Click Clip Gallery Tool

Click the **Clip Gallery** tool on the **Objects** toolbar. Drag your mouse to create a frame of the right size on the page where you want to insert the clip art, or click the page to let Publisher insert the frame. (You can resize it later.)

Click

2 Open MS Clip Gallery

The Microsoft Clip Gallery opens as soon as you release the mouse button. Scroll down and click a category you like.

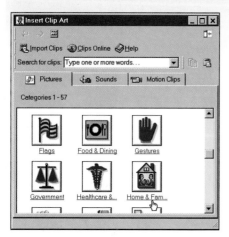

3 Enter Search Term

In the **Search for Clips** text box, you can also enter a descriptive word for the type of clip art you need. You can enter multiple words to narrow the search, separating each word with a space. Press **Enter** to begin the search.

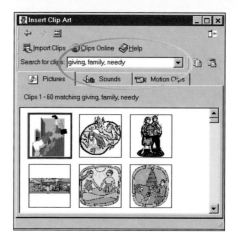

4 Insert the Clip Art

Find the clip art image you want to use and click it, then click **Insert Clip**. Click the **Close** button to remove the dialog box.

5 Preview the Art

If you want to preview the clip before inserting it, click the image and select **Preview Clip**. The image appears in its own window. Click **Close** to return to the Clip Gallery.

6 Moving/Resizing Clip Art

The clip art image is placed in its frame on your page. You can move it or resize it as necessary.

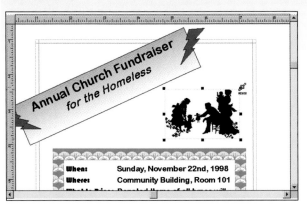

End

How-To Hints

Similar Clips

To find images that are similar to the one you select, click the image and choose **Find similar clips**.

Save Your Favorites

You can copy images to the **Favorites** category to make it easier for you to find the images you use all the time. Just click the image and select **Add clip to Favorites** or other category.

How to Insert Pictures

The Clip Gallery has pictures in addition to clip art, and sometimes one of these photographs provides exactly the illustration you need. If you have pictures from any source available as a file, such as scanned images or downloaded artwork, it's easy to insert them into your publication.

Begin

1 Create A Clip Art Frame

Click the **Clip Gallery** tool on the **Objects** toolbar. Drag your mouse pointer to create a clip art frame, or click the page to let Publisher create the frame for you.

Click

2 Locate Clip Art Picture

When the Clip Gallery opens, select the **Photographs** category on the **Pictures** tab.

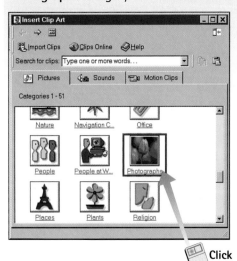

Click

3 Insert Clip Art Picture

Click the photograph you want, then select **Insert clip**. Close the **Insert Clip Art** dialog box.

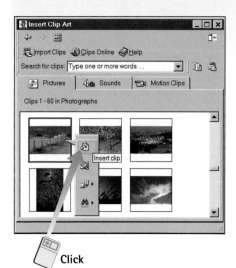

Click

4 Click Picture Frame Tool

To insert a picture file that's not in the **Clip Gallery**, click the **Picture Frame** tool on the **Objects** toolbar.

Click

5 Create Frame and Insert Picture

Drag the frame to the size you need. Then choose **Insert**, **Picture** from the **menu bar**. Choose **From File** to select a picture file from your hard drive.

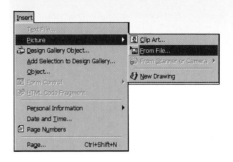

6 Click to Insert Picture

Change to the folder that contains the graphic you want to insert. Click it and select **Insert**.

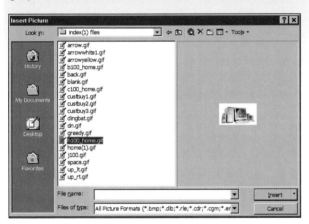

7 Moving/Resizing Pictures

Move or resize the picture as necessary, but be careful not to distort the image (unless you deliberately want the effect of distortion).

End

How-To Hints

Selecting a Replacement

To change a picture to something else in the **Clip Gallery**, just double-click the image to open the **Clip Gallery**.

How to Create Picture Captions

Captions are short phrases that describe illustrations. Sometimes you use captions to explain a graphic; other times you can use a caption to add to the message of a graphic that's very much self-explanatory.

It doesn't really matter where you position the caption in relation to the graphic—there's no absolute rule about whether the caption should be above, below, or next to its illustration. Well, that's not always true—captions for cartoons are traditionally below the cartoon.

Begin

1 Create a Text Frame

Create a text frame above, below, or next to the graphic frame.

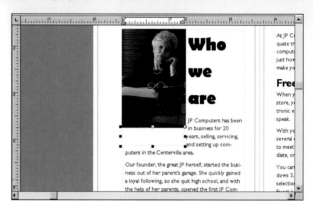

2 Enter Text

Enter your text and format it.

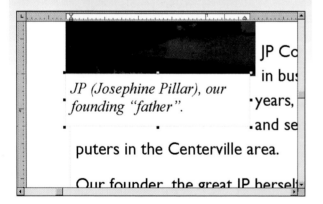

3 Move the Text Frame

Move the text frame, the graphic frame, or both, to put them as close together as possible.

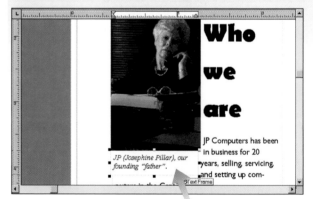

 Drag

4 Click Text Frame Properties Button

Click the text frame to select it and then click the **Text Frame Properties** button on the **Formatting** toolbar.

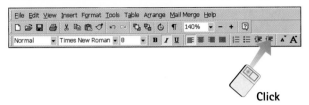

Click

5 Reduce the Margin

In the **Text Frame Properties** dialog box, reduce the margin for the edge of the frame closest to the graphic. Choose **OK**. (This brings the text closer to the graphic frame.)

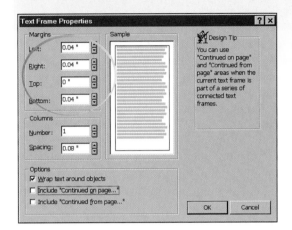

6 Group the Frames

Group the frames by holding down the **Shift** key as you select each frame, or by drawing a line around both frames.

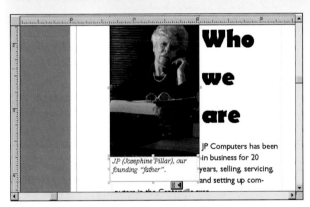

◆Shift

7 Click Group Objects Button

Click the **Group Objects** button on the bottom of the group frame to make the group permanent. Now if you move the picture, you also move the caption (and vice versa).

End

How-To Hints

Learn More About Text Formatting

You can learn about working with text frames and text in Part 2. Look for these tasks:

Task 2, "How to Create a Text Frame," on page **56**

Task 3, "How to Resize and Move Text Frames," on page **58**

Task 4, "How to Format Text Appearance," on page **60**

How to Insert WordArt

WordArt is a way to bend and twist text and graphics, and it's lots of fun! You enter text, but Publisher treats the frame as a graphic.

Begin

1 Click WordArt Frame Tool

Click the **WordArt Frame** tool on the **Objects** toolbar.

Click

2 Create a Frame

Drag to create a frame of the right size.

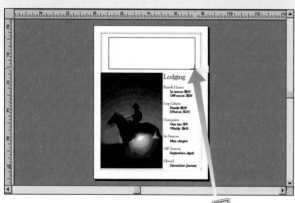

 Drag

3 Release Mouse

When you release the mouse, a **WordArt** text frame is on the page and the **Enter Your Text Here** dialog box sits in front of it.

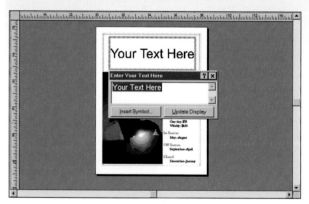

4 Enter Text in WordArt Frame

Enter your text in the dialog box. (Just start typing; your characters replace the selected text automatically.) Keep the text short; this is not a place for long sentences.

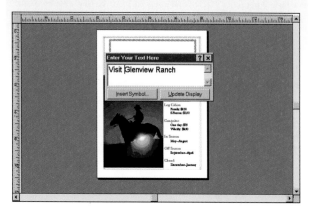

5 Click Update Display

Choose **Update Display** to transfer the text to the **WordArt** frame. Then close the dialog box by clicking the **X** in the upper-right corner. The **WordArt** frame border has a hash-mark look, which means it is in WordArt Edit mode.

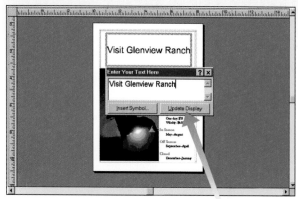

 Click

6 Format WordArt

While WordArt is in Edit mode, you can format your text using any of the WordArt tools—see Task 13 for help. When you're through, click outside the WordArt frame to exit Edit mode (the hash marks disappear).

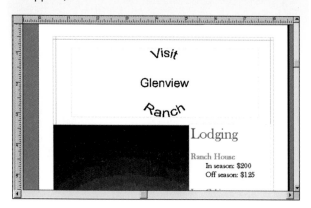

7 Edit WordArt

To edit the WordArt text, double-click anywhere in the frame. The hash-mark frame and the **Enter Your Text Here** dialog box appear so that you can change the text. When you're through, click **Update Display** and close the dialog box.

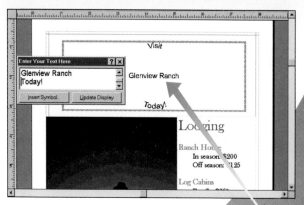

 Double-click

End

How to Format WordArt

Now the fun starts. Formatting WordArt is a cheery, amusing activity. Even better, the results add real pizzazz to your publication. Remember that there are two ways to select a WordArt frame:

✓ Single-click to select the frame, so that you can move or resize the frame.

✓ Double-click to put the WordArt text into Edit mode, so that you can change the text or format it.

Click outside the WordArt frame to deselect either selection mode. When you are in Edit mode, the **WordArt software application** window is on your screen. When you deselect the frame, you return to the **Publisher** window.

Begin

1 Select WordArt Frame

Double-click the **WordArt frame** and then close the **Enter Your Text Here** dialog box (to get it out of the way) by clicking the **X** in the upper-right corner. The frame is bordered with hash marks.

2 Pick a WordArt Shape

Click the **arrow** to the right of the **Style** box in the Formatting toolbar to reveal the available shapes for WordArt. Pick a shape; your text twists to match the shape. This action is referred to as *pouring* your text into the shape.

Click

3 Change WordArt Font

Sometimes pouring the text into a shape makes it a bit more difficult to read. Usually you can fix that by changing the font: Click the **arrow** next to the **Font** box and select a font that works better.

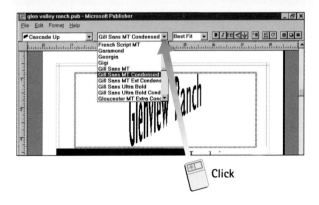

Click

4 Change Letter Size

The **Font Size** box is configured for **Best Fit**. Even though you can click its **arrow** to change the font, you'll find that **Best Fit** almost always fits best. In addition, the **Best Fit** font size changes automatically if you resize the **WordArt** frame.

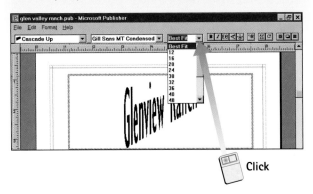

Click

5 Format WordArt Text

Use the **Bold** and **Italic** buttons to format the text. Use the **Even Height** button to make lowercase letters the same height as uppercase letters.

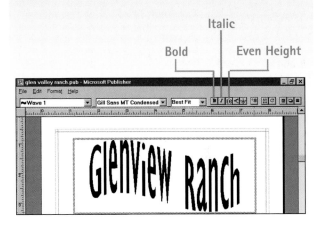

6 Flip Text

Click the **Flip** button to change the direction of your text.

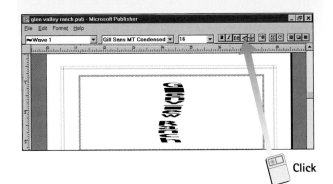

Click

7 Stretch Text

Stretch the text to fit the frame with the **Stretch** button.

Click

Continues

How to Format WordArt Continued

There's no end to the twists, turns, and other manipulations you can apply to the text in your WordArt frame.

Some of the choices involve the spacing of characters, specifically tracking and kerning.

✓ *Tracking* is the amount of space between characters.

✓ *Kerning* is the automatic adjustment of the space between certain pairs of characters, where the second character in the pair can easily be tucked in under (or next to) the first character. An example is any lowercase letter following a *w* because you can move the letter under the right slant of the *w*.

8 Align Text with Frame

Click the **Alignment** button to reposition the text's relationship with the frame.

Click

9 Change Letter Spacing

Click the **Character Spacing** button to change the way the characters are laid out. Specify your selection in the **Spacing Between Characters** dialog box.

Character Spacing

10 Rotate Text

Click the **Special Effects** button to rotate or skew the text. Use the **Rotation** box to specify the number of degrees you want to rotate the WordArt. Use the **Slide** box to type a percentage of skewing. A **50%** value is used as the norm. Anything under 50% skews text to the right; anything over 50% skews text to the left. In effect, you're changing the shape that holds your WordArt.

Special Effects

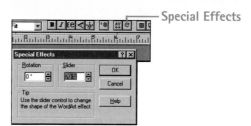

11 Add Texture

Click the **Shading** button to add texture or patterns to the WordArt text. This is unusual; most of the time, you add fill (texture or patterns) to frames, not text.

Shading

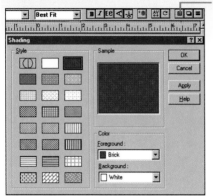

12 Add Shadow

Click the **Shadow** button to add a drop shadow to the text. The **Shadow** dialog box presents an interesting variety of choices. You can also select a color for the drop shadow. Always make the shadow color a lighter version of the text color; usually **Silver** works best regardless of the color of the text.

Shadow

13 Add a Border

Click the **Border** button to add a border to your WordArt text (to the *text*, not to the frame). If you add a border, it won't be seen unless you choose a light color for your text.

Border

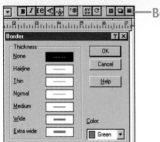

14 Deselect Frame

When you're through making changes, click anywhere outside the frame to deselect it and to exit Edit mode.

End

How-To Hints

Fit the Pattern

To use the **Button (Curve)** or **Button (Pour)** shapes effectively, you must create three lines of text.

How to Use Microsoft Draw

Microsoft Draw is automatically installed with Publisher, and you can use it while you're working in Publisher. As you see in these pages, it launches automatically and disappears when you're finished working on your **MS Draw** frame.

MS Draw contains more tools and AutoShapes than the Formatting toolbar, so you can create more complex art with it.

Begin

1 Select Picture Frame Tool

Start by selecting the **Picture Frame** tool on the **Objects** toolbar.

Click

2 Create New Frame

Drag to create a frame and then choose **Insert, Picture, New Drawing** from the **menu bar**.

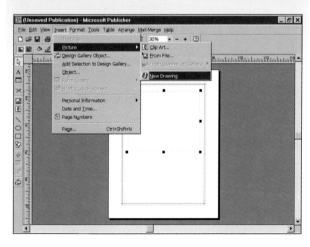

3 Add Elements to Your Frame

Now you're working in Microsoft Draw. The **AutoShapes** toolbar contains tools you can use to create your drawing. The **Drawing** toolbar contains tools similar to those in Publisher.

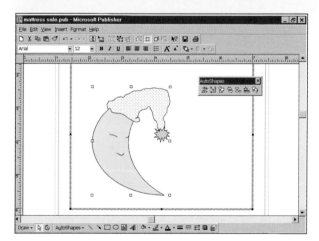

4 Create an Element

Creating an object using the **AutoShapes** or the **Drawing** toolbar is similar to using the drawing tools in Publisher. Click the tool you want to use, than drag to create a shape.

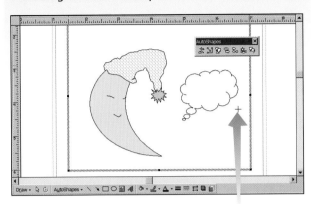

Click & Drag

5 Choose Add Text

If you create a callout shape, the cursor is automatically positioned for you to add text. For other objects, right-click and choose **Add Text** from the **shortcut menu** to place text on a shape. You don't need to add a text frame; just type directly on the shape.

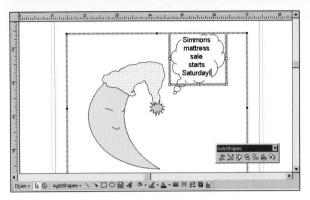

6 Click Insert Clip Art or Picture

To add a graphic to your MS Draw drawing, click the **Insert Clip Art** or **Insert Picture from file** button on the **Standard** toolbar.

End

How-To Hints

Draw Has Its Own Help

When you're working in Microsoft Draw, there's an independent Help system you can use to become more adept with this application.

Toggling Between Publisher and Draw

To leave Microsoft Draw and return to your **Publisher** window, click anywhere outside the Microsoft Draw object. Double-click the object to return to Microsoft Draw.

Zoom Before You Draw

Before you choose **Insert, Picture, New Drawing**, to start MS Draw, make sure that you zoom in on the frame you created so that you can see your work more closely. You cannot adjust the zoom while in MS Draw.

How to Create Borders and Shadows

After your graphic is nestled nicely in its frame, you might want to decorate the frame a bit. A plain border makes the graphic stand out, separating it from the other frames on the page.

A shadow or a decorative border around the frame adds even more luster to your graphic image. This can add to the aesthetics of the frame and also directs the reader's eye to the contents.

Begin

1 Select Graphic Frame

Click the **graphic frame** to select it. The **Formatting** toolbar appears in the **Publisher** window.

2 Click Line/Border Style Button

Click the **Line/Border Style** button on the **Formatting** toolbar.

Click

3 Select a Line

Select one of the lines in the **drop-down menu** to put a simple border around the frame.

4 Select More Styles

For additional choices, choose **More Styles** to open the **Border Style** dialog box. You can select any thickness or change the bottom choice (by default, **10** points) to specify any point value. You can also choose a color if you want one.

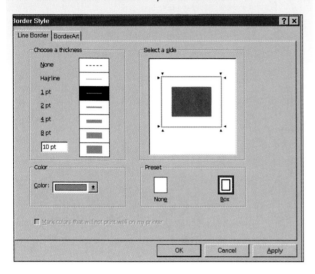

5 Create a Shadow

Create a shadow by holding down the **Shift** key as you click on any two adjacent sides in the **Select a side section** of the dialog box. You can also create a border by placing different-sized borders on sets of sides. (Use **Shift+Click** to deselect any selected side; the clicking action is a toggle.)

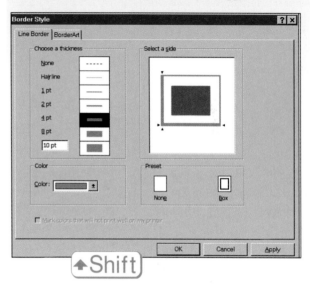

6 Choose a Border

Move to the **BorderArt** tab and scroll through the selections to find a decorative border that suits the graphic. You can adjust the width of the border by specifying the points in the **Border size** box.

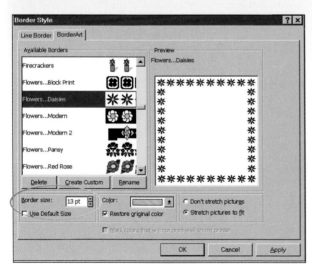

7 Apply Your Border

Choose **OK** to close the dialog box and apply your border.

End

How to Align Objects

Frames that are associated, such as captions and pictures, or groups of like items, should be positioned so that the association is obvious. Additionally, lining up a page's elements in an orderly fashion makes your publication look much more professional.

You can align objects to margins or to each other, depending on the effect you want to produce. Each alignment action must be performed individually, which means that if you want to line up one group of objects in one way, and another in a different way, you must perform two sets of steps.

Begin

1 Select Objects

Select each of the sloppily arranged objects by holding down the **Shift** key as you click each element.

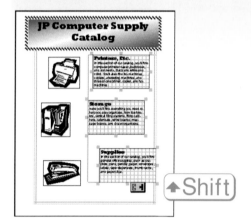

2 Choose Align Objects

Choose **Arrange, Align Objects** from the menu bar.

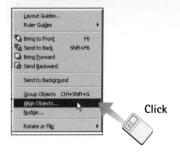

Click

3 Align Objects Vertically

In the **Align Objects** dialog box, use the **Left to right** section to align objects that are positioned vertically on your page. If you want to line up the objects along their frame edges, specify the edge you want to use and choose **OK**.

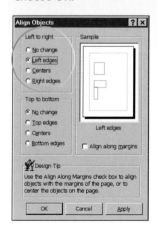

4 Align Objects Horizontally

Use the **Top to bottom** section of the Align Objects dialog box to align objects that are positioned horizontally on your page.

5 Align in Relation to the Margin

Select the **Align along margins** option to line up the elements in relation to the margins instead of in relation to each other. If you choose an edge, the closest margin is used as a guide. If you choose **Center**, the objects are centered between the margins.

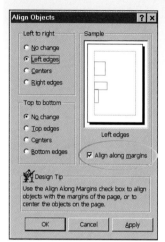

6 Align in Columns

This example shows columns of objects. After you align the objects vertically, you usually have to repeat the process to align them horizontally.

End

How-To Hints

Align Edges for Columns

It's easier to read and understand columns of objects if you align associated items so that their top or bottom edges are on the same line, instead of centering them.

Manual Align

If you want to align objects by hand, set up some guidelines to help you. See the next task and Part 1, Task 13, "How to Use Layout Guides," for help.

How to Use the Snap To Feature

For a professional look, all the pages in your publication should have objects lined up in a similar manner. You can drive yourself nuts moving objects around your pages—or you can let Publisher do it for you automatically. To accomplish this, insert guidelines. Turn on the Snap To feature to place virtual magnets on your objects and the guidelines. As soon as they get close to each other—*bang!*—they line up together.

Rulers provide **Snap To** lines for individual pages where objects should line up in a certain position on the page. **Layout Guides** provides **Snap To** lines for the entire publication.

Begin

1 Create a Ruler Guide

To create a ruler guide, hold down the **Shift** key and position your pointer on either ruler. Your pointer turns into an **Adjust Pointer**.

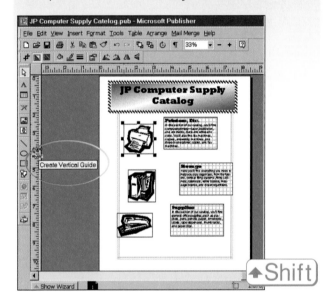

2 Drag Ruler into Position

Continue to hold down the **Shift** key as you drag your pointer to the position on the page where you want to insert a **Snap To** ruler guide. (Don't worry, the green line on your screen doesn't print.) Repeat for as many ruler guides as you need, then skip to step 6.

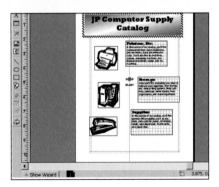

3 Create a Layout Guide

To create a Layout Guide, you must work on the background page, so that the guideline is repeated on every page. Press **Ctrl+M** to move to the background page. The **status bar** replaces your page number with a **background page** icon.

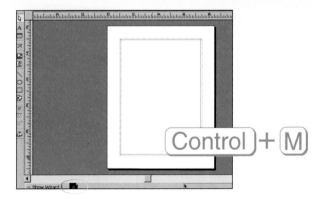

4 Choose Layout Guides

Choose **Arrange, Layout Guides** from the menu bar.

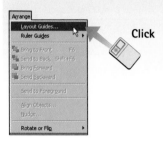

Click

5 Specify Number of Columns/Rows

In the **Layout Guides** dialog box, create a grid with the guidelines you need; do this by specifying the number of **Columns** or **Rows** (or both) it takes to line up all the elements in your publication. Choose **OK** and then press **Ctrl+M** to leave the background page.

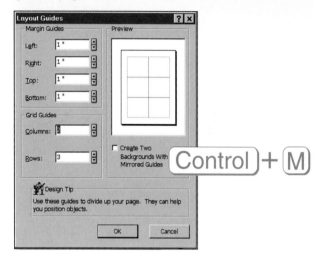

Control + M

6 Turn on Snap To

Make sure the Snap To features you need are enabled on the **Tools** menu. A **check mark** indicates that the feature is enabled.

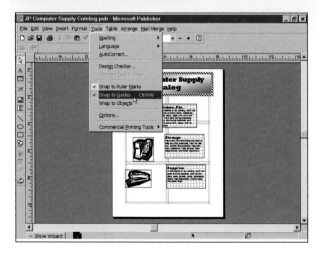

7 Drag Objects to Guidelines

Drag an object toward the appropriate guideline. When you get close, it snaps to the guideline automatically.

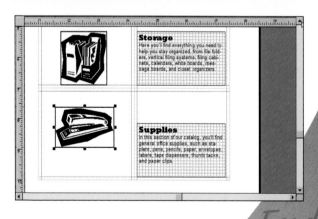

End

How to Wrap Text Around Graphics

If you want to illustrate a story or an article, the illustration should be inserted in the story. This makes your publication look far more professional, because, when you do this, the text automatically moves and rewraps itself to make room for the illustration. The resulting look is called *text wrap*.

Begin

1 Select an Illustration

Create a graphic frame, perhaps **clip art**, inside the text frame. (Select the **Clip Gallery** tool and drag out the frame.) Select the illustration for the frame.

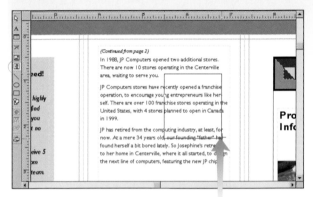

Click & Drag

2 Text Rewraps Automatically

The text rewraps automatically around the graphic frame. The text uses the edge of the frame as a margin.

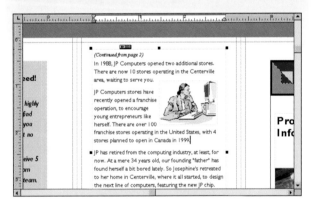

3 Click Object Frame Properties

To force the text to wrap around the picture itself instead of the frame, select the **graphic frame** and click the **Picture Frame Properties** tool on the **Formatting** toolbar.

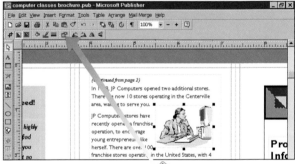

Click

4 Select Picture Only

In the **Picture Frame Properties** dialog box, select the **Picture Only** option; then choose **OK**.

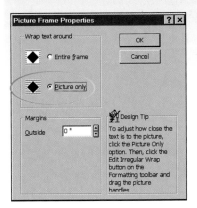

5 Click Irregular Edit Wrap Button

The text rewraps, using the picture itself as a margin. This frequently causes a spillover of words onto the wrong side of the picture.

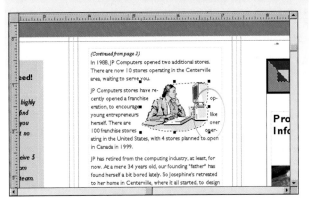

6 Tweak the Margins

To tweak the picture's margins (and therefore the text wrap), click the **Edit Irregular Wrap** button on the **Graphics Formatting** toolbar.

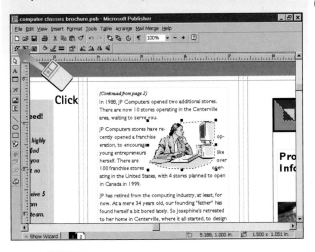

7 Resize Picture's Margins

Sizing handles appear everywhere there is a bend or a curve in the picture. Drag the appropriate sizing handles to fix the text wrap problem. When you're through, click the **Edit Irregular Wrap** button again.

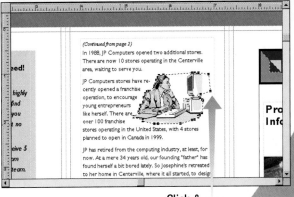

Click & Drag

How-To Hints

Don't Wrap Text on Both Sides

Don't place a graphics frame in the middle of text; it forces the text to wrap on both sides of the illustration. Readers will have to skip over the illustration to complete each sentence—a terribly annoying way to read.

End

TASK *19*

How to Move, Resize, and Crop Graphic Frames

As you work on a publication, you'll find you are constantly rearranging, tweaking, and changing the elements. That's part of the quest for perfection.

Most of your graphics frames can be manipulated without incurring real harm to the general sense of your publication. When you work with text frames, you can't chop a bunch of words out of a sentence or move a couple of sentences to a different location—but graphics are usually more flexible.

1 Select the Frame

To manipulate a graphics frame, select the frame. (You can tell it's selected when you can see the sizing handles.)

2 Move the Graphic

To move the graphic, position your mouse pointer anywhere in the frame. Your pointer turns into a **moving van**. Press and hold the left mouse button and drag the frame in the appropriate direction.

Click & Drag

3 Make Fine Adjustments

If you're making a fine adjustment, you can nudge the frame instead of dragging it. Hold down the **Alt** key and press the appropriate **arrow** key. You can control the distance the frame moves with each nudge by choosing **Arrange**, **Nudge** from the **menu bar** and specifying a measurement in the **Nudge by** box.

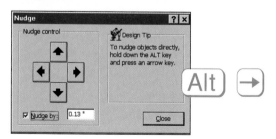

4 Resize a Frame

Drag a sizing handle to resize the frame. Use a corner handle to drag two sides at a time.

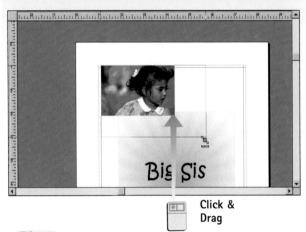

Click & Drag

5 Resize from the Center

To resize the opposite side (or corner) by the same amount, hold down the **Ctrl** key as you drag.

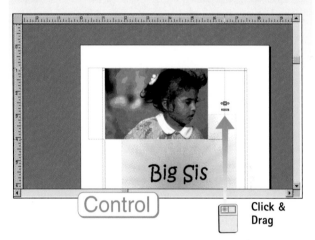

Control

Click & Drag

6 Crop a Picture

To *crop* (cut away parts of) a graphic image, click the **Crop Picture** button on the **Formatting** toolbar. Position your pointer over a sizing handle to have the pointer turn into a cropping tool. Drag your mouse to enclose the portion of the picture you want to keep. Note that you cannot crop shapes you have drawn.

Click & Drag

7 Crop Other Sides

If necessary, repeat the cropping action on another side of the frame. Your pointer remains a cropping tool until you click the **Crop Picture** button again to turn cropping off.

End

Project 1

A Sales Brochure

Here's your chance to practice the skills you've learned so far. In this project, you'll create a sales brochure for your home-based business, *The Simple Chef*. To create a brochure that highlights the cooking products you sell, you'll use the features and functions discussed in Part 1, "Getting Started," through Part 3, "Working with Graphics."

As you follow along with this project, feel free to use your own text and graphics—this is simply a chance for you to put everything you've learned so far to work.

1 Start a New Publication

Open the **File** menu and select **New**.

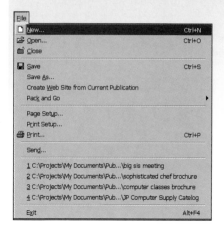

2 Select a Brochure

Expand the list by clicking, **Brochures** in the **Wizards** list. Then click a brochure you like and click **Start Wizard**. (I'm going to use the **Bubbles Informational Brochure**.)

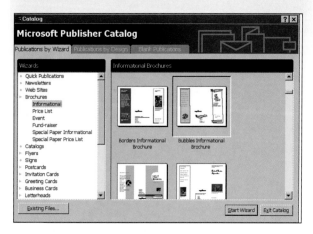

3 Review the Wizard's Selections

The wizard builds the brochure. But before you can begin, you may want to review and change some of the selections. For example, you can click **Next** and select an alternate color scheme for the brochure. Click **Next**.

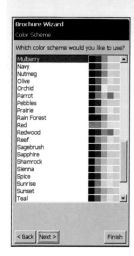

4 Change the Number of Panels

You can change from a tri-fold to a four-panel brochure by clicking **Paper Size (Panels)** and choosing that option. Click **Next**.

5 Create a Customer Placeholder

On the **Customer Address** panel, you can create a space on the brochure for the customer's address (for example, if you plan on mailing it.). Click **Next**.

6 Add a Form

On the **Form** panel, you can add an order, response, or sign-up form, depending on the nature of the brochure. I'm going to add an order form so that my customers can order *Simple Chef* products easily. Click **Next**.

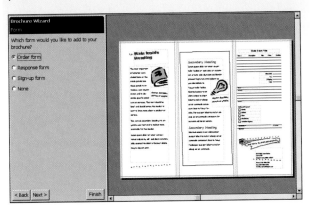

7 Select the Information Set to Use

On the **Personal Information** panel, you can select which Personal Information Set to use. Since this is for a home-based business, I'm going to select the **Home/Family** information set. Click **Finish**.

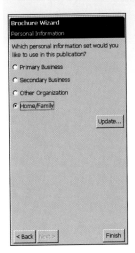

Continues

8 Hide the Wizard

When you're through making selections, click **Hide Wizard** to remove the Wizard panel so that you have more room in which to work.

Click

9 Replace Placeholder Text

Begin by replacing the placeholder text the wizard created. For example, replace **Back Panel Heading The Simple Chef**. (Press **F9** so that you can see what you're typing.)

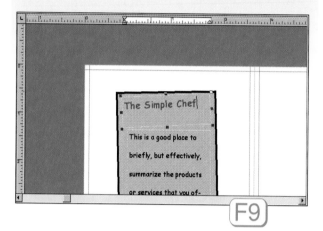

10 Replace Other Text

Click inside the **summary text box** (just below the **Simple Chef** heading) and type a description of your business.

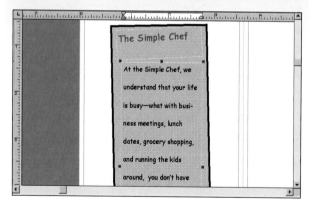

11 Save Your Work

After you complete a task, you should save your work so that you cannot lose what you've just done. Click **Save**.

Click

12 Give Your Publication a Name

Change to the folder in which you want to save the publication. Type a name in the **File name** text box and click **Save**.

13 Continue Replacing Text

Go through both sides of the brochure, replacing text as needed. On the inside of the brochure, you can include details about *Simple Chef* parties and how your products are demonstrated. There's also a place for you to list your products.

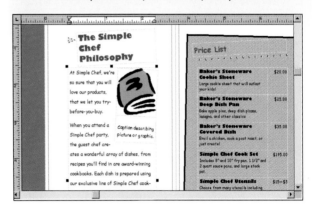

14 Replace Graphics

Now that your text is in place, you can begin to replace the placeholder graphics with something more appropriate. Double-click a graphic to replace it.

Double Click

15 Find an Alternative Graphic

The **Clip Gallery** appears, displaying similar clips to the one you selected. To find what you need, you can type a keyword or two into the text box and press **Enter**.

Continues

16 Insert Your Selection

When you find a piece of clip art you like, click it and select **Insert clip**. Close the **Clip Gallery**.

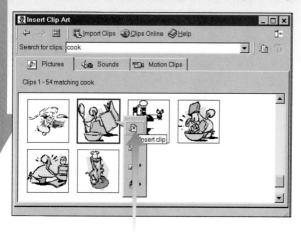

 Click

17 Add a Caption

Type a caption if appropriate. If you don't want a caption, click the **Ungroup Objects** button, select the caption text box, and press **Delete** to remove it.

18 Replace Other Graphics

Follow steps 14 through 17 to replace other graphics in the brochure as needed.

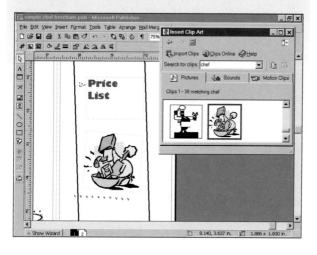

19 Add a Border to a Graphic

You can add a border around a graphic to draw more attention to it. Click the graphic and click the **Line/Border Style** button on the **Formatting** toolbar. Click a style, or for more creative options, click **More Styles**.

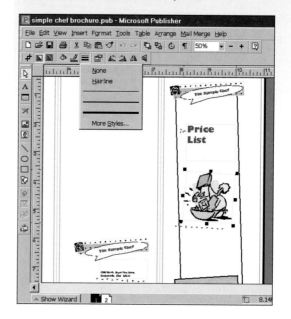

20 Selecting a Unique Border Style

Click **More Styles** from the **Line/Border Style** menu. Click the **Border Art** tab, and select a compatible border. Adjust the **Border size** if needed and then click **OK**.

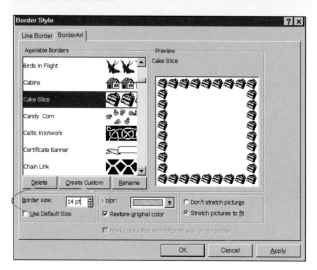

21 Have Fun!

Change other borders if you like, add color, change fonts, and play until the brochure looks the way you want it to look.

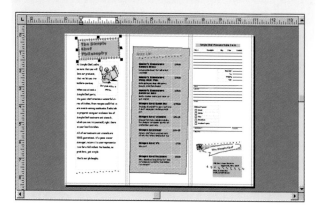

22 Add Finishing Touches

To add your personality to the brochure, consider creating special touches such as WordArt.

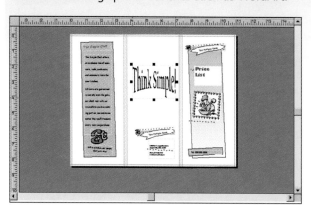

23 Add Your Own Art

Another way to personalize a brochure is to add your own art with Microsoft Draw. This is especially useful for creating your own logos. (See Part 3, Task 14 for help.)

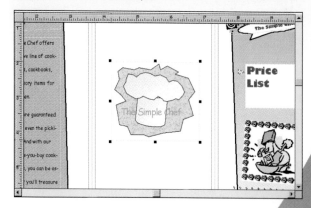

End

Task

1 How to Add a Table 132

2 How to Format a Table 134

3 How to Use the Design Gallery 136

4 How to Create Your Own Design Gallery 138

5 How to Create Background Elements 140

6 How to Insert Elements from Documents 144

7 How to Use Mail Merge 146

Adding Special Elements

*T*o make your publication even more professional and more interesting to readers, Publisher offers some fascinating features and tools.

You can use these tools to add elements to your publication that would be terribly difficult (or, in some cases, impossible) to create from scratch.

Whether you need a stunning, eye-catching design or a complicated spreadsheet that was developed in another software program, Publisher makes it easy to add special elements to your publication. In this part, you learn about a number of these special features. ●

How to Add a Table

A table is a terrific way to present lists of information, such as a catalog of products and their prices; a list of classes, meetings, and other scheduled events; and other things.

Begin

1 Create a Frame

Click the **Table Frame** tool on the **Objects** toolbar. Drag to create a table frame of the size you need.

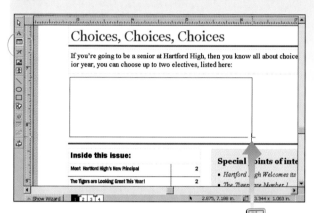

Click & Drag

2 Specify Rows and Columns

When you release the mouse, the **Create Table** dialog box opens so that you can configure the table. Start by specifying the **Number of rows** and **Number of columns**.

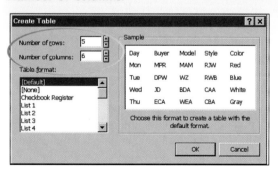

3 Pick a Table Format

Scroll through the **Table format** list to find the layout design that fits your table. The **Sample** box shows you what the format looks like.

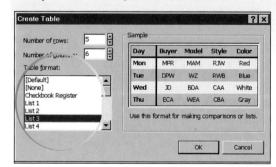

4 Resize Table If Necessary

If the frame you dragged isn't large enough to hold the desired number of rows and columns, Publisher offers to resize the table. Of course, you should accept the offer by clicking the **Yes** button.

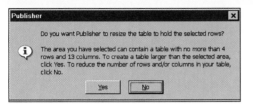

Publisher

Do you want Publisher to resize the table to hold the selected rows?

The area you have selected can contain a table with no more than 4 rows and 13 columns. To create a table larger than the selected area, click Yes. To reduce the number of rows and/or columns in your table, click No.

Yes   No

5 Enter Data Into the Cells

Enter data and use the **Tab** key to move between cells. (Use **Shift+Tab** to move backwards.)

	Mon	Tues	Wed	Thurs	Fri
Choir	2-3		2-3	2-3	
Wood working	4-5	4-5	7-8	7-8	4-5
Metal working		6-7	6-7		6-8
Cooking	10-12		10-12		10

6 Format the Data in the Cells

Each individual cell is a text frame; and you can use the tools on the **Formatting** toolbar to change the text's appearance.

	Mon	Tues	Wed	Thurs	Fri
Choir	2-3		2-3	2-3	
Wood working	4-5	4-5	7-8	7-8	4-5
Metal working		6-7	6-7		6-8
Cooking	10-12		10-12		10-13

End

How-To Hints

Other Things to Read

For more information about formatting frames, read Task 4, "How to Format Text Appearance," in Part 2.

Just a Frame

A table is just like anything else in a frame—it can be moved, resized, and so on. By using the **Delete Object** command, you can remove a table.

How to Format a Table

You can tweak a table to make it look interesting, attractive, and slick. You can merge cells, add rows or columns, and create borders.

Because a table is a collection of text boxes (*cells*) arranged in rows and columns, the formatting changes you make can be applied to a variety of elements:

✓ You can change the formatting of an individual cell or a group of selected cells.

✓ You can change the formatting of a row or a column.

✓ You can change the formatting of the entire table.

Some common formatting changes for tables include the following:

✓ Format the row that holds titles for center alignment.

✓ Format columns that contain numbers for right alignment.

✓ Merge cells to create title rows at the top of the table or a total row at the bottom.

Begin

1 Use Table Autoformat

You selected a table format when you created your table, but to change it, click anywhere in the table to select it and choose **Table**, **Table AutoFormat** from the **menu bar**. Choose a new design.

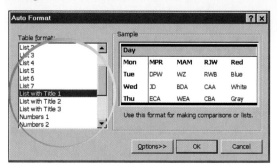

2 Merging Cells

To merge cells (to create one cell from multiple cells), select the cells you want to merge and choose **Table**, **Merge Cells**. You can select cells by dragging your mouse across them, by holding down the Shift key while you press an arrow key, by selecting a column or row selector (the shaded area next to a row or above a column), or by clicking in the first cell, then clicking in the last cell while you hold down the **Shift** key.

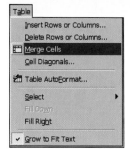

_3_ Formatting Columns and Rows

To change the formatting for a column or row, click the column or row selector. (The heading row is selected in this example.) Then use the tools on the **Formatting** toolbar to apply changes such as alignment, color, fill, or font.

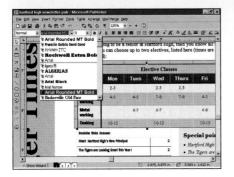

_4_ Adding Columns or Rows

To add rows or columns, click in a cell in the row or column next to where you want the new addition. Then choose **Table**, **Insert Rows or Columns** from the **menu bar**. In the **Insert** dialog box, specify how many new rows or columns you want to add and where they should be placed.

_5_ Removing Columns or Rows

To remove rows or columns, click anywhere in the row or column you want to get rid of and choose **Table**, **Delete Rows or Columns** from the **menu bar**. Select the option you want and click **OK**.

_6_ AutoFill Data in Cells

To fill in data automatically (for data that is the same in multiple cells), select the cell that has the data you want to copy and drag your mouse to select the cells below or to the right of where you want to copy the data. Choose **Table**, **Fill Down** or **Fill Right** to copy the data.

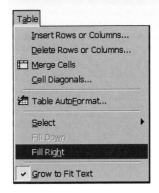

_7_ Formatting the Entire Table

To make a formatting change to the entire table quickly, select the table by clicking the table selector (the gray box in the upper-left corner). Use the tools on the **Formatting** toolbar to apply changes such as alignment, color, fill, or font.

Elective Classes					
	Mon	Tues	Wed	Thurs	Fri
Choir	2-3		2-3	2-3	2-3
Wood working	4-5	4-5	7-8	7-8	4-5
Metal working		6-7	6-7		6-8
Cooking	10-12		10-12		10-13

End

How to Use the Design Gallery

There's a little gallery tucked into Publisher, and you can visit it to insert decorative and functional items such as calendars, tear-off strips, and borders. The Design Gallery's options cover a wide range of design types, from generic things (such as ornamental graphics) to specific items (such as pull quotes, calendars, coupons, and order forms).

Some of the designs can be dropped into your publication without any additional work. Other designs, such as calendars and coupons, require configuration and perhaps some text entry. All the designs have wizards if you don't want to make changes manually.

Begin

1 Click the Design Gallery Toolbar

Click the **Design Gallery Object** button on the **Objects** toolbar.

Click

2 Review the Design Gallery

When the Design Gallery opens, the **Objects by Category** tab is in the foreground. The window's left pane lists the categories; when you select a category, the available designs are displayed in the right pane.

3 Click the Objects by Design Tab

Click the **Objects by Design** tab to see the items listed by design. The left pane displays a list of the designs; when you select a design, you'll see a variety of objects that use that design. This is a good way to make sure that any item you insert will match those already in your publication.

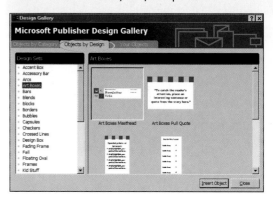

4 Select a Design Element

Select a design element and choose **Insert Object** to place it on your page (alternatively, double-click the element).

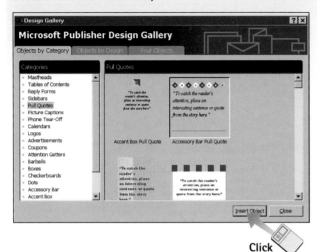

Click

5 Customize the Design Element

A button appears at the bottom of the design when the design is selected. Click the button to launch the wizard specific to this design. For most designs, the wizard merely permits you to change the design color scheme. For more complicated design elements (such as a calendar), the wizard helps you configure the design. Picking the month and year for a calendar is an example.

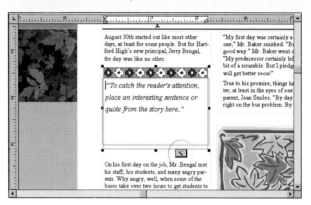

6 Customize the Illustration

If the design has an illustration, and you want to substitute a different illustration, double-click it and then select a new picture from the **Clip Gallery**.

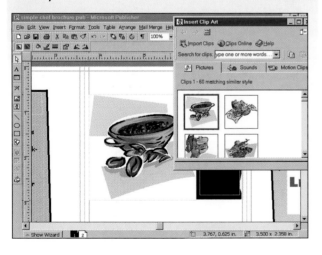

7 Customize Text

If the design has text (as do the attention-getter objects), you must select the text before you can replace it with your own words. To replace the text, just click and type.

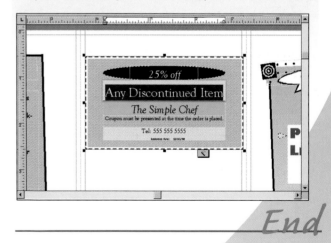

End

How to Create Your Own Design Gallery

In the Design Gallery, you can store the fancy stuff you've created on your own. Later, you can open the gallery to use one of your own creations in a current publication. Just like the designs offered by Publisher, your designs must have a category and name. To make it easy, Publisher walks you through each step of placing your design in the gallery.

Your own designs are placed in the Design Gallery on a publication-by-publication basis; there is no way to save all the designs from multiple publications in one place. However, there is a way to get to a design from one publication while you're working in another one.

Begin

1 Select the Design Element

After you've created a magnificent design element on your own, select it. If it's made up of multiple elements (as are most of the Publisher designs in the gallery), create a group and select it.

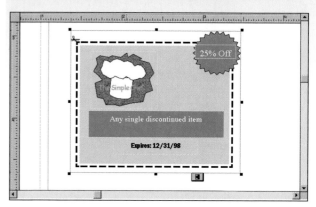

2 Click Design Gallery Object Tool

Click the **Design Gallery Object** button on the **Objects** toolbar.

Click

3 Choose Add Selection to Design

When the **Design Gallery** opens, move to the **Your Objects** tab and click the **Options** button. Choose **Add Selection to Design Gallery**.

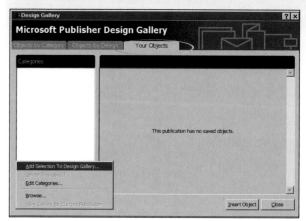

4 Enter Object's Name

In the **Add Object** dialog box, enter an **Object name** and a **Category** and click **OK**. (As you continue to add designs to the gallery for this publication, you can use the category names you've already created.)

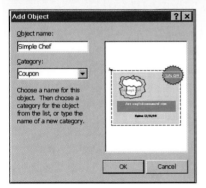

5 Insert Your Design

When you want to use this design element again in the same publication, open the **Design Gallery** and move to the **Your Objects** tab. Select the category and design you want to use.

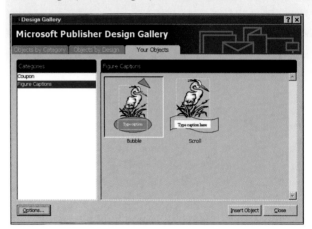

6 Work in a Different Publication

If you want to use your designs from one publication when you're working in another publication, open the **Design Gallery** and move to the **Your Objects** tab. Click the **Options** button and choose **Browse**.

7 Locate and Double-Click to Insert

In the **Other Designs** dialog box, select the publication that has your designs saved in its **Design Gallery**. Double-click it to open its designs in the **Design Gallery**; select the design you want to use and click **OK**.

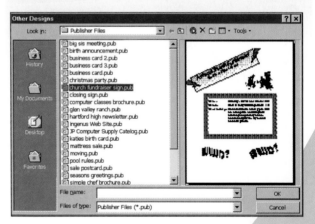

End

How to Create Background Elements

The publication's **background** lurks behind the pages you use to create elements for your publication. There are two characteristics of the background that make it an ideal location for page numbers, titles, company logo designs, and other elements that you want throughout your publication. You can place elements on the background and they're visible when you work on the foreground pages. Of course, they're also visible when you print your publication. Whatever you place on the background is seen on every foreground page.

Begin

1 Go to the Background

To work on the background, choose **View, Go to Background** from the menu bar. The background page looks like a blank page, but there's a visual reminder on the status bar: The **background page** icon replaces the **page number** buttons.

2 Add Guide Lines

To add guide lines, choose **Arrange, Layout Guides** from the **menu bar**. If your publication will be printed like a book with separate background pages, select **Create Two Backgrounds With Mirrored Guides**.

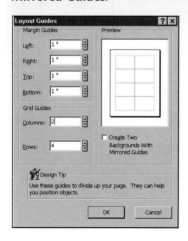

3 Insert Page Numbers

To insert page numbers, create a text box in the appropriate position on the background. To make sure that the page number shows through, choose a position that's outside the margins you're using on the foreground pages.

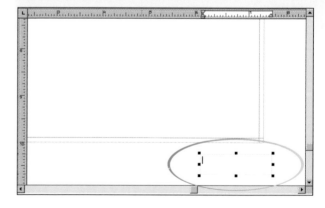

4 Insert Page Numbers

Select the text box and choose **Insert, Page Numbers** from the **menu bar**. Publisher inserts a pound sign (#) in the text box, which represents the code that it uses for the page number. (The actual page number appears on the foreground pages.)

5 Format Page Numbers

You may want to add text (such as the word "Page") before the pound sign. You can also format the text and the page code using the tools available on the **Formatting** toolbar.

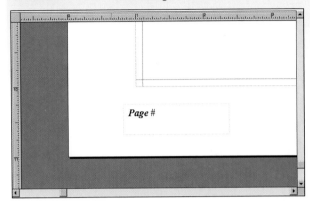

6 Repeat Page Number if Using

If you have mirrored background pages, move to the other page by clicking its icon on the status bar (unless you're working in a Two-Page Spread view, where you can scroll over to the other page). Repeat the procedure on the other background page, remembering to put the text box for the page number on the opposite corner. (Never use the inside edge of the page for a page number.)

7 Add Text Boxes to Publication

Create text boxes on the background for any text you want to appear on every page of your publication. You can format the text on the background in exactly the same way you format text on the foreground pages.

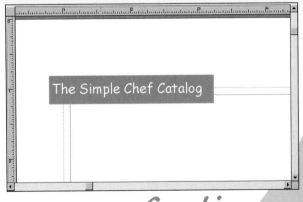

Continues

8 Add Graphics

To create a colorful graphic, create a shape on the background page. Some shapes lend themselves well to page numbers, chapter numbers, or other text. Place a text frame on the shape and make it transparent (press **Ctrl+T**).

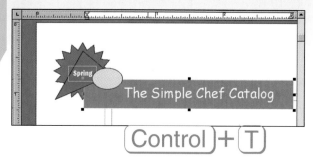

9 Click Clip Gallery

To create a picture watermark, click the **Clip Gallery** tool on the **Objects** toolbar and drag to create a frame.

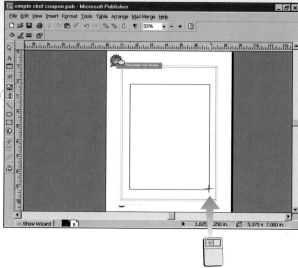

Click & Drag

10 Choose an Image

Select an appropriate graphic image from the **Clip Gallery**. Don't choose anything with a lot of detail or with colors that create the detail (watermarks are not multicolored). Click **Insert clip** (or double-click) to put the image on the background.

Click

11 Recolor Image

Now that the graphic is on your publication's page, choose **Format, Recolor Picture** from the **menu bar**.

12 Choose Fill Effects

In the **Recolor Picture** dialog box, click the arrow next to the **Color** box to see the drop-down menu. Choose **Fill Effects**.

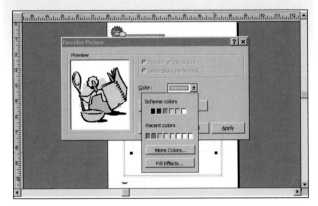

13 Choose Light Gray

In the **Fill Effects** dialog box, choose a light tint (such as 10%). You may also want to change the color in the **Base Color** box. Choose **OK** twice to close the dialog boxes and recolor the graphic.

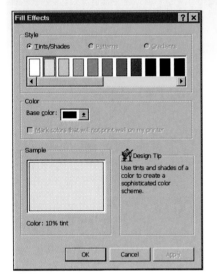

14 Press Ctrl+T

Choose **View, Go to Foreground** to return to the foreground page and check your work. If the watermark is hidden by the text frame, select the text frame and press **Ctrl+T** to make it transparent.

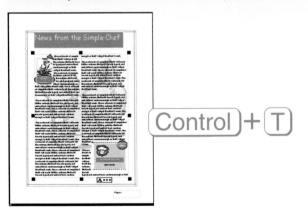

End

How-To Hints

Use WordArt for Text Watermarks

A *watermark* is a graphic, so if you want to use text within your watermark you must create a WordArt graphic or create an MS Draw graphic with text. Learn more about WordArt by reading Part 3, Task 12, "How to Insert WordArt," and Task 13, "How to Format WordArt." To learn more about MS Draw, see Part 3, Task 14, "How to Use Microsoft Draw."

More About Layout Guides

For more help on placing layout guide lines on the background, turn to Part 1, Task 13, "How to Use Layout Guides."

How to Insert Elements from Documents

It's not unusual to need data in your publication that's the same as what's already entered in another software package. A report you wrote might belong in the company newsletter, or a spreadsheet might be needed for the annual report. Publisher provides a way to insert that information directly into your publication, so that you don't have to spend time retyping it.

Publisher supports file types for most popular applications. (If you use Microsoft programs, you can be assured that your data will import.) Check the Publisher documentation or contact Microsoft for an up-to-date list. For information on handling overflow text, see Task 10 in Part 2, "How to Work with Overflow Text."

Begin

1 Create a Text Frame

Click the **Text Frame** tool on the **Objects** toolbar and create a text frame to hold your imported document.

Click

2 Insert a Text File

Choose **Insert, Text File** from the **menu bar**.

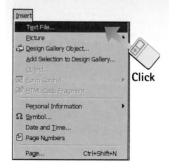

Click

3 Select the File You Need

When the **Insert Text File** dialog box opens, move to the folder on your hard drive that contains the document you need. Select the file by double-clicking on the file.

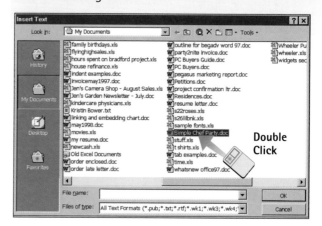

Double Click

4 Placing Excess Text

Very often, the document is too large for the text frame you created. You can have Publisher automate the process of placing the excess text throughout your publication, or you can do it yourself.

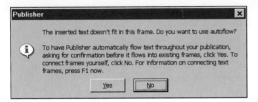

5 Importing Spreadsheets

Spreadsheet application documents are imported in the same manner as text. (Publisher catches on, but you still begin by using the **Insert, Text File** command.) When you select the spreadsheet document, Publisher wants to know if you want the entire document, a worksheet, or a named range. (Click the arrows to select workbook sheets or named ranges.) Choose **OK** after you've made your selection.

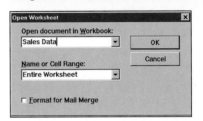

6 Publisher Imports a Spreadsheet

Publisher imports the spreadsheet and recognizes it, creating a table in your text frame.

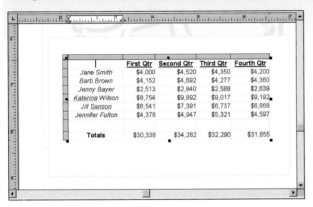

7 Add Text to a Text Frame

You can also use the Clipboard to move data into a Publisher text frame. Open the original document, select the data, and copy it. Move to your Publisher text frame and choose **Paste**.

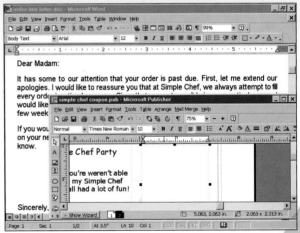

End

How-To Hints

Using Database Reports

If you want to use reports from your database or accounting software, create those reports as disk files—be sure to specify the file type as text—then bring that text file into your word processor so that you can import it into Publisher.

How to Use Mail Merge

A great many publications are meant to be distributed by mail. Perhaps you create brochures, flyers, and price lists that must be mailed to customers. Perhaps you use Publisher at home and want to create your own holiday greeting cards or send a change-of-address notice—Publisher will print each individual mailing address on your publication so that all you have to do is fold and stamp the paper.

To use Mail Merge, you must prepare the two main ingredients:

- ✓ The mailing list
- ✓ The publication, which is preset with codes to indicate where the various parts of the mailing address are printed (name, address, city, and so on)

There are a limited number of lists Publisher can handle automatically (lists created in Access, Excel, or Word usually work, and so do Outlook address lists), but sometimes you'll have to create a Publisher address list from scratch.

Begin

1 Create a Publisher Address List

To create a Publisher mailing list, choose **Mail Merge**, **Create Publisher Address List** from the **menu bar**.

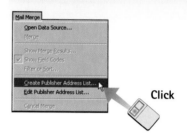

Click

2 Enter Information in Address List

The **New Address List** dialog box opens so that you can begin entering names, addresses, and other information. Press **Tab** to move from field to field; skip those you don't want to use.

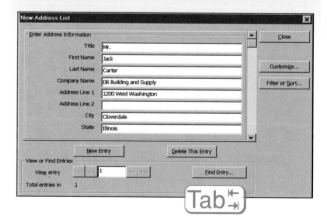

Tab

3 Choose New Entry or Close

Scroll down and enter any additional data you want to keep about this entry. Choose **New Entry** to save this addressee's information and bring up another blank screen so that you can type the next entry in the list. Choose **Close** when you are finished entering addresses.

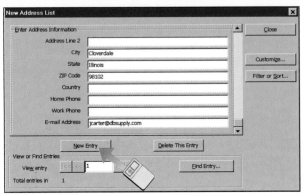

Click

4 Save the Address List

In the **Save As** dialog box that appears, give this mailing list a name and choose **Save**. (Publisher adds the .mdb extension to the filename automatically.)

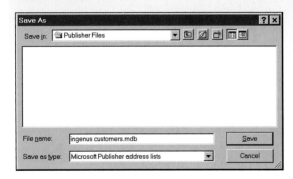

5 Create a Text Frame

After creating your address list, open the publication into which you want the information from the list merged. (You can use the same list with any number of publications.) Select or create the text frame in which you want the mail merge information to appear.

6 Import an Existing Address List

To use a mailing list that exists as a database file, a Microsoft Word file, an Excel file, an Outlook list, or a text file, first select the text frame you are going to use for mailing; then choose **Mail Merge**, **Open Data Source** from the **menu bar**. When the **Open Data Source** dialog box appears, select the option you need.

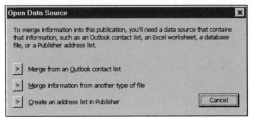

Continues

7 Specify Address List's File Type

The **Open Data Source** dialog box appears so that you can move to the appropriate folder to find your mailing list file. (This dialog box does not appear if you're importing from Outlook—skip to Step 10.) Specify the type of file you're seeking in the **Files of type** box. Double-click the file you want to use.

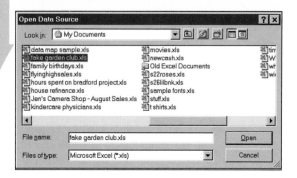

8 Answer Wizard Questions

Publisher usually has a few questions about how you want to use this file and how to recognize the information within it. Your answers depend on the type of file and its layout, which is information you should know before importing the list.

9 Open the Address List

If necessary choose **Mail Merge, Open Data Source, Merge information from another type of file**. On the dialog box that appears, choose the Publisher address list file (the **.mdb** file) you saved earlier.

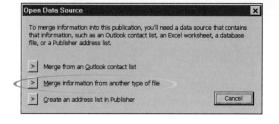

10 Insert Fields

The **Insert Fields** dialog box opens. Select a field—**First Name, Last Name**, and so on—and click **Insert**. The field name appears in the text frame, surrounded by double carats (<< >>). The field you see is a *placeholder* for the real information that will be inserted automatically in Step 11. (The double carats tell you it's a merge field; they won't appear when you print.) After inserting a field, you can either insert another field or click **Close** to close the **Insert Fields** box. (To open it again to insert more fields, choose **Mail Merge, Insert Field**.)

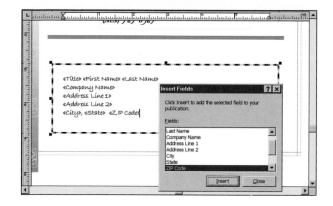

11 Merge the List and Publication

Choose **Mail Merge**, **Merge** from the **menu bar**. In the text frame, you'll see the field names replaced by information from the first entry in the list. To examine the other entries in their place in the page, use the buttons on the **Preview Data** dialog box to move through your mailing list. Close the **Preview Data** box when finished previewing.

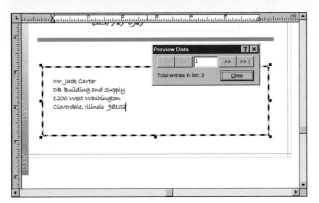

12 Print the Mail Merge

To print all copies of the publication, each containing one list entry's data in place of the field name placeholders, choose **File**, **Print Merge** from the **menu bar,** then click **OK** on the **Print Merge** dialog box. Optionally, you can click **Test** on the **Print Merge** dialog box to print just one copy of the publication (showing just one list entry) to make sure that the Mail Merge data is formatted and positioned the way you want it without having to print the whole list.

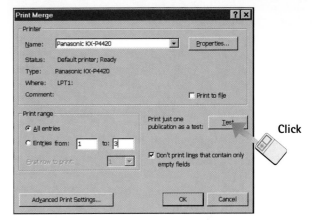

Click

End

How-To Hints

Design Your Merge Text!

You can apply formatting—fonts, sizes, and so on—to the Mail Merge field names in the text frame. When you merge or print, the list data will be displayed or printed with that formatting.

Remember Spaces!

When inserting the merge fields in Step 10, remember to insert spaces where they would normally occur (for example, between the **First Name** and **Last Name** fields). Add commas, too (for example, between the **City** and the **State** fields).

Task

1 How to Tweak Margins **152**

2 How to Spell Check Your Publication **154**

3 How to Check the Design **158**

4 How to Copyfit Your Text **160**

5 How to Control Tracking, Kerning, and Leading **162**

6 How to Perfect Hyphenation **164**

7 How to Work with Bindings **177**

8 How to Work with Crop and Registration Marks **168**

Project 2: A Flyer from Scratch **170**

Tweaking Your Publication

*T*here are publications and then there are **publications**. The difference is measured in slickness, which is slang for "Hey, this really looks professional."

It's not an accident that magazines, newspapers, greeting cards, and other published documents look good enough to incite people to pay for them—a lot of attention is paid to detail.

Publisher has tools that help you pay the same amount of attention to detail, from the mundane chore of checking spelling to advanced tweaking techniques such as copyfitting.

You learn about these techniques in the following tasks. ●

How to Tweak Margins

Your publication is chock-full of margins. There are margins for the foreground and background of each page and for each frame in the publication.

To give you one more thing to worry about, there are even margins for your printer. All laser and deskjet printers need to grab a small part of the paper in order to pull the paper through the printer. Nothing prints in that "grab" area. (Check your Printer Properties dialog box to learn the size of the unprintable area.)

But if your publication's size is smaller than the paper it's printed on, you can forget margins altogether and bleed color right off the edge of the publication itself.

Begin

1 Set Page Margins

To set the page margins for your publication, choose **Arrange, Layout Guides** from the **menu bar** to bring up the **Layout Guides** dialog box. Make the margins smaller to increase the amount of space you can use for printing.

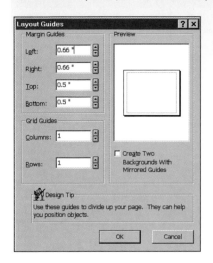

2 Set Page Margins for Background

To set the page margins for the background, press **Ctrl+M** to move to the background. Then choose **Arrange, Layout Guides** from the **menu bar** to bring up the **Layout Guides** dialog box. Make the margins smaller to increase the amount of space you can use for printing. For example, you might want to make the background larger so that it shows behind the foreground text. Learn about using the background in Part 4's Task 5, "How to Create Background Elements."

3 Set Margins for Frames

To set margins for frames, select the frame and click the **Frame Properties** button on the **Formatting** toolbar, which opens the **Layout Guides** dialog box. By default, text frames have margins set; graphic frames (including WordArt) are set for no margin space. You can make changes to margins to alter the look of the frame.

Click

4 Check Publication Size

Some publications are smaller than the paper that's used to print them. For example, here an 8-inch by 10-inch flyer is being printed on 8.5-inch by 11-inch paper; the excess is trimmed away after printing. To check the publication size, check its dimension in the **Page Setup** dialog box. If the publication is smaller than the paper on which you will print it, you have the option of eliminating margins altogether and using *bleeds*, as described next.

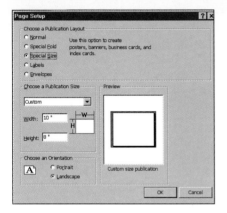

6 Create Bleed Overruns

In fact, you can create frames that overrun the bleed edges. You can bleed color, but you must set the appropriate text margins to make sure that you don't lose any characters.

5 Creating a Bleed

If the page is smaller than the paper, you can set the margins that are not at the end of the paper to **0** (creating a bleed).

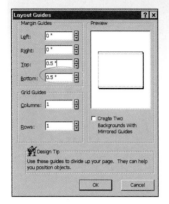

7 Cut Paper with Bleeds

When you print publications with bleeds, you must cut the paper after you finish printing. Sometimes this means that the publication is a good candidate for outside printing services (where cutting is done automatically on machines).

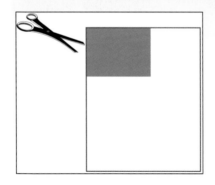

End

How-To Hints

Create Color that Runs to the Edge

Color that prints past the margin is called *bleed*. You can add bleeds to any publication that's smaller than the paper it's printed on.

How to Spell Check Your Publication

Sometimes the fates seem determined to make sure that if you spell a word wrong, it's a word in a headline—a headline printed in a very large font—the sort of thing that makes you wake up in the middle of the night in a cold sweat.

To save you from the agonies of making your mistakes so graphically public, Publisher has a spelling checker. You can configure the spelling checker to show you mistakes as you make them, or wait until you finish your story and then check the spelling.

Begin

1 Select Spell Checking

If you want to change any of the spelling options, choose **Tools**, **Spelling**, **Spelling Options** from the **menu bar**. For example, if you use a lot of acronyms, especially in technical articles, you might want to tell Publisher to skip words that are in uppercase. By default, Publisher checks your spelling as you type.

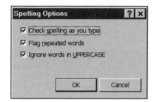

2 Publisher's Misspell Indication

As soon as you press the Spacebar or a punctuation character to indicate the end of a word, Publisher underlines any word not in its dictionary. Publisher automatically corrects the spelling. For example, if you type "somtimes," it will be automatically changed to "sometimes."

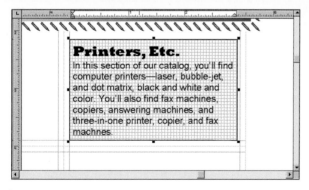

3 Right-Click to Correct Misspellings

Right-click any word that has a red squiggly line beneath it to see a list of suggested replacements. Choose the correct word. If no accurate suggestions are available, choose **Check Spelling** for more options (as covered in the next steps).

Right-click

4 Spell Check at End of Story

If you prefer to ignore the squiggly lines and want to wait until you've finished typing your publication, you can check a story by selecting its first frame and pressing **F7**. The spelling checker stops at the first word that isn't in the Publisher dictionary.

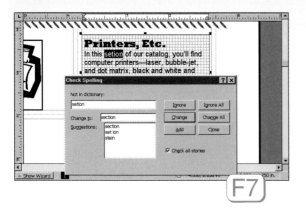

5 Choose Change

To accept one of Publisher's suggestions, highlight the correct suggested word and choose **Change**. To accept the same change throughout the story, choose **Change All**.

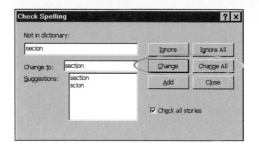

6 Choose Ignore

If the word is just fine (although not in the Publisher dictionary), choose **Ignore** to let your word remain this time, or choose **Ignore All** to let your word remain as is throughout the document.

To make the spelling check more useful and efficient, Publisher gives you some control over the feature's behavior and the dictionary it uses.

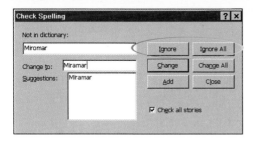

7 Choose Add

If your word is fine and you expect to use it in other stories, choose **Add** to put your word in the dictionary. This means that the spelling checker won't stop on that word again.

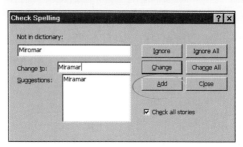

Continues

8 Spell Check Multiple Frames

The spelling checker continues through your story, over multiple frames, until it reaches the end of the story. (You can stop the spell check at any time by choosing **Close**.) As long as the **Check All Stories** option is selected in the **Check Spelling** dialog box, the spelling checker will continue on, checking the rest of the stories in your publication.

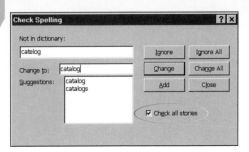

9 Click OK

When the spelling checker finishes its work, it announces the fact. Click **OK**.

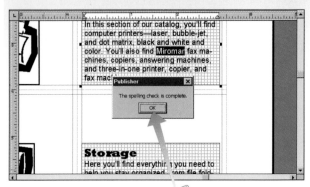

 Click

10 Skipping Spell Check

If you create a paragraph or a story that is replete with technical terms, proper names, or even deliberate misspellings, you can have Publisher skip blocks of text during the spell check. Select the text you want to skip and choose **Tools**, **Language**, **Set Language** from the **menu bar**.

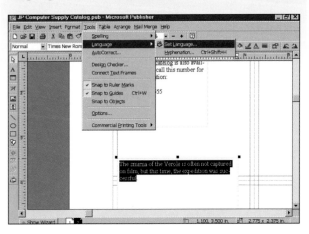

11 Choose No Proofing

In the **Language** dialog box, scroll to the top of the list to find **(no proofing)**. Select it and choose **OK**. (The **All Text** button sets the language for the entire publication.)

12 Adding Your Own Words

Publisher has a list of commonly misspelled words (remember that it corrected "sometimes" automatically) and their correct spellings; it uses the list to autocorrect your spelling. You can add your own frequently misspelled words to the list by choosing **Tools**, **AutoCorrect** from the **menu bar**. When the **AutoCorrect** dialog box opens, enter the wrong and right spelling, then choose **Add**.

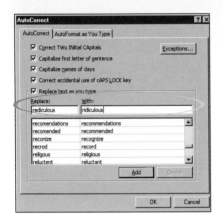

13 Adding Your Own Phrases

You can also use AutoCorrect to substitute frequently used phrases for a code you type (be sure that the code you enter in the **Replace** box isn't a real word). As soon as you press the **Spacebar** or a punctuation character, your code disappears and the phrase appears.

End

How-To Hints

Check Your Web Publication Elements

If you're publishing to the Web, the spelling checker can also check the text you place on buttons or the text you use for labels. Information about preparing publications for the Web is found in Part 6, "Creating a Web Publication."

Check Your Own WordArt

You're not totally safe from errors—the spelling checker can only check text (text frames and tables). You're on your own with your WordArt frames.

Repeated Words Are Fixed, Too

The spelling checker is configured, by default, to catch repeated words such as "put the the pen on the table." This feature is very handy.

Watch Your Grammar!

Even if your publication has no spelling errors, it may have grammatical errors that you can correct only by hand, during a thorough read-through.

How to Check the Design

Your publication's design is almost as important as the messages within it. There are all sorts of research studies that indicate that if it's hard to follow text, the average reader doesn't bother to read it. Too much eye movement is annoying (for example, encountering a graphic in the middle of a text column), too many things to look at on a page is exasperating (for example, a page filled with numerous small text frames).

Publisher has a feature that looks at your publication's overall design and makes suggestions to improve it. It's like having a publishing consultant stop in and give you a no-charge opinion!

Begin

1 Choose Design Checker

To check your design, choose **Tools**, **Design Checker** from the **menu bar**.

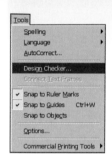

2 Select Pages to Be Reviewed

In the **Design Checker** dialog box, specify whether you want to check **All** or specific **Pages**. (If you have a background design, you should check it out, too.)

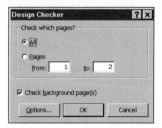

3 Design Checker Dialog Box

The Design Checker starts with the background and then moves through your pages. When a problem is perceived, a dialog box notifies you. Notice that the frame involved in the problem is selected for you by the Design Checker so that you can work on the problem if you want to.

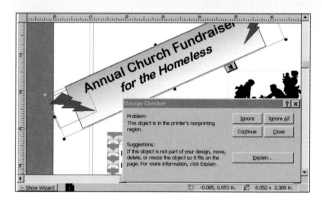

4 Ignore or Fix Problems

Choose **Ignore** if you want to leave the design the way it is, or **Ignore All** if you want all instances of this type of design problem ignored. Otherwise, you must fix the problem. Choose **Continue** to move on. (If you try to choose **Continue** without fixing or ignoring the problem, the Design Checker stubbornly refuses to move on.)

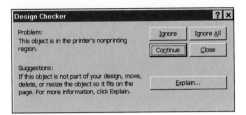

5 Click OK

When everything is fixed (or ignored), the Design Checker tells you it has completed its job. Quick! Click **OK**.

6 Choose Options

You can control the design elements that are checked by choosing **Options** the initial **Design Checker** dialog box. Click to deselect any problem you know you don't care about.

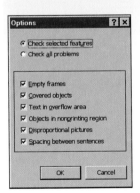

End

How-To Hints

Use Your Judgement

Many of the Design Checker's suggestions are really a matter of taste, and you should feel free to ignore its comments about those items you created for a deliberate reason.

Changed Graphics Are Okay

The most common fault the Design Checker finds is that graphic images are not in their original proportion (you've stretched or shrunken a clip art image). If the image isn't distorted, feel free to ignore this warning.

Don't Print That!

Another common problem is graphics or text placed outside the margins, in the "non-print area." This is usually not a problem you can ignore. You must change the text to fit or create another frame and continue the text.

How to Copyfit Your Text

Copyfitting is the art of fitting text into a specific amount of space. For years in advertising agencies, publishing houses, and printing companies, the person who could compute the necessary copyfitting numbers was highly regarded. That person used special rulers and guides (a circle with a slot on top of a background circle—you twirled the circles to compute the space you had available against the font sizes needed). In the face of computerized publishing, copyfitting as a manual task is becoming a lost art.

Begin

1 Hold Control and Resize Frame

If a headline uses two lines, and you prefer one-line headlines, try expanding the width of the text frame. Hold down the **Ctrl** key while you drag the sizing handle to change both sides at once.

Click & Drag

Control

2 Turn Bold On/Off

Very often, removing bold formatting from a headline copyfits the headline perfectly. The only difference between the two text frames shown here is that the **Bold** icon on the **Formatting** toolbar is clicked to toggle off the **Bold** attribute for the text in the top frame.

3 Reduce/Increase Font Size

You can also reduce the font size. If the text frame has a headline or a list, you can try reducing just one section of text to fit everything into your frame. Select the text you want to change and choose a new size from the **Font Size** box on the **Formatting** toolbar.

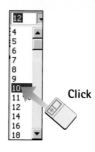

Click

4 Click Best Fit

To let Publisher copyfit the text frame automatically, select the frame and choose **Format**, **AutoFit Text**, **Best Fit**.

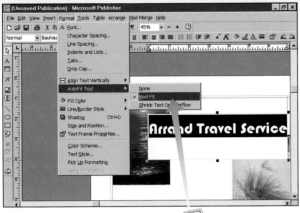

Click

5 Best Fit and Text Frames

As long as the **Best Fit** option is on, Publisher continues to refit the text when you change the size of the text frame.

Click & Drag

6 Best Fit and Font Size

Changing the font size of any part of the text doesn't work when automatic copyfitting is enabled—the text jumps right back to the size best suited for copyfitting.

7 Reducing Overflow Text

To make sure that there is no overflow text in a text frame, choose **Format**, **AutoFit Text**, **Shrink Text on Overflow**. The automatic copyfitting goes into effect by reducing font size as soon as you type past the bottom of the frame into the overflow area.

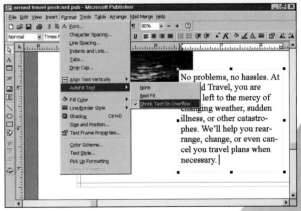

End

How-To Hints

Don't Enlarge the Frame to Force Copyfitting

It's usually easier to solve a copyfitting problem for a single text frame by enlarging the frame, but if you do that often enough, you may have trouble fitting everything you need into your publication. Combine manual tweaking with the copyfitting tools Publisher offers.

How to Control Tracking, Kerning, and Leading

You can control the way text fits and looks by changing the spacing. There are four ways to control spacing in publishing:

- ✓ Scaling—Shrinking or expanding the width of the characters.
- ✓ Tracking—Changing the size of the spaces between characters.
- ✓ Kerning—Changing the size of spaces between specific pairs of characters, such as the letters **A** and **V**.
- ✓ Leading (pronounced *ledding*)—Changing the spacing between lines.

Begin

1 Character Spacing Dialog Box

To change tracking or kerning, select the paragraph(s) you want to tweak and choose **Format, Character Spacing** from the **menu bar** to bring up the **Character Spacing** dialog box. If you have a lot of experience tracking and kerning text, you may prefer the toolbar: Click **Show Toolbar** to display it.

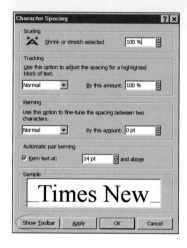

2 Select a Tracking Method

In the **Tracking** section of the dialog box, select a tracking method. The **By this amount** percentage specification changes automatically, but you can change it if you want to fine-tune the tracking.

3 Enable Automatic Pair

To automate kerning, make sure that the **Automatic** pair kerning section of the dialog box is enabled with a check mark in the box named **Kern text at**. Then specify the size of the font at which automatic kerning is applied. Kerning below 14 points usually doesn't work well.

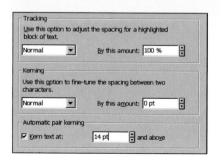

4 Choose a Kerning Option

If you want to force kerning manually (for type that's smaller than the point at which kerning is automatic), choose a kerning option from the drop-down list. Then check the **Sample** box to see how it looks. You can tweak the kerning by changing the percentage in the **By this amount** box.

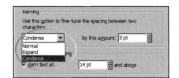

5 Try a Scaling Option

The top of the **Character Spacing** dialog box offers a scaling option, which doesn't change the spacing, but instead shrinks or expands the characters. Sometimes this works when you have just a bit too much text for a text frame. (However, depending on the font you're using, you may not like the condensed look of the text.)

6 Choose Line Spacing

To adjust the leading, select the paragraph(s) you want to change and choose **Format**, **Line Spacing**.

 Click

7 Adjust Default on Line Spacing

In the **Line Spacing** dialog box, adjust the default of **1** space in the **Between lines** box. Make the number smaller for tighter copyfitting, or larger to fill an unfilled frame.

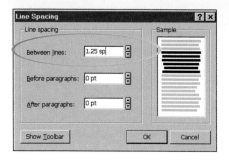

End

How-To Hints

Track and Kern WordArt

You can also track and kern the character spacing in WordArt frames with the tools on the **WordArt Formatting** toolbar.

How to Perfect Hyphenation

By default, Publisher automatically hyphenates words to make your text look neater. Without hyphenation, words that don't completely fit on a line are pushed in their entirety to the next line. This can create a lot of whitespace on the right side of your text frame, which is not very professional-looking.

Checking hyphenation is important because there are situations in which hyphenation stops helping and begins harming the look of your text. For instance, consecutive lines that end with hyphens look unprofessional, as does a hyphen at the end of the last line in a text frame (for those stories that are continued in another frame).

Begin

1 Configuring Hyphehenation

To configure hyphenation, choose **Tools, Options** from the **menu bar**. When the **Options** dialog box opens, select the **Edit** tab.

2 Setting Hyphenation Zone

You can change the way hyphenation works by changing the **Hyphenation zone** specification. The number indicates how much whitespace can exist at the end of each line before hyphenation is used. Make the number larger to decrease hyphens. You can also deselect automatic hyphenation by clicking the **Automatically hyphenate in new text frames** option, but this is not usually a good idea.

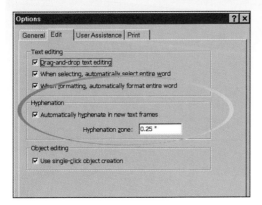

3 Hyphenating Frames

To configure hyphenation for a specific text frame, select the frame and choose **Tools, Language, Hyphenation** from the **menu bar**. When the **Hyphenation** dialog box appears, change the zone for this story (any connected frames are also changed). If you want to turn off all hyphenation in this story, click the **Automatically hyphenate this story** option to remove the check mark.

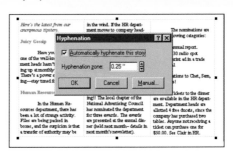

4 Click Manual Hyphenation

Click the **Manual** button in the **Hyphenation** dialog box to approve, change, or eliminate the hyphens that were inserted automatically. Each hyphenated word is displayed with all the possible hyphens. Choose **Yes** to leave the hyphenation as-is, or click a different hyphenation point for the word and choose **Yes**. Choose **No** if you don't want the word hyphenated. The next hyphenated word is displayed, and this continues throughout the story unless you click the **Close** button.

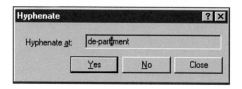

5 Adding a Hyphenated Phrase

If you have a hyphenated phrase, you can tell Publisher you don't want the hyphen used at the end of a line (which means the words must be kept together on one line, such as Mary-Quite-Contrary). Hold **Ctrl+Shift** as you type the hyphens, which tells Publisher that these are non-breaking hyphens.

> Stop by the production department to meet the new graphics manager. The gossip editor of this company newsletter thinks it's important to tell everyone that at her previous company the sign on her door read "Mary-Quite-Contrary". Somebody should find the courage to ask the obvious question.

6 Hyphenating a Word

To change the hyphenation for an individual word, select the word and press **Ctrl+Shift+H** to bring up the **Hyphenate** dialog box. Then click at the alternate hyphenation point and choose **Yes**. If there is no alternate hyphenation point, the **Hyphenate** dialog box offers the options available in Step 4.

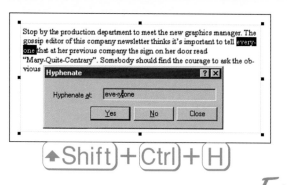

End

How-To Hints

Hyphens in Headlines Are Unprofessional

Never, never permit hyphens in a headline. Widen the text frame, reduce the size of the font, or change the wording—do whatever is necessary to avoid hyphenated headlines.

How to Work with Bindings

Most of the time, a bound publication is printed on two sides, resulting in a *verso* (left) page for the even-numbered pages, and a *recto* (right) page for the odd-numbered pages. However, you can bind a publication that's designed to print only on one side of the paper.

No matter which binding method you use, you have to design your publication around it. Otherwise, the binding might cover text or graphics. The left page needs binding space (called a *gutter*) on the right side and the right page has its gutter on the left side.

Begin

1 Choose Layout Guides

To force empty space for binding, choose **Arrange**, **Layout Guides** from the **menu bar**.

2 Change Inside Margin

If you're printing on both sides of the paper, be sure that the **Create Two Backgrounds With Mirrored Guides** option is selected on the **Layout Guides** dialog box. Change the size of the **Inside** margin to match the gutter size you need for your binding method.

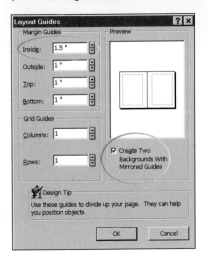

3 Increase Left Margin

If you're printing on only one side of the paper (you might want to leave a blank page on one side of the publication for readers to use for notes), increase the margin for the side of the paper that will be bound. It's most common to have the printed page on the right side of the publication, so adjust the left margin.

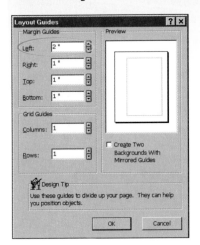

4 Change Background

If you're using the background for page numbers or titles, design the gutter for the background page. If you've already designed the background, you probably need to adjust the graphic to match the new margin. For more information about using the background, see "How to Create Background Elements" in Part 4, "Adding Special Elements."

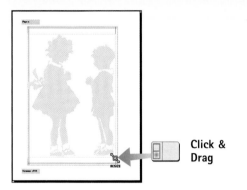

Click & Drag

5 Adjust Mirror Pages

If you're working with mirrored pages, you'll need to adjust the background picture on both the left and right pages. Use ruler guides to help you align the images perfectly.

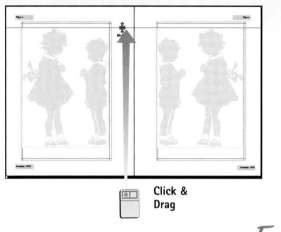

Click & Drag

End

How-To Hints

How to Staple the Middle of Newsletters

If you produce newsletters, you can fold the paper and staple into the fold. You'll need a long stapler, which is available at most office supply stores.

Set the Binding Margins First

If your publication has columns (as does a newspaper or a newsletter), remember that the columns grow thinner as you expand the gutter. If you wait until you've finished your publication to set these binding margins, you may find that some text overflows the frames. That's why you should set your binding margins before you begin work on the publication.

Some Options for Binding Your Publication

There are lots of ways to bind a publication, from stapling to attaching professionally glued covers. For a thick publication or a fancy cover, you'll probably want to contact a professional printing service or a bindery.

Mirrored Background Graphics

If you place a graphic on your background and use mirrored pages, you may want to flip one graphic to reverse its image.

How to Work with Crop and Registration Marks

Crop marks are special markings that must be printed (outside the margins of the publication) when the paper and your publication are not the same size. They provide the guidelines for cutting the paper.

Registration marks are also printed outside the margins of the publication; they indicate the place at which the pages line up as they pass through the printer. This device is used by outside printing companies for printing in multiple-color passes. The printing company needs a separate printed page from Publisher for each color in your publication.

Begin

1 Choose Print

Crop marks are inserted automatically during the printing process. To print the crop marks for your publication, choose **File**, **Print** from the **menu bar** (or press **Ctrl+P**). Click the **Advanced Print Settings** button in the **Print** dialog box.

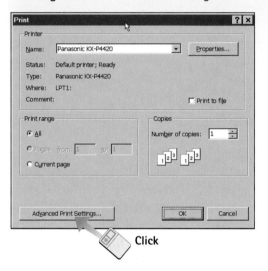

Click

2 Select Print Crop Marks

In the **Print Settings** dialog box, make sure that the **Crop Marks** option is selected.

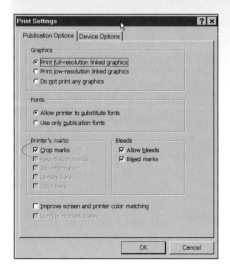

3 Notice Crop Marks

The printed copy displays the crop marks needed to cut the paper accurately.

4 Select Show All Printer Marks

When you set up your publication for outside printing, additional printing marks become available on the **Print Settings** dialog box. All the information you need about printing to an outside printing service is found in Part 8, "Printing Your Publication."

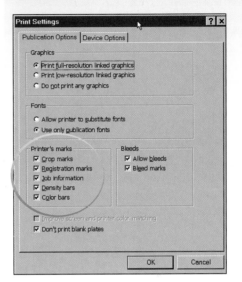

5 Notice Registration Marks

When you print a proof copy (and when the printer prints the publication), the registration marks are printed along with the crop marks.

6 Line Up Registration Marks

Notice that the registration mark provides a way to make very precise connections. The lines and the circles must both line up on at least two registration marks to ensure crisp printing.

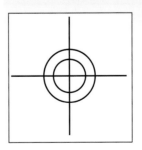

End

Project 2

A Flyer from Scratch

This project will help you practice all the skills you've learned since the last project. In this exercise, we'll move along a little faster than in the first project—the steps assume that you've learned and practiced some of the basic stuff.

In this project, you'll be flying "without a net"—building a publication from scratch, without a wizard. As the owner of a small clothing resale shop called The Attic, you'll use Publisher to create a two-page flyer promoting your business.

1 Start with a Blank Page

When Publisher opens to the Catalog, click **Exit Catalog** to display a blank page. (If Publisher is already started, click the **New** button instead.) Click the **Hide Wizard** button.

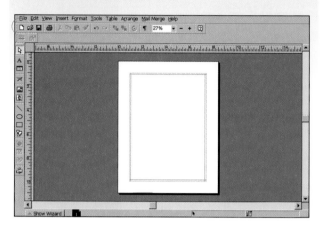

2 Change the Margins

You're going to have this flyer professionally bound and printed, so change the inside margin to **1.25"** using the **Arrange, Layout Guide** command. Be sure to select the **Create Two Backgrounds with Mirrored Guides** option.

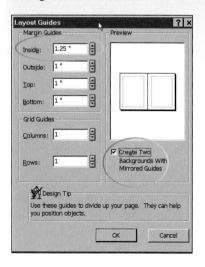

3 Create a Background

Press **Ctrl+M** to view the background. Create a text box and type **Peace** in it, using **Ravie** font, **28 point**. Select the text and change its color to a very light gray.

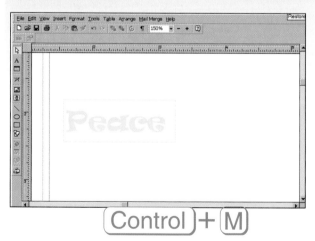

4 Create More Phrases

Create similar text boxes using other 60's catch phrases such as **Love**, **Groovy**, and **Far Out**.

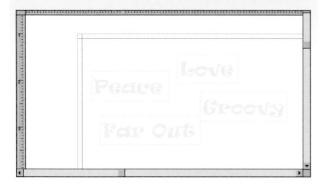

5 Copy and Rotate the Text Boxes

Copy each phrase at least once to create several text boxes. Then press **Alt** as you move the mouse to a corner of one of the text boxes. Rotate the box to create a pleasing effect. Repeat with the other text boxes.

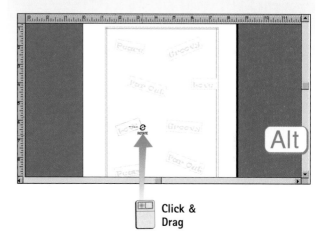

Click & Drag

6 Insert Pages

Return to the foreground by pressing **Ctrl+M**. Then add three pages to the document with the **Insert, Page** command.

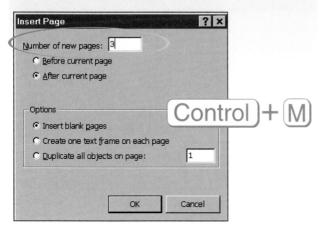

Control + M

7 Add a Title

Flip to page 1 and add a text box for the words **The Attic**. Use the font **Ravie**, **48 point** and **centered**. Size and position the title as shown in the example.

Continues

8 Add a Rectangular Bleed

Draw a rectangle; size and position it over the text box as shown in the example. Use a **Gradient** fill effect and your choice of "groovy" colors to color the text box.

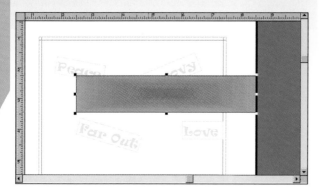

9 Finish the Title

Click **Send to Back** to place the rectangle behind the text box. Next, select the text box and choose **No Fill** so that the background shows through.

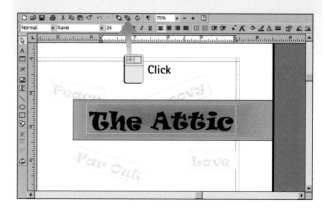

10 Add a Subtitle

Create a text box as shown with the text, **Your 60's Clothier**. Use **Ravie**, **24 point**. Use a gradient fill, with a different pair of colors than the ones you used in Step 8, to fill the text box.

11 Add Clip Art

Add some clip art to the front page—your choice. If you can't find any clip art that you like, feel free to create some using the skills you learned in Part 3, "Working with Graphics."

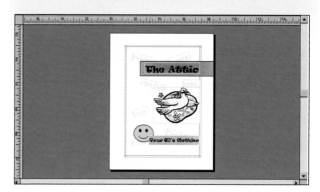

12 Copy the Background Pages

Change to page 2. Press **Ctrl+M** to view the background. Copy the text you created for the odd pages to the even pages (2 and 4) as well.

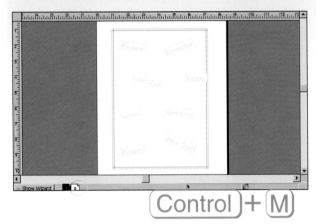

Control + M

13 Add a Headline to Page 2

Press **Ctrl+M** to view the foreground. Create a text box that says, "Turn Your Trash to Treasure." Use **Berlin Sans FB, 40 point** text.

14 Rotate the Headline

Add another colorful gradient fill to the text box—your choice of colors. Then press **Alt** and use the mouse to rotate the text box by its corner.

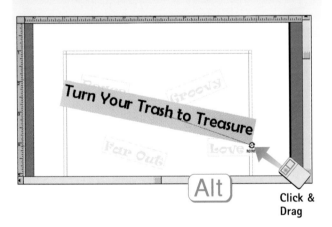

Alt

Click & Drag

15 Add a Bulleted List

Create a text box and add the bulleted list shown in the example. Use **Berlin Sans FB, 28 point, Bold text**. Use the **Format, Align Text Vertically, Center** command to center the text in the frame.

Continues

16 Change the Bullets

Select the list, and use the **Format, Indents and Lists** command to change the bullets to happy faces (you'll find one in the first Wingdings font). Change the size of the bullet to **24 point**, and indent the list by **0.45**.

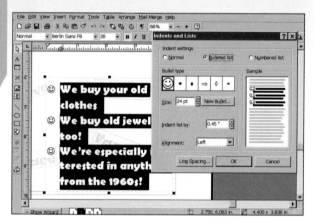

17 Add Final Touches

Fill the text box with the color **yellow**. Then add another piece of clip art or draw your own (such as the Peace symbol shown here.)

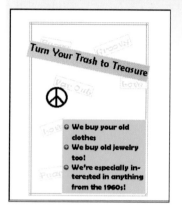

18 Include the Hours of Operation

Create another text box on page 3 that lists the store's hours of operation, as shown. Use **Berlin Sans FB, 48 point, Bold, Underline** text for the heading; use **Berlin Sans FB, 20 point, Bold** text for the rest.

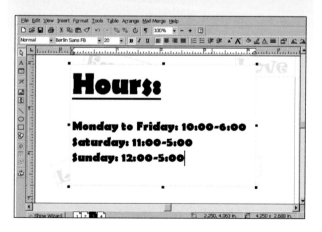

19 Center the Text

Center the text both vertically and horizontally. Fill the text box with the color **yellow**. Rotate the text box as shown in the example.

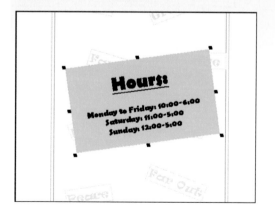

20 Add Some Clip Art

Add more "groovy" clip art to page 3. Then turn to page 4.

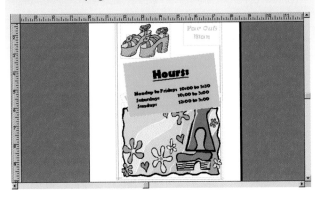

21 Add a Heading

Add a text box that says, "Come Visit Us Soon." Use **Ravie, 36 point, centered** text. Add a colorful gradient fill.

22 A Final Enticement

As an enticement to get customers to visit, include a **Coupon** from the **Design Gallery**. Add lots of color and you've got a great-looking flyer!

End

How-To Hints

Save Often

Don't forget to save your project often as you work through this task.

Select It All

If you want to select a large group of objects, use the **Pointer** tool to draw a box around them. Then click the **Group Objects** button to group them together.

Task

1 How to Set Up a Web Publication 178

2 How to Add Pages to a Web Publication 180

3 How to Add Sounds and Animation to Web Pages 182

4 How to Create Navigation Bars 184

5 How to Add Hyperlinks 186

6 How to Add Hot Spots 188

7 How to Check the Web Design 190

8 How to Preview Your Web Publication 192

9 How to Convert Publications to Web Pages 194

10 How to Publish Your Publication to the Web 196

PART 6

Creating a Web Publication

*I*t doesn't matter how big your mailing list is or how many copies of your publication you think you can give away: You'll never reach as many potential readers as you can if you publish your masterpiece on the World Wide Web.

However, you can't just deliver a printed publication to a Web site and ask for it to be displayed. There are programming rules, programming codes, and graphic conversion programs that have to be used when creating a Web publication. It's all terribly complicated—unless you use Publisher.

In this part, you learn how easy it is to tell Publisher what you want in your Web publication. Publisher does all that techy stuff for you, behind the scenes. You can use these handy tools to create a Web page from scratch or to convert your favorite publications to Web pages.

After your Web publication is ready, you can contact a local Internet Service Provider (ISP) for help in publishing it to the Internet. Or you can publish your information locally, to your company's intranet (a local Internet at work). ●

How to Set Up a Web Publication

Even if you're not in charge of your company's Web site, as you become adept in Publisher, you'll be producing such great graphical publications that somebody will eventually say "We need that on the Web site."

Creating publications for the Web requires some special steps and distinctive design approaches, but don't worry: Publisher is equipped to provide an incredible amount of assistance.

Begin

1 Choose the Web Site Wizard

Choose **Web Sites** in the Catalog's **Publications by Wizard** tab. (The Catalog appears automatically when you first start Publisher, but if you're already working in the software, choose **File, New** from the **menu bar** to open the Catalog.)

2 Select a Design

In the right pane, scroll through the available Web page design layouts and select the one you like; then choose **Start Wizard**.

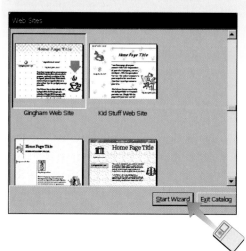

Click

3 Provide Information for the Wizard

Make changes as needed to the **Web Site Wizard** pane. When you're through, hide the wizard by clicking **Hide Wizard**.

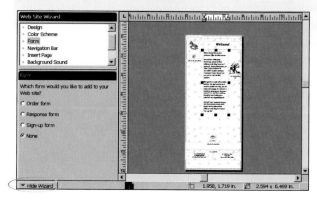

4 Enter Text

Select the text frames in the Web page and substitute your own words for the placeholder text.

5 Replace the Art Work

Double-click any graphic to replace it with artwork that's more suitable for your message.

Double Click

6 Use a Blank Web Page

If you want to build your Web page from scratch, use the Catalog's **Blank Publications** tab and select **Web Page**. Choose **Create** to begin building your Web publication. Create text and graphic frames as you need them.

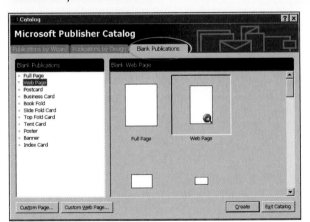

End

How-To Hints

Use the Wizard Until You're Comfortable

You can choose either a predesigned page (with a wizard) or a blank page (and add each element yourself) for your Web publication. It's probably a good idea to use the wizard for your first experiment in creating Web pages.

Already Done?

If you have already created a publication, you can easily convert it to a series of Web pages. See Part 6, Task 9, "How to Convert Publications to Web Pages," for help.

How to Add Pages to a Web Publication

Whether you use a wizard-designed publication or create your own Web page from scratch, you probably will add pages to your Web masterpiece as additional information needs to be disseminated.

Begin

1 Use the Insert Command

Choose **Insert**, **Page** from the **menu bar**.

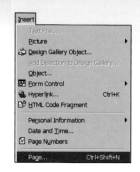

2 Choose a Page Type

The **Insert Page** dialog box for Web pages offers choices specifically for Web publications. Start by clicking the arrow next to the **Available page types** box and picking the type of page you need. If you want this page listed on your navigation bar, make sure that the option is selected at the bottom of the dialog box.

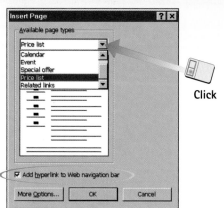

Click

3 Specify Other Options

Choose **More Options** on the **Insert Page** dialog box to see additional choices for inserting this new page. Select the options you want, then choose **OK** twice to insert the page into your publication.

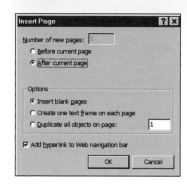

4 Put a Title on the Page

It's always a good idea to add a title to every page. Unlike printed publications, Web documents aren't treated as a continuous story; each page exists for specific information. Don't forget to format the text and frame; plain text is dull on the Web.

5 The Navigation Link Changes

After you insert the new page, notice that the navigation link to your new page has a matching title. This title helps your visitors quickly find the page they want to view.

6 Add Other Text and Graphics

Change other placeholder text in the publication and add graphics and other elements as needed to complete your new page.

End

How-To Hints

Put Everything on the Navigation Bar

Although Publisher offers an option for listing a new page on the navigation bar, don't think of it as optional. *Always* select this link so that your readers can navigate easily through all your publication's pages.

How to Add Sounds and Animation to Web Pages

Some of the fun of visiting Web sites is hearing music or sound effects and watching stuff prance around the screen in a frenzy of animation. You can provide those elements for your Web visitors, too.

Background sound is music (or noise, if you prefer) that you attach to a Web page and it becomes an element of the *page*, not of a particular object.

Begin

1 Open the Web Properties

To add sound that's attached to the Web page (it starts when the Web page opens in a browser), you need to configure the properties for the Web page. With your Web page in the Publisher window, choose **File, Web Properties** from the **menu bar**.

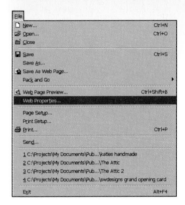

2 Specify a Sound File

In the **Web Properties** dialog box, move to the **Page** tab. In the dialog box's **Background sound** section, enter the name of the sound file you want to use in the **File name** box. Click the **Browse** button to locate the sound file if you don't have the folder and filename memorized. Choose to *loop* (replay) the sound file incessantly while the reader is viewing this page, or choose to have it play a specific number of times. Click **OK**. (Nothing happens; you won't hear the sound in Publisher, just when you're viewing the page in a browser.)

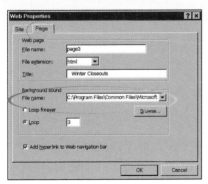

3 Insert Animations

Click the **Clip Gallery** button on the **Objects** toolbar and drag your mouse to create a frame for your graphic animation.

Click

4 Choose the Picture File

The **Clip Gallery** opens automatically when you release the mouse. Move to the **Motion Clips** tab. Select a category or type a key word to search. Click to select a picture, then click **Insert Clip** to insert it in the frame.

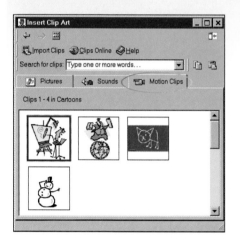

5 Position the Picture Frame

Move the picture frame so that it isn't on any part of a text frame. (That prevents the animation on the Web and you'll have a static picture.) If necessary, resize the picture frame.

6 Preview the Publication on the Web

Because neither the sound nor the animation works in Publisher, choose **File, Web Page Preview** from the **menu bar**. When your browser opens, you hear your sounds and see your animation.

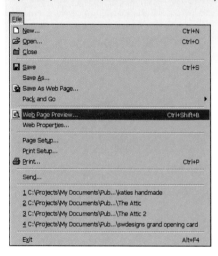

How-To Hints

Sound Files Can Be Very Large

Some sound files are quite large; if your page is filled with lots of elements and graphics, adding sound may make the process of loading it into the browser window slow enough to annoy your reader. Preview the page for friends and co-workers and see what they think.

End

How to Create Navigation Bars

Navigation bars are those parts of a Web page that you use to move to other parts of the Web site.

A true navigation bar is called a *vertical navigation bar*. You can also insert a *horizontal navigation bar*, which is really a text frame with text that is configured as a hyperlink. (If you use the Web Page Wizard, you're offered the choice of a vertical or horizontal navigation bar, or you can choose both.)

You can create your own navigation bar or edit the one placed there by the wizard. See Task 5 for information about creating the actual hyperlinks.

Begin

1 Select the Navigation Bar

If you used the Web Page Wizard for your publication, click the vertical navigation bar that was inserted automatically. When it's selected, a Wizard button appears on the bottom of the frame; you can click it to change the bar's design scheme.

Click

2 Select a Different Scheme

Select a different scheme from the list. The new navigation bar appears in your Web page.

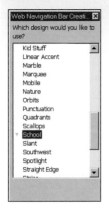

3 Create Your Own Navigation Bar

If you're creating your Web site from scratch, you can add a navigation bar to give your page it a polished look. To create a navigation bar, click the **Design Gallery Object** tool on the **Objects** toolbar.

Click

4 Choose a Navigation Bar Design

When the **Design Gallery** opens, choose **Web Navigation Bars** as the category, and then choose the design you want to use for your main (vertical) bar from the offerings in the right pane. Click **Insert Object** to put the bar on your page.

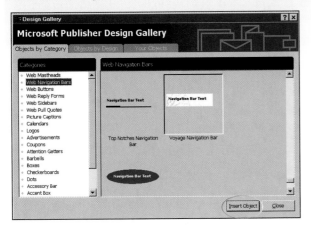

5 Position the Navigation Bar

When the navigation bar appears, move it to an appropriate spot on your page. Usually, it's best to put the bar in the page's upper-left section—Web users have learned to look there for navigation bars.

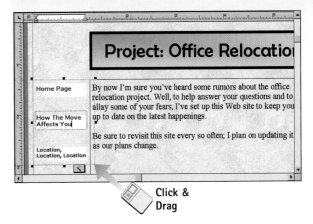

Click & Drag

6 Insert Navigation Bar Text

Select the placeholder text on the navigation bar elements and replace it with something more specific (and more creative). For example, if you're linking to a story about the UFO you saw the last time you took a walk in the swamp, call it *My UFO Sighting*.

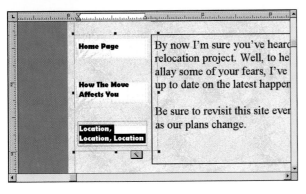

7 Format the Text

Even though you're creating a Web publication, this is still a text frame and you can use all the text formatting tools available. For example, you can change the font, make the text bold, or fill the frame with a color.

End

How-To Hints

Navigation Bars Easier for Audience

You can use a single word or a short phrase within a regular text frame as a hyperlink to other pages on your site, but if you have a lot of links, it's a good idea to provide a navigation bar in one section of your home page.

How to Add Hyperlinks

When your publication is on the Web, readers can't go through the exercise of moistening a finger and turning the page. You have to give them a device to get to the next page. That device is a *hyperlink*, and you can add a hyperlink to text or to a graphic object.

Begin

1 Select Text

To add a hyperlink to text, select the word(s) for the hyperlink.

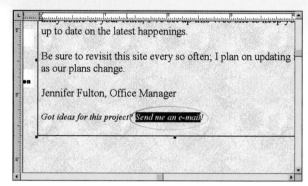

2 Choose the Hyperlink Command

Click the **Insert Hyperlink** button on the **Standard** toolbar (or press **Ctrl+K** for a keyboard shortcut).

Ctrl + K

Click

3 Select the Hyperlink Options

In the **Hyperlink** dialog box, select the options you need to link your text and its target. Choose **OK**.

4 Hyperlinked Text Is Underlined

When you return to your text frame, the text you selected for the hyperlink is underlined.

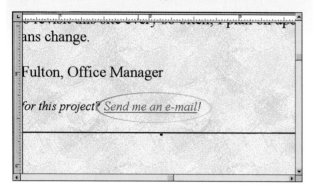

5 Use a Graphic

To add a hyperlink to a graphic image, right-click anywhere in the graphic frame and choose **Hyperlink**; then specify the options you need in the **Hyperlink** dialog box.

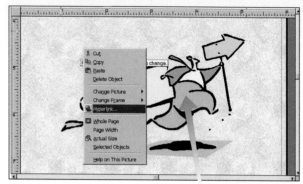

Right Click

6 Check the Graphic Link

When you choose **OK** to close the **Hyperlink** dialog box, check the graphic (it's not underlined the way text is) by placing your mouse pointer anywhere on the frame. You should see a **ScreenTip** that displays the link.

End

How-To Hints

Hyperlinks Can Do Lots of Things

You can create a hyperlink to another page in your Web site or to any page out on the Internet or on your company's local intranet. You can also link to a file (so that a user can download it), or to an email address (so that a use can send an email message).

How to Add Hot Spots

A *hot spot* is a place on an object that holds a hyperlink. You can have numerous hot spots on one object.

If you've played with any children's story CD-ROMs, you've probably clicked specific parts of a picture to launch another story—click the cow and see a cow story, click the tree and see birds flying. Those are examples of hot spots.

Begin

1 Click the Hot Spot Tool

Click the **Hot Spot** button on the **Objects** toolbar.

Click

2 Draw the Hot Spot

Position your pointer where the upper-left corner of the hot spot belongs and drag down and to the right to create a hot spot. In this example, the hot spot is being positioned around central Europe.

Click & Drag

3 Configure the Hyperlink

The **Hyperlink** dialog box opens automatically when you release the mouse button. Select the options you need for this hyperlink and choose **OK**.

4 Check the Hyperlink

Position your pointer over the hot spot to check the hyperlink displayed in the ToolTip.

5 Create Multiple Hot Spots

You can repeat Steps 1 through 4 to create multiple hot spots. While you work in Publisher, you'll see the frame for each hot spot on your page. (The frames aren't displayed when your publication is on the Web, but your reader's pointer changes to a **hand** to indicate a link.)

6 Create a Hot Spot with an Object

Another way to add a hot spot to a picture is to add an element you can use for the hot spot, such as a shape or a text box. (This is not technically a hot spot, but it works the same way.) Click a shape tool on the **Objects** toolbar and add a shape to the picture. Then place a hotspot on the shape, following Steps 1 through 4.

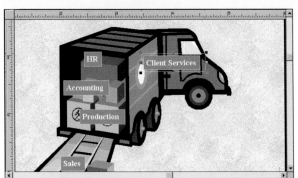

End

How-To Hints

Don't Use Unnecessary Hot Spots

Don't use hot spots on standard Web navigation objects such as **Next** or **Previous** buttons. The entire object should be the hot spot in these cases.

How to Check the Web Design

There are a number of design issues you have to think about when you publish for the Web. Do you have all the correct elements to make your hyperlinks work properly? Are your text and graphic frames placed for easy reading? (Web readers don't expect to see page after page of text-based articles.)

Worry not! Publisher has a built-in design checker that goes over your publication with a critical attitude. This nit-picking expert should be consulted before you begin thinking about publishing to the Web.

Begin

1 Open the Design Checker

Choose **Tools, Design Checker** from the menu bar.

2 Select the Pages to Check

When the **Design Checker** dialog box opens, you can either choose **All** to check the entire publication or select **Pages** and specify a range. If you have only one page you think you should check, set the **from** and **to** pages to the same number.

3 Set the Terms

Choose **Options** on the **Design Checker** dialog box to specify what you want the design checker to cover. Choose **Check selected features** and then click the appropriate check boxes to de-select the items you don't care about. Click **OK** to return to the **Design Checker** dialog box, and then click **OK** again to start the check.

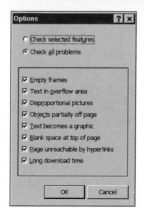

4 Read the Problem Dialog Box

When the design checker encounters a problem, a dialog box appears. Follow one of the solutions offered in the dialog box to fix the problem and then click **Continue**. Click **Ignore** to ignore the problem and continue checking the design.

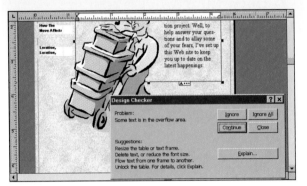

5 Continue the Checkup

After you fix the problem, choose **Continue** to move on to the next problem.

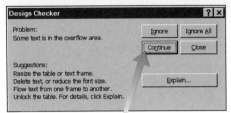

Click

6 Check Your Speed

When a reader opens your publication, the process involved is really a download (from your Web site to the reader's screen). Publisher offers to check the download speed. It reports that it's worried if it finds large, complicated graphics and suggests that you change them. Choose **Yes** to look for problems; click **No** if you don't care about this issue.

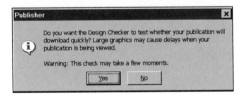

7 Finish the Checkup

When the design checker is finished, it announces that fact. Click **OK** to tell it to go away.

End

How-To Hints

Hints to Use the Design Checker

The **Continue** button in the design checker doesn't work until you've fixed the problem. The checker moves on automatically if you opt to ignore the problem.

✓ Choose **Close** to stop the design checker at any time.

✓ Choose **Explain** to open a **Help** page that explains what's wrong and how to fix it. (You may have to drag the **Design Checker** dialog box before you can see the bottom of the **Help** page.)

How to Preview Your Web Publication

Don't send your publication to your Web site without making sure that it looks the way you think it will. Working in the **Publisher** window does not provide you with a real look at a Web publication—you need to test the way things work as well as the way everything looks.

Begin

1 Open the Preview Program

Choose **File**, **Web Page Preview** from the **menu bar**. If you want to preview only one page, move to that page before selecting this command.

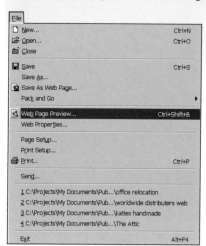

2 Choose the Pages to Preview

When the **Web Page Preview** dialog box opens, it offers a choice of previewing the **Web site** (all the pages in your publication) or the **Current page**. Make your choice and choose **OK**.

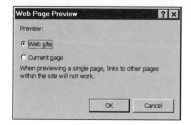

3 Publisher Converts Your Publication

Publisher prepares your publication for the Web. Depending on your machine's speed and your publication's complexity, this process can take a couple of seconds or a minute-plus.

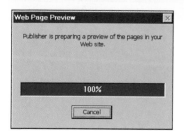

4 Examine the Browser Window

Your default **browser** opens with your publication in the window. The first thing to check is any object you placed a hyperlink in; make sure that your pointer turns into a hand when it is on the object.

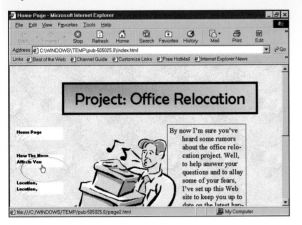

5 Test the Hyperlinks

Click each hyperlink object to make sure that you jump to the right place. In this case, the hyperlink moved me to the right page and I noticed that the main body text, when viewed in the **browser** window, is too close to the **navigation bar**.

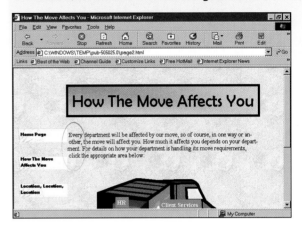

6 Close the Browser

Close the **browser** window (click the **X** in the upper-right corner) to return to the **Publisher** window. Now you can fix any problems you found.

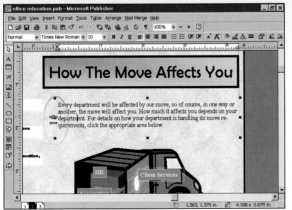

End

How-To Hints

You Can Check One Page at a Time

You can choose to preview a single page, which is helpful if you want to do a fast check of a page you think might have problems. However, a single-page Web preview does not activate your hyperlinks, so you won't be able to see if they work.

How to Convert Publications to Web Pages

If you've created a really terrific publication, it might be suitable for your Web site. You don't have to reconstruct it as a Web publication—you can convert it.

Begin

1 Open the Conversion Program

Open the publication you want to convert, then choose **File, Create Web Site from Current Publication** from the **menu bar**.

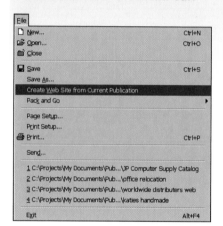

2 Check the Design

The design checker steps right up and offers to check the design before the conversion is complete. Say **Yes** and tell the checker to check **All pages**. Deal with each problem as it is presented. For more information about using the design checker, see Task 7, "How to Check the Web Design."

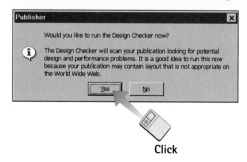

Click

3 Insert Hyperlinks if Needed

If the design checker tells you that a page in your publication cannot be reached, you must create a hyperlink to it. This is always a problem if your publication has more than one page, and it's a good idea to choose **Close** to stop the design checker to take care of this detail.

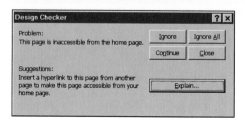

4 Create Links to All Pages

It's easiest to create a navigation bar from the **Design Gallery**. For details about inserting a navigation bar, see Task 4, "How to Create Navigation Bars," in this part. Start the design checker again and solve any remaining problems.

5 Preview the Publication on the Web

After you've fixed any problems, choose **File**, **Web Page Preview** from the **menu bar**. Tell Publisher you want to preview the entire publication by choosing **Web site** in the **Web Page Preview** dialog box.

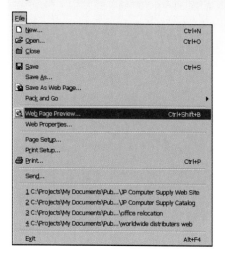

6 Check Everything in Your Browser

When your **browser** opens, check your publication carefully. If you think it will look just fine to the people who will visit your site, you've just saved yourself all the work of creating it again. Save your publication with a new filename.

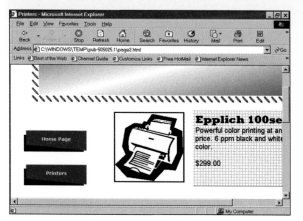

End

How-To Hints

A Converted Document Is New

When you choose the command to convert a publication to a Web publication, you're really creating a new document. You have to save it again with a new filename.

Conversion Isn't Always the Answer

Conversion doesn't always work well because many elements that are created for printed publications don't translate properly to a Web page (especially lots of text), but it's always worth trying. If the end result looks so yechy you're embarrassed when it displays in your browser window, you'll just have to redo it as a Web publication.

How to Publish Your Publication to the Web

There are several methods you can use to publish your publication to the Internet or to a local intranet. But before you begin, check with your company's system administrator or your Internet Service Provider (ISP) before proceeding. (Every ISP and intranet system manager will want you to submit Web pages in a particular manner.) Your options include publishing your site to a Web folder, an FTP site, or your local hard drive (where you share the folder with users on your company's network.)

Web folders allow you to publish your publication to an `http://` location (such as `http://bigcompany.com/myfolder`), but your ISP (or your local intranet) must support FrontPage Server Extensions in order to use the publication.

Begin

1 Create a Web Folder Link

Log on to the Internet (or your intranet). Open **Windows Explorer** and open the **Web Folders** folder. Double-click the **Add Web Folder** icon and follow the steps in the wizard.

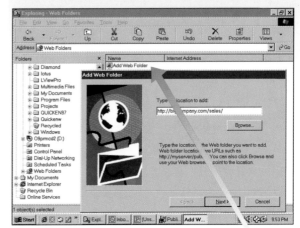

Double Click

2 Save Your Publication

After you create the link to the Web folder, you're ready to publish your site. Select **File, Save as Web Page** from the **menu bar**.

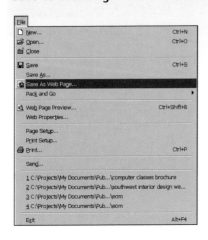

3 Publish to the Web Folder

Click **Web Folders**, and select the Web folder to which you want to publish. Click **OK**. If prompted, enter your **user id** and **password**.

Click

4 Create an FTP Link

Another way to publish your creation is to use FTP. To add the FTP site to your list, select **File, Save as Web Page**. Choose **Add/Modify FTP Location** from the **Look in** list at the top of the dialog box. The **Add/Modify FTP Locations** dialog box appears.

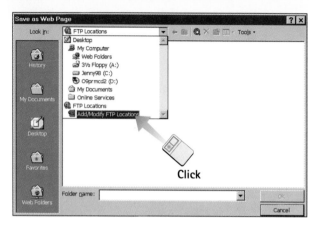

Click

5 Enter the FTP Information

Type the FTP address to which you want to publish in the **Name of FTP site** text box. Enter your login information and click **Add**. Click **OK** to return to the **Save as Web Page** dialog box.

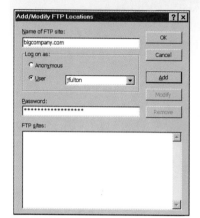

6 Publish to the FTP Site

In the **Save as Web Page** dialog box, select the FTP location you just added and click **OK**.

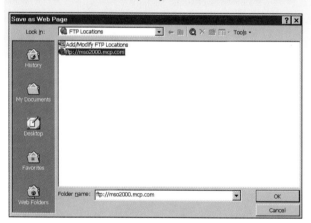

End

How-To Hints

Publishing to Your Hard Drive

To publish a publication to a local hard drive, just select the hard drive from the **Look in** list in the **Save as Web Page** dialog box.

Publishing with the Wizard

You can use the Web Publishing Wizard to help you publish your Web site. Start the wizard by selecting **Start, Programs, Internet Explorer, Web Publishing Wizard** (alternatively, select **Start, Programs, Microsoft Web Publishing**). (If the wizard does not exist on your system, you can install it using Windows Setup or Internet Explorer 5 Setup.)

What's in a Name?

Normally, the first page of your Web site is published under the name index.html. The second page is page2.html, and so on. You can change the name of any page in your publication before you publish it with the **File, Web Properties** command.

Task

1 How to Use Special Paper **200**

2 How to Create Signs **202**

3 How to Create Greeting Cards **204**

4 How to Create Business Forms **206**

5 How to Create a Banner **208**

6 How to Create Calendars **210**

7 How to Create Ads **212**

8 How to Create an Award Certificate **214**

9 How to Create a Gift Certificate **216**

10 How to Create a Program **218**

11 How to Build an Airplane **220**

12 How to Create Origami **222**

Creating Specialty Publications

Your list of things to do includes ordering stationery for the company, sending a greeting card to a friend who should be congratulated for passing the bar exam, and finding something relaxing to do during your lunch hour.

Publisher can take care of everything. There are a host of specialty publications available in Publisher (done with the help of some very clever wizards). You can design matching stationery (everything from business cards to the expense report forms you have to fill in to get those parking fees back). You can create greeting cards. You can make wonderful paper airplanes, complete with instructions on how to fold and fly them.

In this part, you have fun working with some of the Publisher publications that provide relief from the usual daily grind. ●

How to Use Special Paper

Publisher provides information about obtaining special, preprinted paper (with colors or patterns). This is a great way to get colorful designs on your publications without having to use an outside printing service or a color printer.

The company that provides the templates and designs is PaperDirect, which has a catalog available if you want to see all the paper stock it carries; the catalog items are more numerous than the designs displayed in Publisher. The catalog is in your Publisher package.

Begin

1 Choose Special Paper

The quickest way to see the special paper offerings is to move to the **Publications by Design** tab in the **Catalog** and select **Special Paper**. Choose a design and then select a publication from the right pane. Click **Start Wizard** to begin working on the publication.

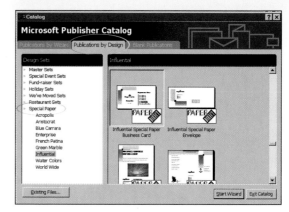

2 Design Through Wizard's Questions

The options that appear in the Wizard pane vary, based on the publication you select. Change the options you want, then click **Hide Wizard**. (You can select a different paper with the **Design** option.)

3 Press Ctrl+M for Background Design

The text and graphic frames on the publication page are carefully positioned so that you don't print over the designs on the paper. (Publisher uses the **background** to hold the paper design; press **Ctrl+M** if you want to see it.) See Task 5, "How to Create Background Elements," in Part 4 for information on using the background.

Control + M

4 Customize Special Paper

Either select text frames to add or change text or format the text. If there are graphic images on the form, double-click them to put a different graphic in the frame.

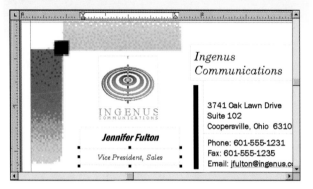

5 Print Special Paper

Put the special paper into your printer's paper tray. Choose **File**, **Print** to bring up the **Print** dialog box. Specify the number of copies you need and click **OK**.

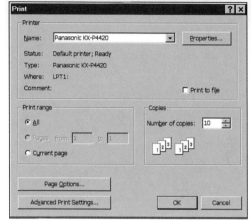

End

How-To Hints

You Can Use any Predesigned Paper

If you have your own source of predesigned paper stock, you can adjust the PaperDirect templates you find in Publisher to fit those patterns or use a blank publication template and design your own. Just use ruler guides to mark off the areas in which the design exists so that you don't try to place graphics or text on top of those design areas.

Take It for a Test Drive

If you're using special paper of your own (not from PaperDirect), print one copy of your completed publication as a test before you print multiple copies That way, you can make any necessary adjustments before you waste a lot of paper.

How to Create Signs

I have a friend with a two-car garage and three cars in the family. Parking on the driveway in front of the garage always creates a problem. She has a sign that says **Park Here and Die**. You can't buy signs like that; you have to make them.

You probably need signs that are less original, but whether you need to put up notices for employees, place signs on rooms to indicate their numbers or names, or warn people that you have a killer cat, you can save money by creating your own signs.

Begin

1 Choose Signs

In the **Catalog**, choose **Signs** (in the **Publications by Wizard** tab) and then scroll through the signs in the right pane to find the style that comes closest to your own needs; then choose **Start Wizard**.

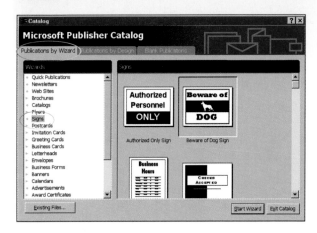

2 Select a Color Scheme

The only decision the wizard requests of you is the color scheme. Select the hues you want to use and then hide the wizard so that you can work on your sign.

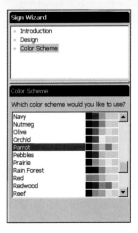

3 Ungroup Sign Elements

Some elements in the sign are grouped. If you want to change one element in the group, click the **Ungroup Objects** button to separate the elements. Learn about working with groups by reading Task 7, "How to Group and Ungroup Objects," in Part 3.

4 Customize the Graphics

Change the picture in a graphic frame by double-clicking it and selecting new art work.

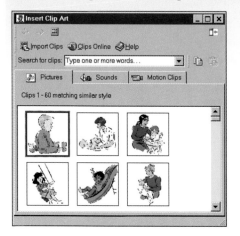

5 Customize the Text

Change text by selecting the text frame and making the appropriate edits.

6 Click Print

Click the **Print** button on the **Standard** toolbar to print your sign.

Click

End

How-To Hints

Print Without Turning the Paper Around The Rollers

If you use heavier paper for your signs, it's a good idea to either go to the printer and push whatever buttons have to be pushed or open whatever panels have to be opened to provide a straight-through path for the paper. If your printer cannot print without turning the paper, print on regular paper and then glue the paper to a heavier material.

How to Create Greeting Cards

There's nothing more embarrassing than forgetting an important occasion. No problem—with Publisher, you can create any cards you need at a moment's notice. And think of the money you'll save! More important (and more fun), your cards will be original and personal.

Most greeting cards have four pages (one is usually blank), even though you only need one piece of paper to print the card.

Begin

1 Choose Greeting Cards

Bring up the **Catalog** by choosing **File, New** from the **menu bar**. (If you just launched Publisher, the Catalog appears automatically.) Click the **Greeting Cards** entry on the **Publications by Wizard** tab to expand it.

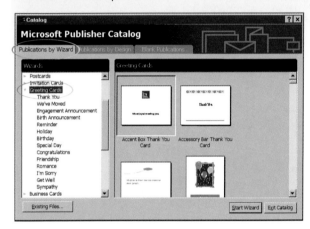

2 Choose Specific Card

Choose the specific type of card you need from the expanded list, and then select a style from the right pane. Click **Start Wizard** to begin.

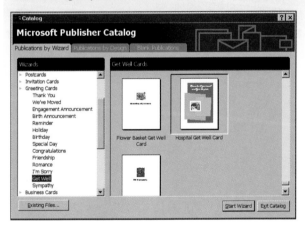

3 Select a Layout

When the Wizard pane opens, begin making decisions. The first determination is the layout. As you select a layout, the card changes so that you can see the results. When you find one you like, move to the next option.

4 Change the Size and Color

If needed, change to a different card size using the **Size and Fold** option. Select a complimentary **Color Scheme** as well.

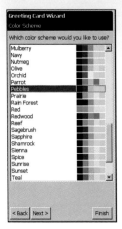

5 Add a Sentiment

To add a sentiment, click **Browse** to see the sentiments available. If you see anything you like, select it and choose **OK** (you can change it later). If you want to write original sentiments, skip this step.

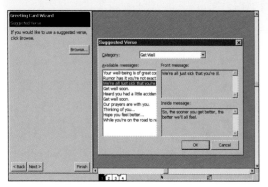

6 Touch Up the Card

Click **Finish** and then click **Hide Wizard** to create new text or replace graphics (some are on the background).

7 Choose Print

Choose **File**, **Print** to print your card; notice that it's ready for folding. The stuff that's upside down will look just fine after you fold it.

How-To Hints

Choosing a Filename

After you've created a greeting card, save the file with a name that indicates the recipient. I know someone who sent the same card to the same person a couple of times. Very embarrassing!

How to Create Business Forms

Some businesses have an incredible number of forms, (although probably nobody has as many as the government). It can be expensive to design and print forms. To top it off, every time there's a change in company policy, there's a good chance there has to be a change in some form.

Businesses that don't have forms aren't in better shape because of that lack; it means that expense accounts are handed in by putting rubber bands around receipts, and sales orders are scribbled on Post-It notes (or napkins, if the sale was made at lunch).

The solution? Create forms in Publisher. You'll have all the forms you need for good record keeping, and you won't spend a fortune on printing.

Begin

1 Choose Business Forms

In the **Catalog**, click **Business Forms** (on the **Publications by Wizard** tab) to expand the list of available forms. Select the type of form you need, and then choose a design from the right pane. Click the **Start Wizard** button to begin designing your form.

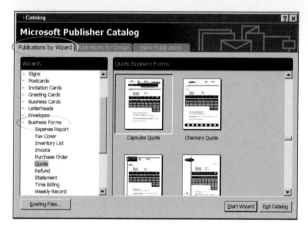

2 Select Custom Form Options

Make your selections in the **Wizard** pane (which vary depending on the form you chose). Then hide the wizard so that you can work on the publication.

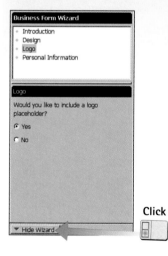

Click

3 Click Publications by Design Tab

If you need a variety of forms, move to the Catalog's **Publications by Design** tab. Choose a design that pleases you and then choose the forms you need. They'll all have the same design, which is a nice, professional approach.

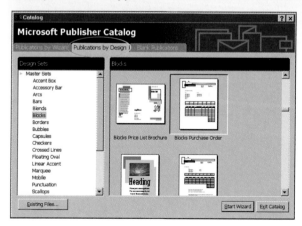

4 Customize Forms

Edit the form, adding or changing the text and graphics that Publisher provides. If you're creating a generic form that you will use over and over, enter only the common text. You can also create a complete form (with customer information, for example) and print it from Publisher.

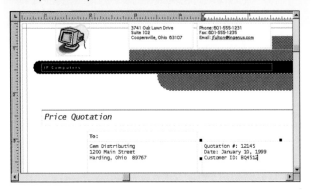

5 Print Forms

Print the form and distribute it, or send it to your printer for outside printing.

Click

End

How-To Hints

Special Needs May Require an Outside Printer

It's not always possible to print the forms you design in Publisher in-house, especially if you use non-standard paper, need duplicate copies (pink, white, and so on), or want the forms bound into a pad. However, creating the design for the printer (called a *mechanical* or a *camera-ready* hard copy) can save you money and time.

Add a Form to Your Web Site

In its Design Gallery, Publisher has many forms (such as order forms) that you can add to your Web site.

How to Create a Banner

If someone in your office just won a Nobel prize (or just a local contest), you should celebrate. At home, perhaps a family member or a neighbor just returned from the Oscar awards clutching her statue.

The celebration is much more fun with a banner. Luckily, you don't have to draw one (banners are a lot of work) because you have Publisher.

Begin

1 Choose Banner

Choose **File**, **New** from the **menu bar** to bring up the **Catalog**. (The **Catalog** appears automatically if you're just opening Publisher.) Choose **Banners** from the **Publications by Wizard** tab to expand the list of banners.

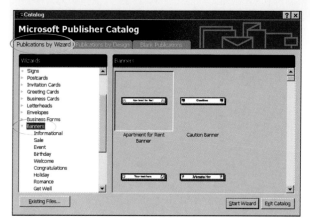

2 Choose a Specific Banner

Select the type of banner you want. Select the specific banner you want from the right pane. Choose **Start Wizard**.

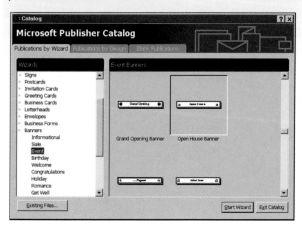

3 Change Banner Options

Select from various options in the **Wizard** pane. For example, you may want to change the length of the banner.

4 Choose Finish

Choose **Finish**, and then click **Hide Wizard** so that you can work on your banner. You can change the text, the graphics, or the border.

5 Choose Print

Banners are printed on multiple pieces of paper. Choose **File**, **Print** from the **menu bar**. When the **Print** dialog box opens, choose **Tile Printing Options**.

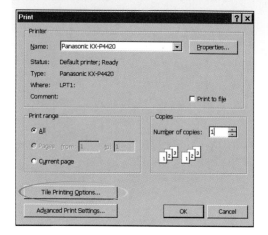

6 Select Options

Check the paper use in the **Poster and Banner Printing Options** dialog box. If only a tiny portion of the last piece of paper is being used, you can reduce the size of the overlap to eliminate it. (Most of the time, it's best to leave everything the way Publisher set it up.) Choose **OK** to return to the **Print** dialog box. Print your banner, get out the tape or glue, and put it together.

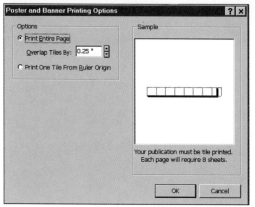

How-To Hints

Add a Personal Touch

Every banner I've ever created in Publisher or helped clients create had decorations added after it was printed and assembled. Having people sign their names (along with a sweet or funny sentiment) is part of the fun of banners.

End

How to Create Calendars

Sending calendars to your customers is a great idea. Every time the customer enters an appointment or checks the date, there's a reminder of your company.

Calendars are also effective when you add all sorts of personal touches and send them to friends and relatives.

Begin

1 Choose a Calendar

Open the **Catalog** and click the **Calendars** entry to expand it. Then select **Full Page** or **Wallet Size**. In the right pane, select the layout you want to use and then choose **Start Wizard**.

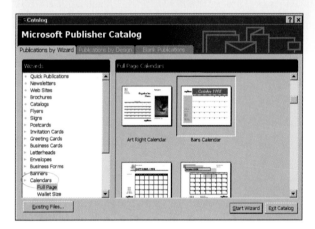

2 Choose a Monthly or Yearly Calendar

In the **Wizard** pane, select a different color scheme and orientation if needed. Then select either a monthly or a yearly calendar.

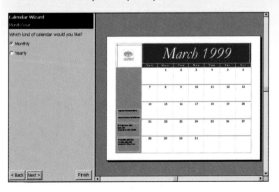

3 Change the Dates

By default, Publisher uses the current month and year for your calendar. Click **Change Dates** to select a different date.

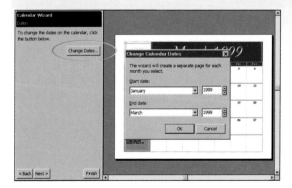

4 Add a Schedule of Events

You can add a schedule of events to your calendar. A blank event section looks silly, so choose **No** if you don't have any events.

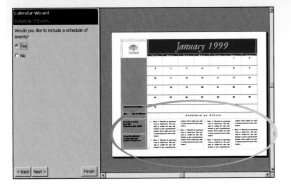

5 Customize Your Calendar

Click **Finish** and hide the wizard to begin working on your publication. Select the frames you need to work in and change the text as necessary. For example, if you have a schedule of events for the month the calendar covers, add them to the schedule frame. Notice that the schedule is a bullet list. (Read all about creating bulleted lists in Task 8, "How to Create Lists," in Part 2.

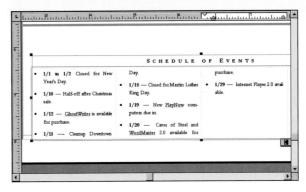

6 Add Special Dates

It's a good idea to annotate special dates right on the **date block**, which is a text frame.

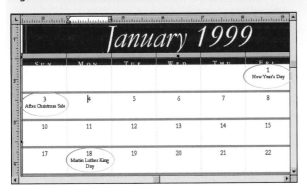

7 Print Your Calendar

Click the **Print** icon on the **standard** toolbar to print your calendar.

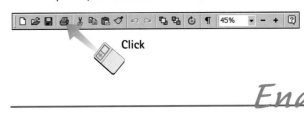

Click

End

How-To Hints

Add Text to Monthly Calendars

If you want to personalize dates, choose a monthly calendar instead of a yearly calendar.

How to Get Presents

A nifty trick is to enter your own birthday on calendars you send to friends and relatives.

How to Create Ads

If you're in business, you probably advertise that business. If you buy space in a newspaper or magazine, you have to provide the ad (or pay the paper or magazine to produce one, which is frequently not worth the money).

Use Publisher to create your ads—you'll end up with a polished, professional look without paying an agency big bucks.

Begin

1 Choose Advertisements

In the **Catalog**, choose **Advertisements** (in the **Publications by Wizard** tab) and then scroll through the designs in the right pane to find the one that comes closest to the format you need.

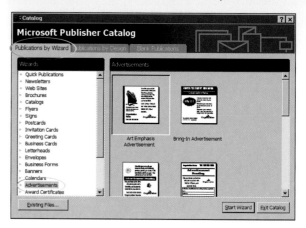

2 Choose Ad Size

Choose **Start Wizard** to begin configuring your ad. One of the first options concerns the ad's size; standard sizes are offered. If the space you bought doesn't match the wizard's choices, click the **Custom** button to open the **Page Setup** dialog box, which has the **Special Size** option selected.

3 Customize Ad Size

Enter the **Width** and **Height** you need for your custom size and choose **OK**.

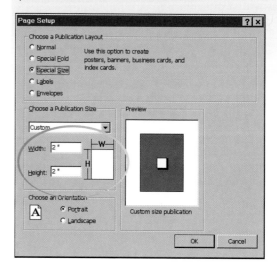

4 Select Other Options

If you want, you can include your company logo with your ad. If your advertisement is small, you can print multiple copies (which is useful if you're buying space in multiple publications) using the **Print Tiling** option.

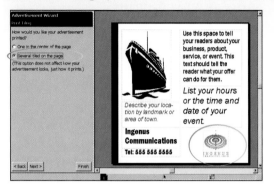

5 Customize the Ad

Hide the wizard to start working on your ad. Select frames and replace the placeholder contents with your own text and graphics.

6 Print Ad

Click the **Print** button on the **standard** toolbar to produce a printed ad. It's a good idea to use coated paper to make sure that the image stays crisp as it goes through production (and is printed on the cheap paper used by newspapers).

Click

End

How-To Hints

Black and White

Design ads in black and white, even if the printed ad will be colorized—the paper's/magazine's production department will handle the colorization. Provide color swatches or chips. (You can buy books of standard colors with tear-out squares you can give to the production department.)

How to Create an Award Certificate

Everyone likes his or her work to be acknowledged, and with Publisher, it's easy to give someone else the credit they deserve. The next time a co-worker makes the "Golden Circle" or a friend hits a hole-in-one, you can whip up a nice certificate that says *Great job!*

Begin

1 Choose a Certificate

In the **Catalog**, click **Award Certificates** (on the **Publications by Wizard** tab) to expand the listing. Select from **Plain Paper** or **Special Paper** certificates (Special Paper certificates are available from PaperDirect) and select the design you want to use from the right pane. Click **Start Wizard** to begin designing your certificate.

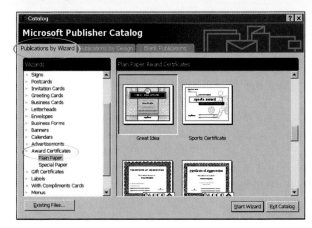

2 Change the Wizard Options

Change the wizard options as needed. For example, you may want to use a different **Color Scheme**.

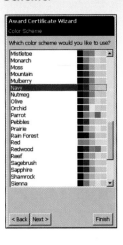

3 Customize the Text

Click **Hide Wizard** to maximize your work area and begin working on the certificate. Replace the placeholder text with your own words.

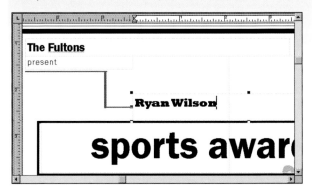

4 Replace Graphics

Double-click to replace any graphics with your own designs or those available from the **Insert Clip Art** dialog box.

5 Add Special Touches

Don't be afraid to add extra text and graphics to make the certificate a one-of-a-kind publication.

6 Print the Certificate

If you're using a Special Paper certificate, load the special paper into your printer. Then open the **File** menu and select **Print**; from the **Print** dialog box, select the appropriate options to print the certificate.

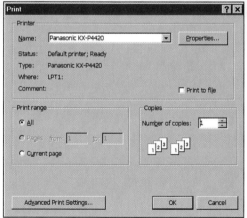

End

How-To Hints

Save That Paper!

If you're using special preprinted paper for your certificate, you may want to print a test copy on plain paper first so that you can make any necessary adjustments before using the more expensive paper.

Additional Embellishments

Stationery stores carry many items you can use to embellish your certificate—such as gold ribbons, stickers, and gold or black calligraphy pens.

How to Create a Gift Certificate

One way to entice your customers to spend more time and money with you is to offer gift certificates. These promotional pieces are great for last-minute gifts ideas, weddings, birthdays, and so on.

Because a gift certificate is like a miniature ad for your store, you want it to look as professional as possible—and with Publisher, that's easy to do.

Begin

1 Choose a Certificate

In the **Catalog**, click **Gift Certificates** (on the **Publications by Wizard** tab). Select a design you like from the right pane and then click **Start Wizard** to begin.

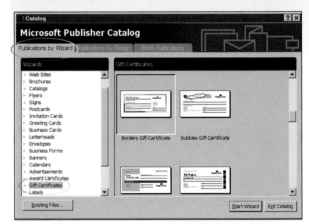

2 Select Your Options

Change options as needed in the **Wizard** pane. For example, you may want to use the **Print Tiling** option to print multiple certificates on one piece of paper. Click **Finish**, and then click **Hide Wizard**.

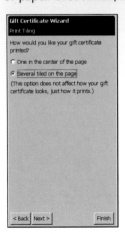

3 Replace the Text

Replace any placeholder text as needed. Feel free to change the font and size of text as well.

4 Change Placeholder Graphics

Replace any placeholder graphics with images of your own. If you don't have a company logo, select a nice piece of clip art instead.

5 Add Final Touches

Add personal touches such as an expiration date and a certificate number (if you're printing only one copy of the certificate, that is).

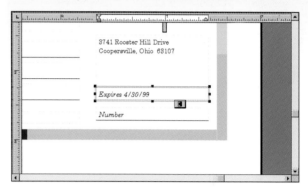

6 Print the Certificate

To print your certificate(s), select **File, Print** from the **menu bar**. In the **Print** dialog box, choose the number of **Copies** you want and click **OK**. Print enough so that your employees will always have some gift certificates on hand.

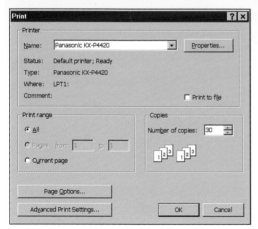

End

How-To Hints

Add a Value

Some gift certificates have a value limitation, so be sure to include that if it's appropriate. To place the value on the background, press **Ctrl+M** and then create a text box that contains the dollar value for your certificate (for example, you may want to print $20 certificates). Position the text box so that it shows through the foreground design (for example, in all four corners).

Another Idea

Gift certificates can be used to award personal gifts to friends and neighbors. For example, you can create a certificate for some new parents good for a night of baby-sitting services.

How to Create a Program

It wasn't enough to volunteer to help with the school bake sale, the Girl Scout camping trip, and the church fish fry. No, you also had to volunteer to create the program for your son's school pageant. Well, this time you're in luck because Publisher comes with a wide variety of programs predesigned for your immediate use.

Begin

1 Choose a Program

On the **Publications by Wizard** tab in the **Catalog**, click **Programs**. Select the type of program you need from the right pane and click **Start Wizard** to begin.

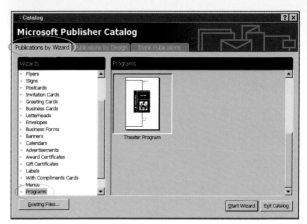

2 Select the Wizard Options

Select a color scheme from the **Wizard** pane. Change other options as needed and then click **Finish** and **Hide Wizard** to maximize your work area.

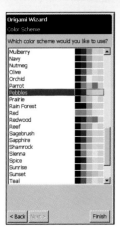

3 Add Your Text

Use the placeholders to help you add your own text, including the list of program participants.

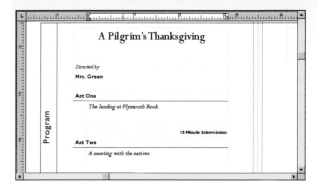

4 Change the Graphics

Replace the program's original graphics with ones that fit the program's theme. You can use original art or choose from the myriad pieces of clip art that come with Publisher.

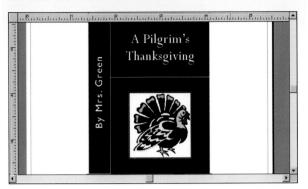

5 Add Splashes of Color

Don't be afraid to add additional graphics and splashes of color to dress up a plain program. (If you're printing in black and white, use gray-toned graphics to add interest.)

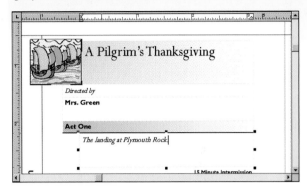

6 Print the Program

To print your program, open the **File** menu and select **Print**. In the **Print** dialog box, choose the number of **Copies** you want and click **OK**.

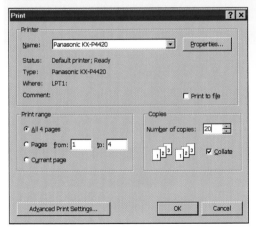

End

How-To Hints

Special Paper

You may want to print the program on special paper—for example, paper heavier than your printer can handle. Your local copier can help you with your selection.

Many Copies?

Another reason you may want to consider having the local copy shop print your program is if you need a lot of copies or special binding. See Part 8, "Printing Your Publication," for more information on these options.

How to Build an Airplane

Don't laugh. Think about it: An airplane isn't just a toy; it can be a great marketing device. Send an airplane to your customers to announce your new catalog, a price reduction, a new phone number (or email address).

Or, for personal messages, send an airplane to announce a new address; use it as a greeting card.

Begin

1 Choose Airplanes

Open the **Catalog** and choose **Airplanes** (in the **Publications by Wizard** tab) to see the available selections. Select the airplane you want to create and choose **Start Wizard**.

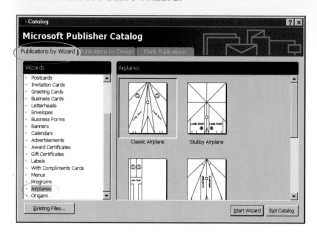

2 Change Options

Select from various options in the **Wizard** pane. For example, you may want to change the color scheme (use black and white if you're going to print on colored paper) and make other decisions.

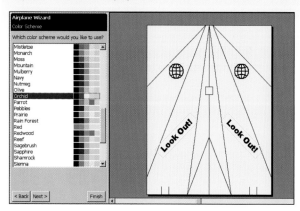

3 Customize Airplane Text

Click **Finish** and hide the wizard to begin working on your design. Start by selecting a text frame and replacing the placeholder text with your own words. Notice that the copyfitting feature is turned on, so the font gets smaller if you use more words. (Learn about copyfitting text in Task 4, "How to Copyfit Your Text," in Part 5.

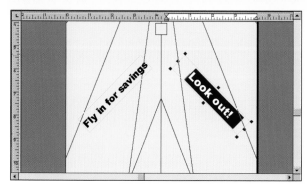

4 Customize Airplane Graphics

Double-click the picture frames to replace the clip art with a design of your own choosing. There is information about clip art in Task 9, "How to Insert Clip Art," in Part 3.

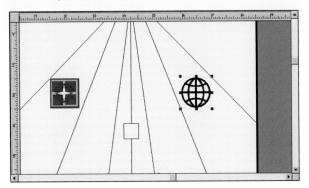

5 Customize Folding Instructions

Move to the second page if you want to add a personal note in the instructions.

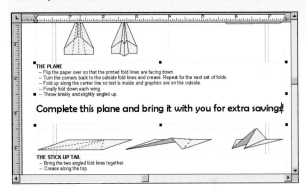

6 Make Other Changes

Add custom touches with additional text boxes and graphics.

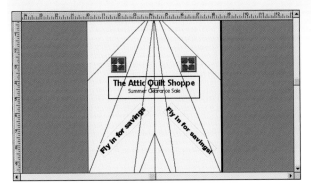

7 Print Airplane

Click the **Print** icon on the **Standard** toolbar to print your airplane and its instructions.

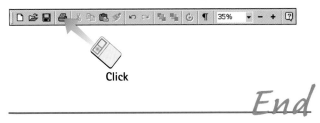

Click

End

How-To Hints

Add Pizzazz to Your Aircraft

Airplanes are more fun if you print them on special paper, especially shiny (even metallic) paper.

How to Create Origami

Origami is the ancient Japanese art of folding a piece of paper so that it becomes a recognizable object. Most of the time, origami produces graceful paper sculptures of birds, but you can build almost anything you want to—unless you don't know the art and have to rely on the choices available in Publisher.

Origami is another specialty publication that has multiple uses. You can create origami for fun, as greeting cards, or as a marketing promotion.

Begin

1 Choose Origami

Choose **Origami** from the **Catalog** (in the **Publications by Wizard** tab) and then select the specific origami shape you want to create. Choose **Start Wizard** to begin.

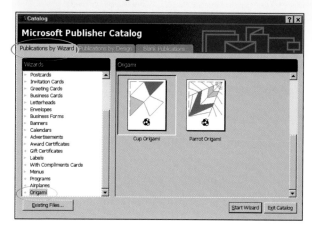

2 Select a Color Scheme

The only decision to make in origami is the color scheme. The default is usually muted colors (traditional with this art), but you might want to use a company's logo colors or some other more colorful scheme.

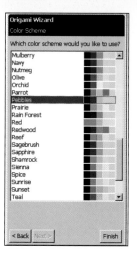

3 Choose Finish

Click **Finish** and hide the wizard so that you can begin working on your origami publication. Only the boat origami (not shown in Step 1) uses the entire piece of paper, so if you've selected anything else, you see a second graphic (a recycle symbol) at the bottom of your page.

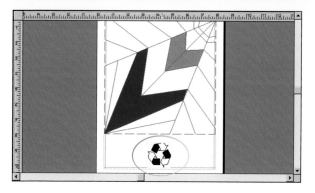

4 Customize Origami

Select the graphic of the recycle symbol and change the art work (perhaps you want to insert your company logo).

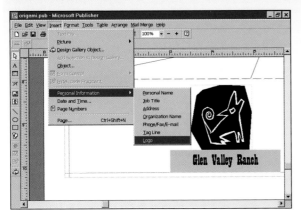

5 Customize Folding Instructions

The second page of the origami publication contains directions for folding. These are usually graphic frames, so the only way to personalize this page is to add a small text frame if there's room for it. Don't disturb the size or shape of the instructions—they're hard enough to follow when they're the proper size.

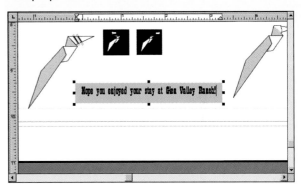

6 Click Print

Click the **Print** icon on the **Standard** toolbar to print your origami publication.

Click

End

How-To Hints

Use Plain Paper

Origami folds better if the paper you use isn't slick or coated. Use inexpensive laser/copier paper for best results.

Task

1   How to Print Your Publication   **226**

2   How to Print Special Publications   **228**

3   How to Use an Outside Printing Service   **230**

Project 3: A Web Site   **236**

Printing Your Publication

*P*rinting a publication is frequently far more complicated than printing a document from your word processor. In fact, there will be many occasions in which you'll find your printer just won't do an adequate job—you'll want the services of a professional printing company.

If your publication requires special handling when you send it to your own printer, Publisher helps you make the right decisions and choose the right options.

If you have to use an outside company, Publisher walks you through the process so that the experience doesn't turn into a nightmare.

In this part, you learn how to print your publication in-house and out-of-house. ●

How to Print Your Publication

After you've done all the work involved in creating a masterpiece of a publication, you'll certainly want people to read it. Unless you're planning to gather all those people in front of your monitor, you have to print your publication.

Begin

1 Print the Entire Publication

To send your publication to your printer quickly and with no muss, no fuss, click the **Print** button on the **Standard** toolbar. It's quick but there is a downside—you have no choices about what pages to print or which printer to use. The entire publication prints to the currently selected printer. (Or, even worse, if you printed with the **Print** dialog box before you click the **Print** button, the settings you left behind are used for this print job.)

Click

2 Configure the Printer

You can change the printer options to match your publication, including resolution, paper, graphics, and so on. Choose **File**, **Print Setup** from the **menu bar** to see the **Print Setup** dialog box, where you can change the paper size and the orientation. Click the **Properties** button to make any needed adjustments to the printer's configuration. (Each printer has its own set of properties.)

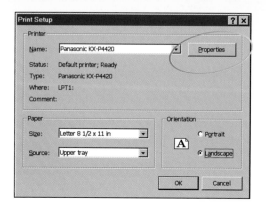

3 Set Printer Options

From the publication, press **Ctrl+P** to open the **Print** dialog box so that you can set the printing options. Choose the pages you want to print, the number of copies, and so on. You can also change printers if you have more than one printer available.

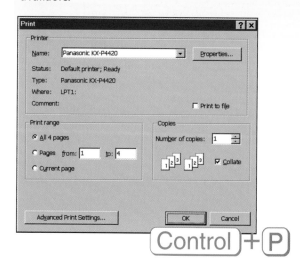

Control + P

4 Set Advanced Settings

Click **Advanced Print Settings** in the **Print** dialog box to set advanced options such as graphics resolution. Click **OK** to return to the **Print** dialog box.

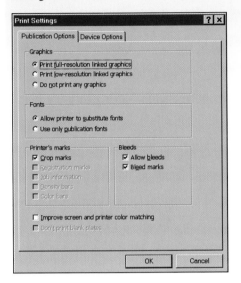

5 Print the Publication

Click **OK** on the **Print** dialog box to send your publication to the printer. If your publication is large and has a lot of graphics, you'll probably have to wait a bit to see the printed image. This is normal and you shouldn't assume that there's a problem.

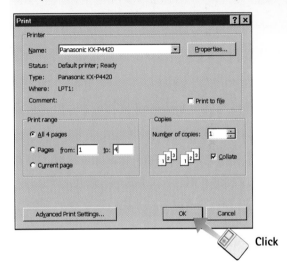

Click

6 Save Some Trees

If your publication is small enough that more than one copy will fit on a page, a **Page Options** button appears on the **Print** dialog box. Click this button to display the **Page Options** dialog box, from which you can choose the number of copies to print on each page.

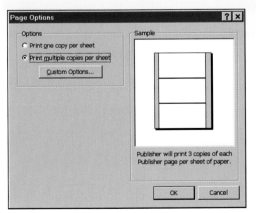

How-To Hints

Troubleshooting Printing

If you need help with a printing problem, select **Troubleshooting** from the **Contents** list in Publisher Help, and select **Desktop Printing**. Select a topic, and help for that problem is displayed.

End

How to Print Special Publications

Many of Publisher's publications require special printing techniques. For example, your publication may need a special paper size or it may be extremely small (such as a business card or a postcard). If so, you need to plan and to set up the printing process.

If your publication is configured for a size that's smaller than standard letter paper, you can either feed that paper into the printer or print on letter paper. If you choose the latter, you must print crop marks so that you'll know where to cut the paper.

1 Printing Small Publications on Regular Paper

To print a small publication on regular paper, add crop marks so that you know where to cut. In the **Print** dialog box, click **Advanced Print Settings** and select **Crop marks**. Use the crop marks to cut the paper evenly.

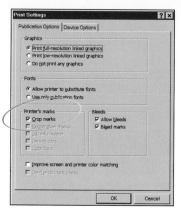

2 Printing To Unique Paper Sizes

If you want to print directly on paper that matches the size of your publication, choose **Properties** in the **Print** dialog box and select the paper size. If your printer doesn't offer the size you need, you may be able to enter a custom size (if not, choose the closest size). If the printer doesn't have a paper tray for the size you need, choose the manual feed option.

3 Printing Multiple Business Cards

If you want to print a bunch of business cards on a single sheet of paper, choose **Page Options** from the **Print** dialog box to open the **Page Options** dialog box. Select **Print multiple copies per sheet**, then choose **OK** to return to the **Print** dialog box. Click **Advanced Print Options**, select **Crop marks**, and click **OK** twice to print; use the crop marks to cut.

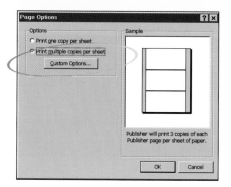

4 Configuring Multiple Cards

You can configure the way multiple cards are printed (business cards, placecards, or any other very small publication). Open the **Page Options** dialog box as described in Step 3 and choose **Custom Options**. In the **Custom Options** dialog box, change the margins and the *gaps* (the space between each printed section). You may have to experiment a bit, but usually these options make printing more economical.

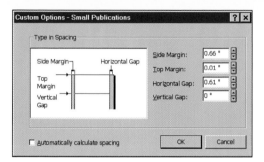

6 Other Tricks for Quick Printing

There are other ways to speed printing for all the draft copies you must print until your publication is approved and you can print the final masterpiece. Open the **Print** dialog box and choose **Properties**. Change the graphics resolution to a lower number—this speeds printing substantially. (Don't forget to skip the pictures.)

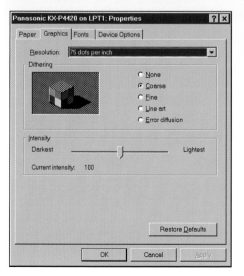

5 Print a Draft Copy

If you want to see what your layout looks like in print, you can speed printing by skipping the pictures. Open the **Print** dialog box and click **Advanced Print Settings**. Select **Do not print any graphics**. The printed copy will indicate the placement of all the pictures with dotted lines.

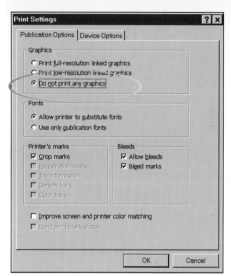

How-To Hints

Use Draft Printing to Create a Paste-Up

You can also use the draft printing technique described in Step 5 to paste pictures in those dotted lines and take the printout to a professional printer. If you prefer not to do the pasting yourself, indicate the picture number with a pencil mark and then mark the real pictures with the corresponding numbers. (Let the printer handle the paste-up.)

How to Use an Outside Printing Service

If your publication is in color, or if you need a lot of copies, you should consider using an outside printing service. You'll get the professional results you need for important publications such as annual reports, sales brochures, and product catalogs.

Before you begin designing, however, discuss your project with your printing service to decide what files they will need from you—and in what format. You can provide information to the printing service in Publisher, PostScript, or EPS format using Microsoft Publisher.

2 Option 1: Select Process Color

In the **Color Printing** dialog box, click **Process Color** and then click **OK**. *Process color* is more expensive, but it allows you to include color photos in your publication. (For spot-color printing, jump to Step 4. For black-and-white printing, skip to Step 8.)

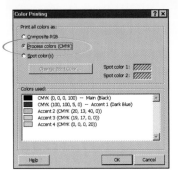

Begin

1 Prepare Your Publication

After your publication has been designed, tweaked, and approved to everyone's satisfaction, prepare it for printing by an outside printing service. Choose **Tools, Commercial Printing Tools, Color Printing** from the **menu bar**.

3 Check Your Colors

Some **RGB colors** (colors displayed on your monitor) cannot be accurately converted to the **CYMK color** model used by commercial printers. Change the color of individual objects as needed: Select the object, click the **Fill Color** button in the **Standard** toolbar, and choose **More Colors**. Select **CMYK** from the **Color model** list and then select a new color. Continue with Step 9.

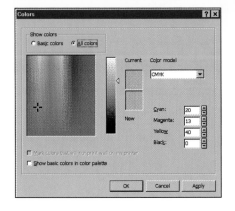

4 Option 2: Select Spot-Color Printing

If you choose **spot-color** printing (instead of process color printing), graphics are in black and white with a "spot" of one or two colors (plus black). To choose this printing option, select **Spot Color(s)** from the **Color Printing** dialog box.

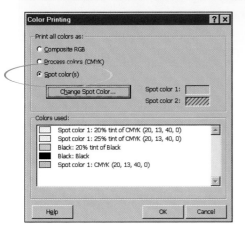

5 Select the Spot Color(s) You Want

Click the **Change Spot Color** button in the **Color Printing** dialog box; in the **Choose Spot Color** dialog box, open the **Spot Color 1** list and choose **More Colors**.

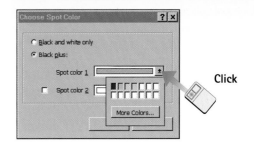

6 Change to PANTONE

In the **Colors** dialog box, choose **All Colors** and then select **PANTONE** from the **Color model** list. Click **Change color** and then select the color you want from the **PANTONE Colors** dialog box. (You can enter the **PANTONE** color number if you know it.)

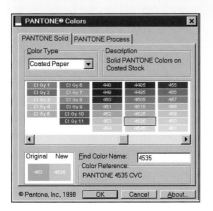

7 Check Your Colors

Repeat Steps 5 and 6 to select a second spot color if you want one. Then check your publication and make any necessary color adjustments. Continue with Step 9.

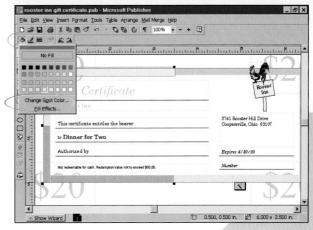

Continues

8 Option 3: Print in Black & White

If your publication will be printed in black and white only, select **Spot color(s)** in the **Color Printing** dialog box; then click **Change Spot Color** and select the **Black and white only** option.

9 Option 1: Save in Publisher Format

Now that you've selected the options for the printing process you want to use, you're ready to save your files. If your printing service can accept Publisher files, that's the easiest way to go: Just select **File, Pack and Go**, and choose **Take to a Commercial Printing Service**. Then follow the steps in the wizard that appears. You are done!

10 Option 2: Save in PostScript Format

If your printing service requires you to submit files in PostScript format, you must install a PostScript printer driver on your system. In the Windows **Control Panel**, double-click the **Printers** icon. Double-click **Add Printer**. Select a generic printer such as the **HP Color LaserJet 5/5M PS**. Select **File** from the **Available ports** list. *Do not let Windows set this as your default printer.* Insert the Windows CD-ROM when prompted.

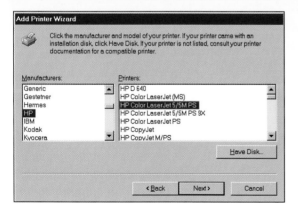

11 Installing a PostScript Printer

Ask your printing service which PostScript Printer Definition (PPD) file you should use and where you can get a copy of it. In a pinch, you can install Publisher's PPD files: In the **Control Panel**, double-click the **Printers** icon. Double-click **Add Printer**. Click **Have Disk** and change to the **C:\Program Files\Microsoft Office\Office** directory. Select either **MSPUB.INF** (for offset printing) or **PRINTER.INF** (for digital color).

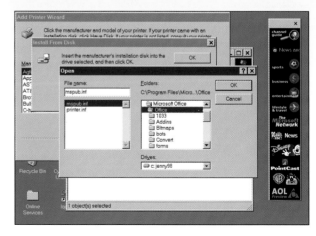

12 Choose Your Color Option

In the **Add Printer Wizard**, select either **MS Publisher Color Printer** (for process color) or **MS Publisher Imagesetter** (for spot color) and click **Next**. Select **File** from the **Available ports** list. *Do not let Windows set this as your default printer.*

13 Optimize for Portability

To optimize the files for transport on a disk, select **File, Print Setup** from the **menu bar**. Select the PostScript printer you want to use and click **Properties**. Click the **PostScript** tab and choose **PostScript (optimize for portability–ADSC)**.

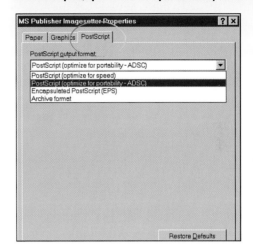

14 Save as a PostScript File

Choose **File, Save As** from the **menu bar**. In the **Save As** dialog box, select **PostScript** from the **Save as type** list and click **Save**.

15 Verify Your Options

In the **Save As PostScript File** dialog box that appears, select the option your printing service requires: **Print composite** or **Print separations**.

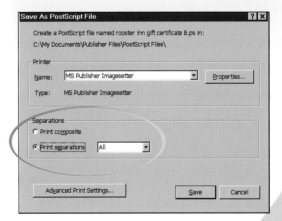

Continues

HOW TO USE AN OUTSIDE PRINTING SERVICE **233**

16 Set Advanced Options

In the **Save As PostScript File** dialog box, click **Advanced Printing Settings** and then set the options you need on the **Publications Options** tab of the **Print Settings** dialog box. (Check with your printing service before setting any options.)

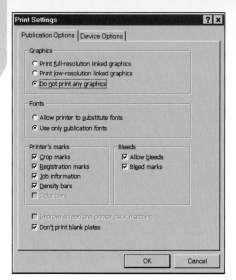

17 Set Device Options

In the **Print Settings** dialog box, click the **Device Options** tab and set any additional options you need. Click **OK**.

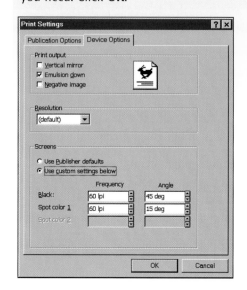

18 Save the File

In the **Save As PostScript File** dialog box, click **Save** to save your publication in PostScript format.

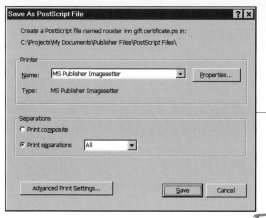

End

How-To Hints

Don't Forget the Graphics!

If you created a PostScript file, don't forget to copy any graphics or fonts used in your publication to the disk you take to your printing service.

I Want EPS!

If you have to create an Encapsulated PostScript (EPS) file for your printing service, you'll have to save each page as a separate file. Follow the steps to create a PostScript file, but in Step 13, select **Encapsulated PostScript (EPS)**. Then, instead of using the **File, Save As** command, choose **File, Print** to "print" the *current page* to a *file*. Repeat for each page in your publication.

Project 3

A Web Site

In this project, you face a new challenge: designing a Human Resources Web site for your company, Southwest Interior Designs. Luckily, you don't plan on publishing all your information at once; instead, you just want to design a nice-looking site with some basic information that employees can access. Additional stuff can be added later.

For now, you want to create the Home page, a page listing upcoming holidays and company events, and some pages honoring the employees of the month. First, you'll create the employee-of-the-month pages, using a template. Then you'll convert that publication to Web pages and create the rest of the Web site.

1 Create Employee-of-Month Pages

In the **Catalog**, on the **Publications by Wizard** tab, select **Award Certificates**. Select **Employee of the Month** from the right pane, and click **Start Wizard** to begin.

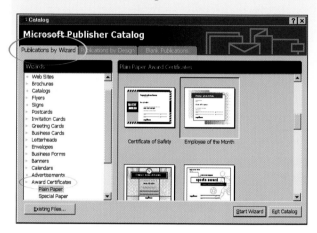

2 Change the Color Scheme

In the **Wizard** pane, select the **Prairie** color scheme. Click the **Hide Wizard** button to maximize your work area and begin customizing the publication.

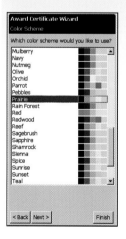

3 Add the Recipient's Name

Add your company name, and the name of the first person, **Tom Carter**, who received the employee-of-the-month award for January 1999. Delete the **signature and date** lines—because this will be posted online, you won't be signing it.

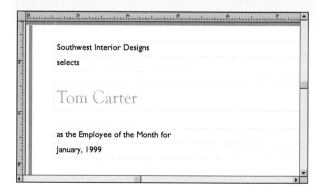

4 Add Custom Touches

Insert a text box with some text explaining why Tom received the award. Change the logo to something matching a company with a southwest theme.

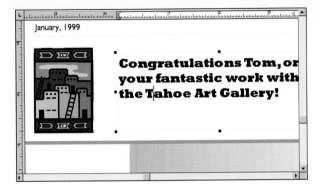

5 Insert a Second Page

You have a February employee of the month as well, so open the **Insert** menu and select **Page** to create page 2. Select the **Duplicate all objects on page** option as well.

6 Change the Placeholder Text

The February employee of the month was **Alice Swann**, who's being recognized for her help with the 1999 Home Show.

7 Convert the Publication to HTML

To convert the employee of the month certificate pages to HTML (the format necessary to display information on the Web), choose **File, Create Web Site from Current Publication** from the **menu bar**. Click **Yes** and choose the **All** option to let the design checker check the publication.

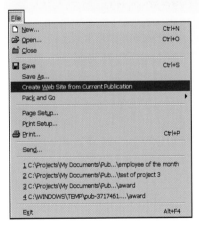

Continues

8 Add Hyperlinks

The design checker will tell you that you need to add a hyperlink to get to the second page. Click the **Design Gallery Object** button in the **Objects** toolbar and select the **Web Navigation Bars** category. Select the **Southwest Navigation Bar** from the right pane and click **Insert Object**.

Click

9 Change the Background

Change the background of your Web site by choosing **Format, Color and Background Scheme**. In the dialog box, under **Background**, click **Browse** and select the file wb007801.gif. Click **Close**. Reselect the **Praire** color scheme.

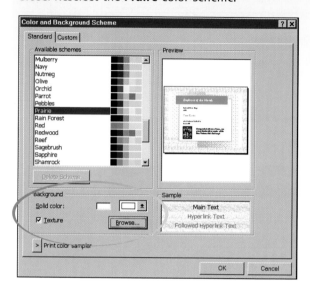

10 Customize the Navigation Bar

Move the navigation bar into an appropriate place on page 1 and change the hyperlink text to **January 1999** and **February 1999**, respectively. Copy the navigation bar to page 2.

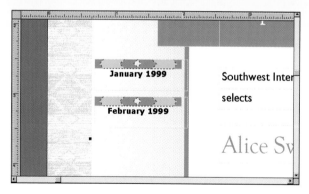

11 Publish the Site

Change the name under which your pages will be published: On page 1, select **File, Web Properties** and click the **Page** tab. Enter **jan** for the **File name** and click **OK**. Move to page 2 and repeat this step to change page 2's filename to **feb**. Select **File, Save as Web Page** and choose the folder in which you want to publish your site: your local hard drive, a network drive, a Web folder, or an FTP site. See Part 6, Task 10 for help.

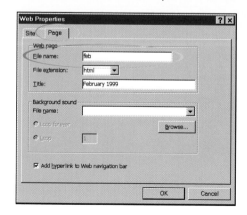

12 Create a Human Resources Page

In the **Catalog**, on the **Publications by Wizard** tab, select **Web Sites**. Choose **Southwest Web Site** from the right pane and click **Start Wizard** to begin.

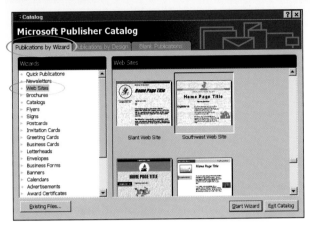

13 Change the Placeholder Text

Select the **Prairie** color scheme and click **Hide Wizard**. Change the company's name to **Southwest Interior Designs**, the page title to **Human Resources**, and the tag line to **Designs that capture the flavor of the old Southwest**. Create a welcome paragraph similar to the one shown here.

14 Add an Email Link

To let employees contact you directly with questions, add an email link. Select your name (which appears at the bottom of the page) and click **Insert Hyperlink**. Choose the **An Internet e-mail address** option and type your email address in the **Internet e-mail address** text box. Click **OK**. (There's also a logo that appears in this area at the bottom of the page; you may want to change it to something more Southwest looking.)

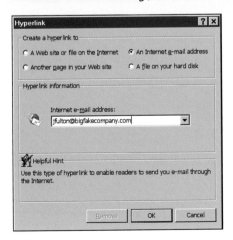

15 Insert a Calendar of Events Page

Choose **Insert, Page** from the **menu bar** and select **Calendar** from the **Available page types** list. Click **OK**.

Continues

16 Add Special Dates for This Month

Change the page title to **Calendar of Events**. Add special dates for this month by typing them into the calendar as shown. (You'll have to change the font size to 6 or 7 points.) You can adjust the size of a row when needed by dragging its border.

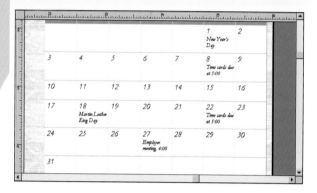

17 Add Events for the Month

Enter the special events for this month in a **Schedule of Events** text box as shown.

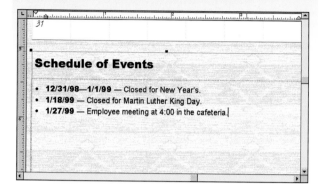

18 Insert an Employee Story

Insert a page that links to your employee-of-the-month Web site by choosing **Insert, Page** from the menu. Select **Story** from the **Available page types** list and click **OK**.

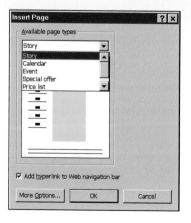

19 Add a Description of the Contest

Change the page title to **Employee of the Month**. Add a description of the employee-of-the-month contest, as shown.

20 Add a Quote

Replace the quote placeholder with the following text: **There is nothing quite so satisfying as a job well done.** (Use **Arial Black, 14 point, italic** formatting.)

21 Create Links to the Site

To create a link to the first page in the employee-of-the-month site, type **Thanks again to our employees of the month**. Underneath that text, type **January 1999**; select the text and click **Insert Hyperlink** in the **Standard** toolbar. Select the **A Web site or file on the Internet** option and type the address to the January page (for example, `http://bigcompany.com/mystuff/jan.html`). Repeat for the February link.

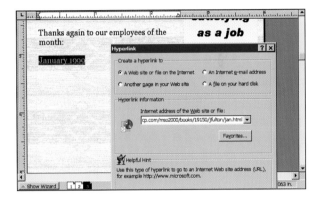

22 Publish Human Resources Site

To publish the Human Resources site, select **File, Save as Web Page**. Choose the folder in which you want to publish your site: your local hard drive, a network drive, a Web folder, or an FTP site. Refer to Part 6, Task 10 for help.

End

How-To Hints

Check It Out!

Be sure to check out your Web site after it's published: Check all the links, see how long the graphics take to display, and so on. If you make changes, simply use the **File, Save as Web Page** command again to republish your site.

Change the Calendar Date

When you insert a calendar page into your Web site, the default is to display a monthly calendar using the current month. You can change the display by right-clicking the calendar, choosing **Calendar Creation Wizard**, and selecting a different design or different dates from the wizard that appears.

Glossary

B

background page   A virtual page that holds elements that you want repeated on every page of your publication.

bleed   Printing past the edge of a margin; used mainly to ensure that color graphics or backgrounds reach the edge of the finished page.

C

camera-ready   A printed document that's ready for an outside printing service to print. The name comes from the fact that a camera is used to take a picture of the document; then the negative is used for printing.

Clip Gallery   A program that contains clip art, pictures, sound files, and video clips that can be used in publications.

copyfit   Size text to fit into a specific amount of space (the space is defined as a *frame* in Publisher).

D

design checker   A program that checks your publication for errors in design.

Design Gallery   A collection of special predesigned and preformated elements you can add to a publication.

dialog box   An information box that appears when the software needs input from the user.

G

gutter   The space on a page left blank for binding (the left edge of a right page, the right edge of a left page).

H

hard copy   Computer jargon for a printed copy of a document file.

hotspot   A special area on a graphic that, when clicked, takes the viewer to another Web page.

hyperlink   A bit of underlined text on a Web page that, when clicked, takes the viewer to another Web page.

I

intranet   A local "mini-internet" network, commonly found in large corporations.

ISP (Internet Service Provider)   A company or organization that provides your computer with access to the Internet.

J

justification   Aligning text so that it fills the area between the left and right margins.

K

kerning   Changing the size of spaces between specific pairs of characters.

L

layout guides   Guide lines you put on the background page, representing boundaries for all pages in your publication. You can also use these guide lines to align objects.

leading   (Pronounced *ledding*) The spacing between lines.

M

mechanical   Printing term for finished art work that's ready to be processed by a printer. See also *camera-ready*.

P

placeholder text   Text that is inserted automatically in a text frame. It is replaced by your own text.

printer properties   Information about your printer and its capabilities. To see the properties, choose **Settings**, **Printers** from the **Start** menu and right-click the icon for your printer. Choose **Properties** from the **shortcut menu** to see the **Properties** dialog box.

process color   A printing process that allows you to include full-color graphics and photos in your publication.

publish   The process of copying files to an Internet or intranet server so that they can be viewed by other users.

R

ruler guides   Guide lines representing ruler positions that you place on a page in order to align objects.

S

scratch area   The portion of the **Publisher** window outside the page display. Use the scratch area to "park" frames you want to move to another page.

ScreenTips   Notes displayed on your screen to explain a function or feature.

Snap To   A feature that forces objects to a specific position on a page by making them snap to a guide line.

spot color   A printing process that results in black-and-white text and photographs with "spots" of one or two colors in the finished publication.

T

Text Overflow icon   A button at the bottom of a text frame; indicates that there is additional text in the frame that is not currently seen because the frame isn't large enough to display it.

tracking   Changing the size of the spaces between characters.

W

watermark   A pale element placed in the background of a document page. Used for graphics or special text.

Index

A

Add Object dialog box, 139
Add Text command (Microsoft Draw), 113
Add/Modify FTP Locations dialog box, 197
adding. *See* inserting
address lists
  creating, 146
  importing, 147
  inserting, 148
  merging, 149
  saving, 147
  text frames, 147
ads
  color, 213
  printing, 213
  size, 212
airplanes, 220-221
Align Objects (Arrange menu), 116
Align Objects dialog box, 116
Align Text Vertically command (Format menu), 65
aligning text, 173-174
alignment
  objects, 116-117
  tables, 135
  text, 61
  text frames, formatting, 65
  WordArt, 110
animation, 182-183
Answer Wizard, 39
applying text styles, 77-81

Arrange menu commands
  Align Objects, 116
  Layout Guides, 19, 28, 119, 152, 166
  Nudge, 122
  Rotate or Flip, 99
  Ruler Guides, 31
articles (online Help), 43
artwork. *See* images
attributes (text), 60
audio, 182-183
AutoCorrect command (Tools menu), 157
AutoCorrect dialog box, 157
AutoShapes toolbar, 112
award certificates, 214-215

B

background pages
  guidelines, 140
  images
    color, 142
    fill effects, 143
    shapes, 142
    watermarks, 142-143
  pagination, 140-141
  text boxes, 141
background sound, 182-183
backgrounds
  changing, 238
  copying, 173
  gutters, 167
  mirrored pages, 167
  special paper, 200-201
  text frames, formatting, 64
  viewing, 170

banners
  creating, 208-209
  printing, 209
binding
  newsletters, 167
  publications, 166
blank design, 16-17
blank pages, 18
  startup, 49
  Web publications, 179
bleeds, 153, 172
bold style
  text, copyfitting, 160
  WordArt, 109
Border Style dialog box, 115
BorderArt, 65, 115
borders
  graphics, 114-115
  text frames, formatting, 65
  WordArt, 111
bullet lists, 68
  bullets, 70
    formatting, 69
    size, changing, 174
  creating, 173
business cards, printing, 228-229
business forms. *See* forms
buttons
  toolbars, 24
  Redo, 55
  Undo (Standard toolbar), 55

C

calendars
  events, 211
  printing, 211

size, 210
text, 211
camera-ready copies, 207
captions, 104-105
catalog
closing, 6, 9
opening, 6, 16
removing, 9
cells
merging, 134
navigating, 133
text, copying, 135
centering
frames, 59
objects, 117
centimeters (guides), 49
certificates
award certificates
printing, 215
text, customizing, 214
gift certificates, 216-217
Change or Apply Style dialog box, 77
Change Style dialog box, 79
changing. *See* **editing**
Character Spacing command (Format menu), 61, 162
Character Spacing dialog box, 61, 162-163
circles, 27, 84
clicking frames, creating, 50
clip art, 100-101. *See also* **images**
Clip Gallery
Tool, 26, 100-103
watermarks, 142-143
Clipboard
copying/pasting data, 145
text, inserting, 72
Close command (File menu), 47
closing
catalog, 6, 9
files, 47
Publisher, 7
color
ads, 213
bleed, 153
color schemes
changing, 236
origami, 222
PISs, 11
images, background, 142

navigation bars, 185
PANTONE, 231
PostScript options, 233
printing
CYMK, 230
RGB, 230
special paper, 9
process, 230
shapes, 90-91
spot, 231
tables, 135
text
formatting, 62
frames, 64
Color Printing dialog box, 230
color schemes
changing, 236
origami, 222
PISs, 11
columns
alignment, objects, 117
guides, 28
overflow text, gutters, 167
tables
creating, 132
deleting, 135
formatting, 135
inserting, 135
text frames
column breaks, 71
spacing, 70
uneven columns, 71
commands
Add Text (Microsoft Draw), 113
Arrange menu
Align Objects, 116
Layout Guides, 19, 28, 119, 152, 166
Nudge, 122
Rotate or Flip, 99
Ruler Guides, 31
Edit menu, Delete Page, 23
File menu
Close, 47
Create Web Site from Current Publication, 194, 237
Exit, 7
New, 8, 14, 208
Page Setup, 18
Print, 168, 209
Print Merge, 149
Print Setup, 226
Save, 46
Save As, 47

Save as Web Page, 196
Web Properties, 182, 197, 238
Web Site Preview, 183, 192
Format menu
Align Text Vertically, 65
Character Spacing, 61, 162
Copyfit Text, 161
Drop Cap, 63
Indents and Lists, 69, 174
Line Spacing, 61, 163
Recolor Object, 142
Text Style, 78-80
Help menu
Microsoft Publisher Help, 34
Microsoft Publisher Web Site, 42
Insert menu
Page, 22, 180
Page Numbers, 75, 141
Pages, 171
Picture, 103, 112
Text File, 144
Mail Merge menu
Create Publisher Address List, 146
Insert Field, 148
Merge, 149
Open Data Source, 147
Start menu
Programs, 6
Run, 4
Table menu
Delete Rows or Columns, 135
Fill Down, 135
Insert Rows or Columns, 135
Merge Cells, 134
Table AutoFormat, 134
Tools menu
AutoCorrect, 157
Design Checker, 158, 190
Language, 156, 164
Options, 48
Spelling, 154
Text Frame Connect, 72
View menu
Go To Background, 29, 140
Go To Foreground, 29, 143
Hide Boundaries and Guides, 32
Picture Display, 33
Show Boundaries and Guides, 32
Two-Page Spread, 21
configuring. *See also* **customizing; editing; formatting**
greeting cards, 205
Help, 50
hyperlinks, hot spots, 188

hyphenation, 50
   hyphenation zone, 164
   non-breaking hyphens, 165
   text frames, 164-165
layout, custom, 19
Office Assistant, 36-37
printers, 226
printing, 51
synchronization, 50
text, editing, 49

Connect Frames toolbar, 73

Contents page
How? link, 38
tutorials, 39

"continued" references, 74-75

converting
filenames, 195
HTML conversion, 237
Web publications to sites, 194-195

copies, 207

Copyfit Text command (Format menu), 161

copyfitting
automatically, 161
bold text, 160
Design Checker, 159
fonts, 160
hyphenation
   configuring, 164
   hyphenation zone, 164
   non-breaking hyphens, 165
   text frames, 164-165
kerning, 162-163
leading, 162-163
overflow text, 159-161
scaling, 162-163
text frames, 160
tracking, 162

copying. *See also* **dragging; pasting**
backgrounds, 173
Clipboard data, 145
formatting, 66-67
frames, 24
text
   styles, 79
   tables, 135
toolbar, 24

Create Publisher Address List command (Mail Merge menu), 146

Create Style by Example dialog box, 77

Create Table dialog box, 132

Create Web Site from Current Publication command (File menu), 194, 237

creating PISs, 10

crop marks, printing, 168-169

cropping graphic frames, 123

crosshair pointer, 56

Ctrl key
Ctrl+D keys (text frame shadows), 65
Ctrl+P keys (Print dialog box), 226
Ctrl+Shift+H keys (hyphenation), 165
Ctrl+T keys (transparency), 95
dragging, 59

cursor, moving, 55

Custom Options dialog box, 229

Custom Rotate dialog box, 25, 63, 99

customizing. *See also* **configuring; editing; formatting**
custom shapes, 86-87
designs, 17, 137
fonts, 48
frames, creating, 50
Help, 50
installation, 5
measurement units, 49
mouse pointers, messages, 51
options, 48, 51
pages
   page layout, 18-19
   pagination, 49
printing, 51
startup, 49
synchronization, 50
text
   hyphenation, 50
   text editing, 49

cutting, toolbar, 24

CYMK color, printing, 230

D

data entry (tables), 133

database reports, importing, 145

Delete Page command (Edit menu), 23

Delete Page dialog box, 23

Delete Rows or Columns command (Table menu), 135

deleting
columns, 135
pages, 23
rows, 135
rulers, 31
text, 55
text styles, 81
Undo/Redo tools, 25

design
blank, 16-17
custom, 17
design sets, 14-15
forms, 206
labels, 17
navigation bars, 185

Design Checker, 191
command (Tools menu), 158, 190
dialog box, 158, 190
copyfitting, 159
graphics, 159

Design Gallery
categories, 136
designs
   adding, 139
   customizing, 137
   inserting, 139
   listing, 136
   text, 137
Object tool, 184
Objects toolbar, 27

design sets, 14-15

desktop shortcuts, startup, 7

dialog boxes. *See also* **wizards**
Add Object, 139
Add/Modify FTP Locations, 197
Align Objects, 116
AutoCorrect, 157
Border Style, 115
Change or Apply Style, 77
Change Style, 79
Character Spacing, 61, 162-163
Color Printing dialog box, 230
Create Style by Example, 77
Create Table, 132
Custom Options, 229
Custom Rotate, 25, 63, 99
Delete Page, 23
Design Checker, 158, 190
Drop Cap, 63
Enter Your Text Here, 106
Fill Effects, 91, 143

Find Clips, 100
Hyperlink, 186
Hyphenation, 164
Import Styles, 78-80
Insert, 135
Insert Clip Art, 102, 215
Insert Fields, 148
Insert Page, 22, 180
Insert Text File, 144
Labels, 17
Language, 156
Layout Guides, 28, 119, 152, 166
Line Spacing, 61, 69, 163
New Address List, 146
Office Assistant, 36
Open Data Source, 147
Options, 48
Other Designs, 139
Page Options, 227-228
Page Setup, 17-18
Personal Information Set, 10
Picture Display, 33
Poster and Banner Printing, 209
Preview Data, 149
Print, 168, 209, 226
Print Merge, 149
Print Setup, 226
Recolor Object, 143
Run, 4
Save As, 46
Save As PostScript File, 233
Save as Web Page, 196
Setup, 5
Shadow, 111
Spacing Between Characters, 110
Text Frame Properties, 70, 74, 105
Text Style, 78-80
Web Properties, 182
Web Site Preview, 192

Dictionary. *See* **spell checker**

displaying. *See* **viewing**

documents, importing, 144-145

drafts, printing, 229

dragging. *See also* **copying; pasting**
    Ctrl key, 59
    frames
        centering, 59
        creating, 50
        sizing handles, 58
    graphic frames, 122
    guides, 29, 118
    rulers, 30-32
    undoing, 59

Draw (Microsoft)
    Add Text command, 113
    AutoShapes toolbar, 112
    Insert Clip Art button, 113
    Picture Frame tool, 112
    toggling with Publisher, 113

drawing tools, 27

Drop Cap command (Format menu), 63

Drop Cap dialog box, 63

drop caps, 63

drop shadows (WordArt), 111

E

Edit menu commands, Delete Page, 23

editing. *See also* **configuring; customizing; formatting**
    "continued" references, 75
    fonts, 60
    guides, 29
    hyphenation
        configuring, 164
        headlines, 165
        hyphenation zone, 164
        non-breaking hyphens, 165
        text frames, 164-165
    text
        customizing, 49
        Design Checker, 159
        spell checker, 154-157
        styles, 77-81
        text wrapping, 121
        troubleshooting overflow, 167
        WordArt, 107
    Undo button, 57

Enter Your Text Here dialog box, 106

envelopes, printing, 51

EPS (Encapsulated PostScript) files, 235

Esc key, 59

events (calendars), 211

Exit command (File menu), 7

F

F6 key (quick layering), 93

FAQs (Frequently Asked Questions), 44

features. *See* **tools**

fields (Mail Merge), formatting, 149

File menu commands
    Close, 47
    Create Web Site from Current Publication, 194, 237
    Exit, 7
    New, 8, 14, 208
    Page Setup, 18
    Print, 168, 209
    Print Merge, 149
    Print Setup, 226
    Save, 46
    Save As, 47
    Save as Web Page, 196
    Web Properties, 182, 197, 238
    Web Site Preview, 183, 192

filenames
    greeting cards, 205
    Web site conversion, 195

files. *See also* **publications**
    ads
        color, 213
        printing, 213
        size, 212
    airplanes, 220-221
    audio, 182-183
    award certificates
        printing, 215
        text, customizing, 214
    calendars
        events, 211
        printing, 211
        size, 210
        text, 211
    closing, 47
    envelopes, printing, 51
    event programs, 218-219
    forms
        design, 206
        printing, 207
    gift certificates, 216-217
    greeting cards
        configuring, 205
        filenames, 205
        images, 205
        layout, 204

printing, 205
text, 205
images (animation), 182-183
importing, 144-147
margins, 152-153
origami
color schemes, 222
folding instructions, 223
images, 223
paper, 223
printing, 223
printing, toolbar, 24
saving, 46-47
for print services, 232
PostScript format, 232-233
reminder message, 46
signs
images, 203
printing, 203
text, 203
ungrouping elements, 202
toolbar buttons, 24

Fill Down command (Table menu), 135

fill effects
Fill Effects dialog box, 91, 143
gradients, 64, 91
patterns, 64
shapes, 91

Find Clips dialog box, 100

finding. See **searching**

flipping
frames, 98-99
objects, 98-99
WordArt, 99, 109

flyer project
background, 170
bleed, 172
bulleted list, 173
bullets, changing, 174
clip art, adding, 172
copying background, 173
inserting pages, 171
margins, 170
rotating
headline, 173
text boxes, 171

folding
airplanes, 221
origami, 223

fonts
copyfitting, 160
customizing, 48
font box, 60

font size box, 60
selecting, 60
size, 60
WordArt, 108

Form Control, 27

Format menu commands
Align Text Vertically, 65
Character Spacing, 61, 162
Copyfit Text, 161
Drop Cap, 63
Indents and Lists command, 69, 174
Line Spacing, 61, 163
Recolor Object, 142
Text Style, 78-80

Format Painter tool, 24, 66-67

formatting. See also **configuring; customizing; editing**
bullets, 69
"continued" references, 75
frames
groups, 97
toolbar, 24
Mail Merge fields, 149
numbered lists, 69
pagination, 141
shapes
color, 90-91
fill effects, 91
size, 88-89
tables, 132-133
columns, 135
merging cells, 134
rows, 135
text
attributes, 60
colors, 62
drop caps, 63
fonts, 60
Format Painter tool, 66-67
letter spacing, 61
line spacing, 61
rotating, 63
size, 60
tables, 133
text frames
alignment, 65
background, 64
BorderArt, 65
borders, 65
color, 64
copying, 66-67
printing, 65
shadows, 65

Web publications, navigation bars, 185
WordArt
alignment, 110
bold, 109
borders, 111
drop shadows, 111
flipping, 109
fonts, 108
italic, 109
kerning, 110
rotating, 110
shading, 111
size, 109
spacing, 110
stretching, 109
texture, 111
tracking, 110

forms
creating, toolbar, 27
design, 206
printing, 207

Frame tool (WordArt), 106-107

frames. See also **objects**
bleeds, 153
centering, 59
creating, options, 50
dragging, 59
flipping, 98-99
formatting, 24
graphic
Clip Gallery Tool, 26
cropping, 123
dragging, 122
margins, 152
Picture Frame Tool, 26
sizing, 123
WordArt Frame Tool, 26
wrapping text, 120-121
grouping, 96-97
HTML, 27
layering, 92-93
margins, 152
navigating, 25
picture frames, 103
resizing, 58-59
rotating, 25, 98-99
sizing
rulers, 33
sizing handles, 58
table, 26, 132
text
address lists, 147
alignment, 65
background, 64

BorderArt, 65
borders, 65
captions, 104-105
color, 64
columns, 70-71
connecting, 72-73
"continued" references, 74-75
copyfitting, 160
copying formatting, 66-67
creating, 56-57
formatting, borders, 65
margins, 152
navigation bars, 184-185
printing, 65
selecting, 58
shadows, 65
sizing, 56-57, 71
sizing handles, 58-59
Text Frame Tool, 26
vertical rectangles, 57
wizards, 57
transparency, 95
undoing, 57
WordArt, 106
editing, 107
formatting, 108-109
pouring, 108

**Frequently Asked Questions
(FAQs), 44**

**FTP links, publishing Web sites,
197**

G

Gallery (Office Assistant), 36

gaps, printing, 229

gift certificates, 216-217

**Go To Background command
(View menu), 29, 140**

**Go To Foreground command (View
menu), 29, 143**

gradients
fill effects, 64
shapes, 91

Graphic Formatting toolbar, 114

graphic frames. *See also* **frames**
Clip Gallery Tool, 26
cropping, 123
dragging, 122
margins, 152
Picture Frame Tool, 26

sizing, 123
text, wrapping, 120-121
WordArt Frame Tool, 26

graphics. *See also* **images; objects;
shapes**
banners
creating, 208-209
printing, 209
borders, 114-115
clip art, 100-101
Design Checker, 159
hyperlinks, adding, 187
pictures, 102-103
shadows, 114-115
shapes
circles, 84
custom, 86-87
lines, 85
ovals, 84
rectangles, 85
WordArt
alignment, 110
bold, 109
borders, 111
drop shadows, 111
flipping, 99, 109
fonts, 108
formatting, 108-109
Frame tool, 106-107
italic, 109
kerning, 110
pouring, 108
rotating, 110
shading, 111
size, 109
spacing, 110
stretching, 109
texture, 111
tracking, 110

greeting cards
configuring, 205
filenames, 205
images, 205
layout, 204
printing, 205
text, 205

grouping
frames, 96-97
signs, 202
text frames, captions, 105

groups
creating, 96-97
formatting, 97
sizing, 97

guidelines. *See* **guides**

guides
creating, 118-119
displaying/hiding, 32
dragging, 29, 118
horizontal, 29
layout
background, 167
left margins, 166
mirrored, 166
overflow text, 167
Layout Guides, creating, 118-119
margins
bleeds, 153
frames, 152
pages, 152-153
measurement units, customizing, 49
mirrored, 29
rulers
adding, 31
deleting, 31
displaying/hiding, 33
dragging, 30-32
sizing frames, 33
vertical, 28

gutters, 166-167

H

**hard drives, publishing Web sites,
197**

headlines
hyphenation, 165
rotating, 173

Help. *See also* **Office Assistant;
troubleshooting**
Answer Wizard, 39
Contents page
How? link, 38
tutorials, 39
customizing, 50
Index, 40
Office Assistant
configuring, 36-37
dialog box, 36
Gallery, 36
Help Contents window, 35
hiding, 36
opening, 34
searches, 34
toolbar, 25
topics, 35

online, 42
 articles, 43
 downloading files, 45
 FAQs, 44
 Personal Support Center, 43
 searching, 43
 printing Help topics, 41

Help Contents window (Office Assistant), 35

Help menu commands
 Microsoft Publisher Help, 34
 Microsoft Publisher Web Site, 42

Hide Boundaries and Guides command (View menu), 32

hiding
 catalog, 9
 Office Assistant, 36
 publication wizards, 13
 Quick Publication wizard, 6
 special characters, toolbar, 25

highlighting. *See* **selecting**

Hot Spot Tool, 27, 188

hot spots
 creating, 27
 Web publications
  configuring, 188
  shapes, 189

How? link (Contents page), 38

HTML (Hypertext Markup Language)
 converting pages, 237
 frames, 27

Human Resources Web site project. *See also* **Web publications**
 background, 238
 Calendar page, 239
 color scheme, 236
 email link, 239
 employee-of-the-month
  pages, 236
  story, 240
 HTML conversion, 237
 hyperlinks, 238, 241
 inserting pages, 237
 navigation bar, 238
 publishing, 238, 241

Hyperlink dialog box, 186

hyperlinks
 adding, 187, 238
 creating, 27, 186, 241
 email, 239
 hot spots, 188-189

text, 186
Web publications
 pages, 181
 testing, 193

Hypertext Markup Language (HTML)
 converting pages, 237
 frames, 27

hyphenation
 configuring, 164
 customizing, 50
 editing, 164-165
 headlines, 165
 hyphenation zone, 164
 non-breaking hyphens, 165
 text frames, 164-165
 zone, 164

Hyphenation dialog box, 164

I

icons (toolbars), 24

images. *See also* **graphics; objects; shapes**
 airplanes, 221
 animation, 182-183
 background
  color, 142
  fill effects, 143
  shapes, 142
  watermarks, 142-143
 captions, 104-105
 cropping, 123
 Design Checker, 159
 Design Gallery
  adding designs, 139
  categories, 136
  customizing, 137
  inserting designs, 139
  listing designs, 136
  text, 137
 displaying/hiding, navigation speed, 33
 greeting cards, 205
 hyperlinks
  creating, 186
  hot spots, 188-189
 Line Tool, 27
 origami, 223
 Oval Tool, 27
 Rectangle Tool, 27
 signs, 203

uploading speed, 191
Web publications, 179

Import Styles dialog box, 78-80

importing
 address lists, 147
 database reports, 145
 files, 144-145
 spreadsheets, 145
 text styles, 77-81

inches (guides), 49

Indents and Lists command (Format menu), 69, 174

Index, 40

Insert Clip Art button (Microsoft Draw), 113

Insert Clip Art dialog box, 102, 215

Insert dialog box, 135

Insert Fields command (Mail Merge menu), 148

Insert Fields dialog box, 148

Insert menu commands
 Page, 22, 171, 180
 Page Numbers, 75, 141
 Picture, 103, 112
 Text File, 144

Insert Page dialog box, 22, 180

Insert Rows or Columns command (Table menu), 135

Insert Text File dialog box, 144

inserting
 address lists, 148
 pages, 22, 171, 237
 pagination, 141
 rulers, 31

inside margins, 166-167

installation, 4-5

installing PostScript printer definition files, 232

italics (WordArt), 109

J-L

kerning
 text, 162-163
 WordArt, 110

keyboard shortcuts
 column breaks, 71
 Ctrl key, 59

Ctrl+D (text frame shadows), 65
Ctrl+P (Print dialog box), 226
Ctrl+Shift+H (hyphenation), 165
Ctrl+T (transparency), 95
Esc key, 59
F6 key (quick layering), 93
selecting text, 61

labels, printing, 17

Labels dialog box, 17

Language command (Tools menu), 156, 164

Language dialog box, 156

launching publication wizards, 12-13

layering frames, 92-93

layout
blank, 16-17
columns, overflow text, 167
crop marks, 168-169
custom, 17-19
Design Checker, 158-159
greeting cards, 204
guides
dragging, 29
horizontal, 29
left margins, 166
mirrored, 29, 166
overflow text, 167
vertical, 28
gutters, 166
labels, 17
margins
background, 167
bleeds, 153
frames, 152
gutters, 166
left, 166
pages, 152-153
registration marks, 168-169
verso pages, 166

Layout Guides. *See also* **guides**
command (Arrange menu), 19,
28, 119, 152, 166
creating, 118-119
dialog box, 28, 119, 152, 166

layouts
design sets, 14-15
Web publications, 178

leading text, 162-163

left margins, 166

Line Spacing
command (Format menu), 61, 163
dialog box, 61, 69, 163

lines
Line Tool, 27, 85
spacing, leading, 162-163
text, spacing, 61

linking
toolbar, 27
Web publications
pages, 181
testing, 193

links, FTP, 197

lists. *See also* **text; text frames**
bullet lists, 68-69, 173
creating, 68
ending, 68
numbered lists, 68-69

locating. *See* **searching**

logos, PISs, 11

looping audio, 182

M

Mail Merge
address lists
creating, 146
formatting, 149
importing, 147
inserting, 148
merging, 149
saving, 147
text frames, 147
menu commands
Create Publisher Address List, 146
Insert Fields, 148
Merge, 149
Open Data Source, 147
printing documents, 149

margins
alignment (objects), 117
bleeds, 153
captions, 105
changing, 170
frames, 152
graphic frames, 152
guides
dragging, 29
horizontal, 29
mirrored, 29
vertical, 28

gutters, 166-167
left, 166
pages, 152-153
text
frames, 152
wrapping, 121

measurement units, customizing, 49

mechanical copies, 207

Merge Cells command (Table menu), 134

Merge command (Mail Merge menu), 149

merging
address lists, 149
cells, 134
mail. *See* Mail Merge

messages (mouse pointers), 51

Microsoft Draw
Add Text command, 113
AutoShapes toolbar, 112
Insert Clip Art button, 113
Picture Frame tool, 112
toggling with Publisher, 113

Microsoft Publisher Help command (Help menu), 34

Microsoft Publisher Web Site command (Help menu), 42

Microsoft Web site, 42-43

mirrored guides, 29, 166

mirrored pages, backgrounds, 167

mouse pointers, messages, 51

moving. *See* **dragging**

moving van pointer, 59

music, 182-183

N

naming text styles, 76

navigating
frames, 25
pages, 20-21
speed (picture display), 33
table cells, 133

navigation bars (Web publications), 184
designing, 185
formatting, 185
linking pages, 181

placement, 185
text, 185

New Address List dialog box, 146

New command (File menu), 8, 14, 208

new pages, 18

newsletters, binding, 167

non-breaking hyphens, 165

Nudge command (Arrange menu), 122

numbered lists, 68-69

O

Object Frame Properties tool, 120

objects
alignment, 116-117
flipping, 98-99
rotating, 98-99

Objects toolbar
Clip Gallery Tool, 26
Design Gallery, 27
Form Control, 27
Hot Spot Tool, 27
HTML Code Fragment, 27
Line Tool, 27
Oval Tool, 27
Picture Frame Tool, 26
Pointer Tool, 26
Rectangle Tool, 27
Table Frame Tool, 26
Text Frame Tool, 26, 56-57
WordArt Frame Tool, 26

Office Assistant. See also Help; troubleshooting
configuring, 36-37
dialog box, 36
Gallery, 36
Help Contents window, 35
hiding, 36
opening, 34
searches, 34
toolbar, 25
topics, 35

online Help, 42. See also Help
articles, 43
downloading files, 45
FAQs, 44
Personal Support Center, 43
searching, 43

Open Data Source command (Mail Merge menu), 147

Open Data Source dialog box, 147

opening
catalog, 6, 16
files, 24
Office Assistant, 34

options
customizing, 48, 51
fonts, 48
frame creation, 50
Help, 50
measurement units, 49
pagination, 49
pointers, messages, 51
printing, 51
startup, 49
synchronization, 50
text
editing, 49
hyphenation, 50

Options command (Tools menu), 48

Options dialog box, 48

origami
color schemes, 222
folding instructions, 223
images, 223
paper, 223
printing, 223

Other Designs dialog box, 139

Oval Tool, 27, 84

ovals, 27, 84

overflow text, 72
copyfitting, 161
Design Checker, 159
pouring into frames, 73

P

Pack and Go wizard, 232

Page command (Insert menu), 22, 171, 180

Page Numbers command (Insert menu), 75, 141

Page Options dialog box, 227-228

Page Setup
command (File menu), 18
dialog box, 17-18

pages
background pages
guidelines, 140
images, 142-143
pagination, 140-141
text boxes, 141
watermarks, 142-143
blank, 18
Web publications, 179
startup, 49
custom, layout, 18-19
deleting, 23
Design Checker, 190
HTML conversion, 237
inserting, 22, 171, 237
margins, 152-153
navigating, 20-21
pagination options, 49
recto, 166
verso, 166
viewing, 32
Web publications, 180
linking, 181
previewing, 192-193
titles, 181

pagination
"continued" references, 75
formatting, 141
inserting, 141
options, 49
text boxes, 140

PANTONE color, 231

paper
airplanes, 221
bleeds, 153
origami, 223
printing
size, 228
special paper, 200-201
special paper wizards, 9

PaperDirect, 9, 200-201

paste-ups, printing, 229

pasting. See also dragging; copying
Clipboard data, 145
toolbar, 24

patterns (fill effects), 64

Personal Information Sets. See PISs

photographs. See pictures

picas (guides), 49

Picture command (Insert menu), 103, 112

Picture Display command (View menu), 33

Picture Display dialog box, 33

Picture Frame Tool, 26, 103, 112

pictures, 102-103. *See also* **graph-ics; images**
 captions, 104-105
 cropping, 123

PISs (Personal Information Sets)
 color schemes, 11
 creating, 10
 dialog box, 10
 logos, 11
 selecting, 11
 synchronization, customizing, 50

pitcher pointer, 73

Pointer Tool, 26

pointers
 crosshair, 56
 messages, 51
 moving van, 59
 pitcher, 73
 Resize pointer, 58

points (guides), 49

Poster and Banner Printing dialog box, 209

PostScript
 color options, 233
 Encapsulated PostScript files, 235
 optimizing for portability, 233
 printer definition file, installing, 232
 saving files in, 232

pouring text, 108

Preview Data dialog box, 149

Print command (File menu), 168, 209

Print dialog box, 168, 209, 226

Print Merge command (File menu), 149

Print Merge dialog box, 149

print services, 230-233

Print Setup command (File menu), 226

Print Setup dialog box, 226

printer definition files (PostScript), installing, 232

printing
 ads, 213
 airplanes, 221
 award certificates, 215
 banners, 209
 bleeds, 153

business cards, 228-229

calendars, 211

color
 CYMK, 230
 RGB, 230
 special paper, 9

copies, 227

crop marks, 168-169

customizing, 51

drafts, 229

envelopes, customizing, 51

forms, 207

gaps, 229

gift certificates, 217

greeting cards, 205

Help topics, 41

labels, 17

Mail Merge documents, 149

origami, 223

paper
 size, 228
 special paper, 200-201

paste-ups, 229

print services, 230-233

printer configuration, 226

printer options, 226

registration marks, 168-169

setup, 226

signs, 203

size (custom pages), 19

speed, 229

standard, 226

text frames, formatting, 65

tiling, 209

toolbar, 24

troubleshooting, 227

process color, 230

programs (event programs), 218-219

Programs command (Start menu), 6

projects (Human Resources Web site). *See also* **Web publications**
 background, 238
 Calendar page, 239
 color scheme, 236
 email link, 239
 employee-of-the-month
  pages, 236
  story, 240
 HTML conversion, 237
 hyperlinks, 238, 241
 inserting pages, 237
 navigation bar, 238
 publishing, 238, 241

proofreading. *See* **editing**

proofs, 168-169

publication wizards
 displaying/hiding, 13
 launching, 12-13

publications. *See also* **files**
 ads
  color, 213
  printing, 213
  size, 212
 airplanes, 220-221
 award certificates
  printing, 215
  text, customizing, 214
 binding, 166
 calendars
  events, 211
  printing, 211
  size, 210
  text, 211
 crop marks, 168-169
 event programs, 218-219
 forms
  design, 206
  printing, 207
 gift certificates, 216-217
 greeting cards
  configuring, 205
  filenames, 205
  images, 205
  layout, 204
  printing, 205
  text, 205
 newsletters, 167
 origami
  color schemes, 222
  folding instructions, 223
  images, 223
  paper, 223
  printing, 223
 printing, print services, 230-233
 registration marks, 168-169
 signs
  images, 203
  printing, 203
  text, 203
  ungrouping elements, 202
 Web publications
  animation, 182-183
  audio, 182-183
  blank pages, 179
  creating, 178-179
  Design Checker, 190-191
  hot spots, 188-189
  hyperlinks, 186
  hyperlinks, testing, 193
  images, 179
  layouts, 178

linking, 181
navigation bars, 184-185
pages, 180-181
previewing, 192-193
publishing, 196-197
text, 179
titles, 181
uploading speed, 191
Web site conversion, 194-195
Publisher, toggling with Microsoft Draw, 113
publishing
to Internet, 238
Web publications, 196-197

Q-R

Quick Publication Wizard, hiding, 6

Recolor Object
command (Format menu), 142
dialog box, 143
rectangles
frames, 57
Rectangle Tool, 27, 85
recto pages, 166
Redo button, 55
registration marks, 168-169
removing. *See* **deleting**
Resize pointer, 58
resolution, printing, 229
RGB colors, printing, 230
Rotate or Flip command (Arrange menu), 99
rotating
frames, 25, 98-99
headlines, 173
objects, 98-99
text, 63
text boxes, 171
WordArt, 110
rough drafts, printing, 229
rows
deleting, 135
formatting, 135
guides, 29
inserting, 135
tables, creating, 132

ruler guides. *See* **guides**
Ruler Guides command (Arrange menu), 31
rulers. *See also* **guides**
adding, 31
deleting, 31
displaying/hiding, 33
dragging, 30-32
sizing frames, 33
Run command (Start menu), 4
Run dialog box, 4

S

sample text, 54
Save As
command (File menu), 47
dialog box, 46
Save As PostScript File dialog box, 233
Save as Web Page command (File menu), 196
Save as Web Page dialog box, 196
Save command (File menu), 46
saving
address lists, 147
files, 47
PostScript format, 232-233
print services, 232
reminder message, 46
toolbar, 24
text styles, 77
scaling text, 162-163
ScreenTips, 25
searching
clip art, 100
Office Assistant, 34
online Help, 43
selecting
fonts, 60
frames, 58
PISs, 11
sample text, 54
text, 60-61
Text Formatting toolbar, 60
setting options, 48, 51
Setup dialog box, 5
shading (WordArt), 111

Shadow dialog box, 111
shadows
graphics, 114-115
text frames, formatting, 65
shapes. *See also* **graphics; images; objects**
background images, 142
color, 90-91
cropping, 123
custom, 86-87
fill effects, 91
frames, 57
hyperlinks, hot spots, 189
layering, 92-93
Line Tool, 27
Oval Tool, 27
Rectangle Tool, 27
size, 88-89
standard
circles, 84
lines, 85
ovals, 84
rectangles, 85
text, 94-95
shortcuts, startup, 7. *See also* **keyboard shortcuts**
Show Boundaries and Guides command (View menu), 32
signs
images, 203
printing, 203
text, 203
ungrouping elements, 202
sites (Web). *See also* **Human Resources Web site project**
converting Web publications, 194-195
Microsoft, 42-43
publishing, 196-197
size
ads, 212
calendars, 210
custom shapes, 87
fonts, 60
frames, rulers, 33
groups, 97
pages
actual size, 32
custom, 19
full page, 32
margins, 153
paper, printing, 228
shapes, 88-89
WordArt, 109

sizing
  frames, 58-59
  graphic frames, 123
  sizing handles, 58-59
  tables, 133
  text frames, 56, 71

Snap To tool, 118-119

sound, 182-183

spacing
  text
    kerning, 162-163
    leading, 162-163
    scaling, 163
    tracking, 162
  text frames, columns, 70
  WordArt, 110

Spacing Between Characters dialog box, 110

special characters, displaying/hiding, 25

special paper, printing, 200-201

special paper wizards, 9

speed
  navigating (picture display), 33
  printing, 229
  uploading Web publications, 191

spell checker, 154
  adding words, 155-157
  Dictionary, 155-157
  disabling, 156
  WordArt, 157

Spelling command (Tools menu), 154

spot color, 231

spreadsheets, importing, 145

squares (Rectangle Tool), 27

standard shapes
  circles, 84
  lines, 85
  ovals, 84
  rectangles, 85

Standard toolbar. *See also* **toolbars**
  buttons (icons), 24
  copying, 24
  cutting, 24
  files, 24
  Format Painter, 24
  frames, 25
  Office Assistant, 25
  pasting, 24
  printing, 24

ScreenTips, displaying/hiding, 25
special characters, displaying/hiding, 25
Undo/Redo
  buttons, 55
  tools, 25
zooming, 25

Start menu
  commands
    Programs, 6
    Run, 4
  Start button, 4

starting wizards, 8-9

startup, 6
  blank page, 49
  catalog, 9
  shortcuts, 7

status bar, 7

stretching (WordArt), 109

styles
  applying, 77-81
  copying, 79
  creating, 76
  deleting, 81
  editing, 77-81
  importing, 77-81
  naming, 76
  saving, 77
  templates, 81
  wizards, 8

symbols (wizards), 8

synchronization, customizing, 50

T

Table AutoFormat command (Table menu), 134

Table Frame Tool, 26, 132

table frames, 26, 132

Table menu commands
  Delete Rows or Columns, 135
  Fill Down, 135
  Insert Rows or Columns, 135
  Merge Cells, 134
  Table AutoFormat, 134

tables
  cells, 133-134
  columns
    creating, 132
    deleting, 135

    formatting, 135
    inserting, 135
  creating, 132
  data entry, 133
  formatting, 132-135
  rows
    creating, 132
    deleting, 135
    formatting, 135
    inserting, 135
  sizing, 133
  text
    copying, 135
    formatting, 133

technical support. *See* **Help**

templates
  PaperDirect, printing, 200-201
  text styles, 81

text. *See also* **lists; text frames**
  adding (Microsoft Draw), 113
  aligning, 61, 173-174
  award certificates, 214
  background pages (text pages), 141
  calendars, 211
  captions, 104-105
  Clipboard, inserting, 72
  copyfitting
    automatically, 161
    bold text, 160
    fonts, 160
    kerning, 162-163
    leading, 162-163
    overflow, 161
    scaling, 162-163
    text frames, 160
    tracking, 162
  deleting, 55
  Design Gallery, 137
  editing, 49
  fonts, 48
  formatting
    attributes, 60
    colors, 62
    drop caps, 63
    fonts, 60
    letter spacing, 61
    line spacing, 61
    rotating, 63
    size, 60
  greeting cards, 205
  hyperlinks, 186
  hyphenation
    configuring, 164
    customizing, 50
    editing, 164-165

headlines, 165
hyphenation zone, 164
non-breaking hyphens, 165
text frames, 164-165
overflow, 72
Design Checker, 159
pouring into frames, 73
troubleshooting, 167
pagination, 141
sample, 54
selecting, 60-61
shapes, 94-95
signs, 203
special characters, 25
spell checker, 154
adding words, 155-157
disabling, 156
styles
applying, 77-81
copying, 79
creating, 76
deleting, 81
editing, 77-81
importing, 77-81
naming, 76
saving, 77
templates, 81
tables, 134
copying, 135
formatting, 133
Web publications, 179, 185
WordArt
alignment, 110
bold, 109
borders, 111
drop shadows, 111
flipping, 99, 109
fonts, 108
formatting, 108-109
Frame tool, 106-107
italic, 109
kerning, 110
pouring, 108
rotating, 110
shading, 111
size, 109
spacing, 110
spell checker, 157
stretching, 109
texture, 111
tracking, 110
wrapping, 120-121

text boxes
background pages, 141
pagination, 140
rotating, 171

Text File command (Insert menu), 144

Text Formatting toolbar, 60

Text Frame Connect command (Tools menu), 72

Text Frame Properties dialog box, 70, 74, 105

Text Frame Tool, 26, 56-57, 94

text frames. *See also* **frames; lists; text**
adding, wizards, 57
address lists, 147
captions, 104-105
centering, 59
columns
column breaks, 71
spacing, 70
uneven, 71
connecting, 72-73
"continued" references, 74-75
copyfitting, 160
creating, 56-57
dragging, 59
formatting
background, 64
BorderArt, 65
borders, 65
color, 64
copying, 66-67
printing, 65
shadows, 65
text alignment, 65
margins, 152
navigation bars, 184-185
resizing, 58-59, 71
selecting, 58
sizing, 56
sizing handles, 58-59
Text Frame Tool, 26
undoing, 57
vertical rectangles, 57

Text in Overflow indicator button, 72

Text Style command (Format menu), 78-80

Text Style dialog box, 78-80

texture (WordArt), 111. *See* **fill effects**

tiling, printing, 209

titles, pages (Web publications), 181

toolbars. *See also* **Standard toolbar**
AutoShapes, 112
Connect Frames, 73

displaying/hiding, 33
Graphic Formatting, 114
Objects
Clip Gallery Tool, 26
Design Gallery, 27
Form Control, 27
Hot Spot Tool, 27
HTML Code Fragment, 27
Line Tool, 27
Oval Tool, 27
Picture Frame Tool, 26
Pointer Tool, 26
Rectangle Tool, 27
Table Frame Tool, 26
Text Frame Tool, 26, 56-57
WordArt Frame Tool, 26
Text Formatting, selecting, 60

tools
Clip Gallery, 26, 100-103, 142-143
Design Checker, 158-159
Design Gallery Object, 184
Form Control, 27
Format Painter, 24, 66-67
Hot Spot Tool, 27, 188
HTML Code Fragment, 27
Line Tool, 27, 85
Object Frame Properties, 120
Oval, 84
Oval Tool, 27
Picture Frame, 103, 112
Picture Frame Tool, 26
Pointer Tool, 26
Rectangle, 85
Rectangle Tool, 27
Snap To, 118-119
spell checker
adding words, 155-157
Dictionary, 155-157
disabling, 156
WordArt, 157
Table Frame, 26, 132
Text Frame, 26, 56-57, 94
Text Frame Tool, 26
WordArt Frame Tool, 26, 106-107

Tools menu commands
AutoCorrect, 157
Design Checker, 158, 190
Language, 156, 164
Options, 48
Spelling, 154
Text Frame Connect, 72

topics (Office Assistant), 35

tracking
text, 162
WordArt, 110

transparency (frames), 95

troubleshooting. *See also* **Help;
Office Assistant**
  overflow text (gutters), 167
  printing, 17, 227
  shapes, size, 89
  Web publications
    Design Checker, 190-191
    uploading speed, 191

tutorials (Contents page), 39

**Two-Page Spread command (View
menu), 21**

two-page spreads
  inserting, 22
  viewing, 21

U–V

Undo button (Standard toolbar),
55

Undo/Redo tools, 25

undoing
  dragging, 59
  frames, 57

uploading speed, 191

verso pages, 166

vertical rectangles, 57

View menu commands
  Go To Background, 29, 140
  Go To Foreground, 29, 143
  Hide Boundaries and Guides, 32
  Picture Display, 33
  Show Boundaries and Guides, 32
  Two-Page Spread, 21

viewing. *See also* **hiding**
  background, 170
  guides, 32
  pages, 20
    actual size, 32
    full page, 32

  two-page spreads, 21
  zooming, 21
pictures, navigation speed, 33
publication wizards, 13
rulers, 33
ScreenTips, 25
special characters, 25
toolbars, 33
zooming, 25

W–Z

watermarks, 142–143

Web pages. *See* **pages; Web publications**

**Web Properties command (File
menu), 182, 197, 238**

Web Properties dialog box, 182

Web publications. *See also* **Human
Resources Web site project**
  audio, 182-183
  blank pages, 179
  creating, 178-179
  Design Checker, 190-191
  hyperlinks
    creating, 186
    hot spots, 188-189
    testing, 193
    text, 186
  images, 179, 182-183
  layouts, 178
  navigation bars, 184-185
  pages, 180-181
  previewing, 192-193
  publishing, 196-197
  text, 179
  uploading speed, 191
  Web site conversion, 194-195

Web Publishing Wizard, 197

**Web Site Preview command (File
menu), 183, 192**

Web Site Preview dialog box, 192

Web Site Wizard, 178–179

Web sites. *See also* **Human Resources
Web site project**
  converting Web publications,
    194-195
  Microsoft, 42-43
  publishing, 196-197

windows, 7

wizards. *See also* **dialog boxes**
  Answer Wizard, 39
  Pack and Go, 232
  publication
    displaying/hiding, 13
    launching, 12-13
  Quick Publication, 6
  special paper, 9
  starting, 8-9
  styles, 8
  symbols, 8
  text frames, 57
  Web Site Wizard, 178-179

WordArt. *See also* **objects**
  alignment, 110
  bold, 109
  borders, 111
  drop shadows, 111
  flipping, 99, 109
  fonts, 108
  formatting, 108-109
  Frame Tool, 26, 106-107
  frames, 106-107
  italics, 109
  kerning, 110
  pouring, 108
  rotating, 110
  shading, 111
  size, 109
  spacing, 110
  spell checker, 157
  stretching, 109
  texture, 111
  tracking, 110

wrapping text, 120–121

zooming
  toolbar, 25
  viewing pages, 21